This new instructive series
has been created
primarily for self-education
but can equally well
be used as
an aid to group study.
However complex the subject,
the reader is taken
step by step,
clearly and methodically
through the course. Each volume
has been prepared by
experts,
using throughout the
Made Simple technique of teaching.
Consequently the gaining
of knowledge now becomes
an experience to be enjoyed.

BIOLOGY   Made Simple

Ethel R. Hanauer, M.A.

Advisory editor
Susan Barnett, B.Sc. (Hons.)

Made Simple Books
W. H. ALLEN   London
A Division of Howard & Wyndham Ltd

Made and printed in Great Britain
by Richard Clay (The Chaucer Press) Ltd., Bungay, Suffolk
for the publishers W. H. Allen & Company, Ltd.,
Essex Street, London WC2R 3JG

First edition, April 1967
Reprinted, May 1969
Reprinted, September 1970
Reprinted, June 1972
Reprinted, October 1973

ISBN 0 491 00500 8 Casebound
ISBN 0 491 00540 7 Paperbound

Foreword

We live in a world largely dominated by science and, whether we like it or not, we cannot escape its consequences. Television and radio, with their excellent educational programmes, present detailed aspects of all the sciences to a very large number of people. So, too, do the magazines written especially for the layman who wants to widen his knowledge. Books on scientific subjects are a different matter. Often they are highly technical, written for the reader who is already an expert, or they are books of 'popular appeal', superficial and over-simplified.

Biology Made Simple comes somewhere between these two extremes. Its purpose is to provide a readable, soundly factual introduction to biology, the science most closely concerning ourselves—the science that seeks to understand the world of all things that live and grow.

The book is ideal for the reader studying alone who is willing to supplement his reading by observation and experiment, for which he need go no farther than his own back garden or local park. Sections of exercises in each chapter act very effectively as test-pieces and help to fix the knowledge acquired. Most questions are supplied with answers, but a number of them ask the student for written paragraphs on certain topics to which there is no set answer. These tests of comprehension can easily be checked by referring back to the text.

Biology Made Simple may also be used for more formal study, particularly by students preparing for examinations such as C.S.E. and G.C.E. where it provides suitable complementary reading to the text-books recommended for class use.

With the help of this book, it is hoped that readers will not only acquire a fundamental knowledge of the subject, but will be encouraged to dig deeper into certain aspects of it, and to obtain greater pleasure from the world around them.

SUSAN BARNETT

Table of Contents

CHAPTER I

BIOLOGY—ITS SCOPE AND METHOD

Biology is the study of all living forms, plants and animals, including man, as individuals and as interdependent entities.

To the biologist, who is above all a natural scientist, the human being is an object of scientific investigation; a very highly specialized protoplasmic structure, reflecting in his life processes the activity of all living animal structures. Biology demonstrates the absolute dependence of man, the human animal, on all other forms of life.

Biology covers so vast a field that, to make for greater accuracy and greater ease of study, it has been divided into subdivisions or branches. Each subdivision is worthy of a lifetime's study in itself.

Depending upon his interests, the biologist specializes in a single phase, if in animals, **Zoology**; if in plant life, **Botany**; if in the development of the individual from the fertilized egg stage through early stages of life, **Embryology**; if in the structure of the living organism, **Anatomy**; if in its functions, **Physiology**.

Another vital biological science is **Genetics,** which explains the phenomena of heredity. For microscope work, there is **Cytology,** the science of cell structure and function or, **Histology,** the science of living tissues. **Protozoology** is a branch of Biology which deals with one-celled animal life; **Bacteriology** is the science of a type of one-celled plant life.

Another important and fascinating branch of Biology is **Ecology,** the study of the relationship of living things to their environment. There are many other branches of Biology, one of which is **Molecular Biology.** This science, in the forefront of research today, investigates the fundamental chemical structure of living cells.

Frequently a person who studies Biology from intellectual curiosity becomes intensely interested in a particular division and makes it his hobby or even his life work, his profession. Biology is the basis of such professions as Medicine, Nursing, Agriculture, Plant and Animal Breeding and even Pharmacy.

How shall we acquaint ourselves with the living world around us? Constant awareness coupled with the curiosity and desire to dig deeper will make our immediate surroundings a field and a laboratory for studying life.

A small patch of back garden, a piece of waste ground, even a window box will provide field for exploration; as will the public park, a local wooded area, or the seashore, crowded with plant and animal life for us to observe.

The city streets, for all their concrete pavements and huge structures, have some trees and foliage to watch as they bud in the spring, blossom in the summer, change colour in the autumn and become bare in the winter.

Even in the heart of the city, there are birds which nest near by or pass through on their migrations. Or one sees an earthworm crawling on the pavement after a heavy rain has driven it out of the soil beneath. Where

1

there are human beings there must be other forms of plant and animal life.

One of the most famous **Entomologists** (a biologist who specializes in the study of insects), JEAN HENRI FABRE, did most of his field work in his own back-garden or in some close-by field. He spent hours watching insects in their daily activities and making notes of his observations.

While some biologists explore the lands, the waters and the skies, others prefer to work in a laboratory, the workshop of the scientist. If well equipped, this will have running water in a sink, connexions for gas, non-corrosive table tops (usually stone) with air pressure, vacuum, and electricity outlets. In addition there will be glass beakers, jars, flasks, test tubes, bottles, porcelain crucibles, and shelves for various basic chemicals. There will probably be an oven or an incubator, a pressure cooker, and even a refrigerator in some handy place. A well-stocked library of reference books in every branch of Biology is essential.

The individual who has no access to such a laboratory can build one of his own, using materials bought in Woolworths, a chemist, a do-it-yourself shop or even found on the kitchen shelf or in the medicine cabinet. Kitchen appliances such as the stove, the pressure cooker, and the refrigerator can be very useful. One can always use cardboard, wooden or metal boxes to house small animals (hamsters, white mice, guinea pigs, insects) for study. One can always plant a window-box garden or even a pocket garden in a drinking glass to study the growth of a seedling or an avocado stone. It is simple to leave a moist piece of bread or fruit in a warm spot in the house so that mould can grow and flourish.

With this simple equipment you can think scientifically and experiment. There are certain steps which a scientist follows, without bias or preconception and in logical order, when thinking scientifically.

1 First recognize and state clearly the problem to be solved or the question to be answered.
2 Concentrate on one part of the problem at a time.
3 Collect accurate and complete information from reliable sources.
4 Test this information with new ideas of your own.
5 Answer the question or draw conclusions.

The scientist forms an hypothesis, a proposition which, although it remains to be tested under controlled, experimental conditions, seems to him the probable explanation of the phenomenon in question. If subsequent experiments support the hypothesis, it will become the basis of a scientific theory, which may in turn be accepted as natural law, if it is observed to occur, without failure or variation, in nature.

In every experiment there are usually different factors involved which determine the results. Some examples of these factors are: material used, temperature, air or water pressure, amount of moisture, sunlight and season of the year.

The scientist cannot draw any conclusions unless he has a control to his experiment. This control is an omission or a change of one of the factors. If there is any difference in the results, the difference must then be due to that one factor which has been omitted or changed. When you perform any experiment at home, you must employ the logical order of the scientific method, and make use of the control.

Let us return to the well-equipped laboratory. Here, in addition to all the equipment that has been mentioned, there must be a microscope. It can open to you a marvellous world of living plants and animals that normally cannot be seen at all or only barely seen with the unaided eye.

The microscope, in a simple lensed form, was used in the seventeenth century by a Dutch lensmaker, ANTON VAN LEEUWENHOEK, who ground and polished a tiny bead of glass until it magnified whatever he looked at. To his great astonishment and awe he found that a drop of stagnant water was teeming with life never before visible to the human eye. For greater convenience, he fashioned a crude microscope of metal in which he inserted and secured this bead of glass.

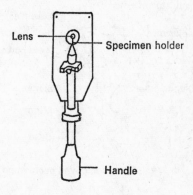

Leeuwenhoek microscope

Figure 1

Since that pioneering discovery of a revolutionary new use of optical lenses, there have been vast improvements and advances in magnifying lenses and microscopes. An Englishman, ROBERT HOOKE, is accredited with the first **compound microscope.** This type is used today; it can magnify objects clearly as much in 1,800 times. Such a microscope contains many lenses which, combined, increase magnification tremendously. See Fig. 2.

Early in this century, it was discovered that **ultra-violet** light could be used instead of light visble to the human eye, to obtain even higher magnification, as much as 4,000 times the life size of the object. This light cannot be seen by the human eye but can be photographed by the **ultra-violet microscope.**

In very recent years, engineers have developed an **electron microscope** which does not look at all like the compound microscope we are familiar with and which can produce a magnification of several million times.

There is no doubt that microscopes of even greater magnification and accuracy can be developed by the large optical companies, and will be in due course.

Because of increasing interest in the use of the microscope by individuals at home, there are companies in this country and elsewhere which make inexpensive but adequate instruments. They do not, of course, have the magnifying power of a scientist's compound microscope but they are adequate for a home laboratory.

In this atomic age, we are all becoming very science-conscious. Our curiosity and interests are constantly stimulated. Many newspapers have a science column, frequently biological in nature. Current science news, science facts

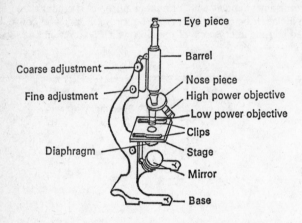

Figure 2   Compound microscope

and advice are presented so that they can be understood and appreciated by the average reader.

There are science digests, science magazines, radio and television broadcasts for the express purpose of informing the average individual. They attempt to whet his desire to seek further information.

Among the greatest storehouses of biological wealth are our museums, our botanical and zoological gardens. In London, the Museum of Natural History houses the story of life from times historic to modern. There are life-size models, life-like and accurate in every minute detail, set in carefully studied, simulated natural habitats. There are miniatures and fossilized remains. In this museum one can learn just by observing the exhibits, reading the labels and listening to the lecturing guides, the entire field of biology with its related subjects. There are such museums in most large cities and universities throughout the country. Zoological gardens such as Regent's Park and Whipsnade are also found all over the country.

Spend a day in the springtime at a Botanical Garden, for example, Kew in London. Take your camera with you and make mental pictures as well of new leaves fresh out of their buds, of pastel-coloured blossoms, especially on the fruit trees, on vines and growing from the moist ground. Walk through the hot houses and see the vast variety of plant life which exists in climates other than yours. Smell the heavily fragrant, moist air. See the mist that haloes the foliage and the damp rich soil from which it grows. Learn about plant life from growing plants.

There are numerous places in which to study flora and fauna in their natural environments and few experiences are more rewarding.

CHAPTER II

THE NATURE OF LIFE

Biology was defined as the study of all living things, both plant and animal, including man. If we specify living things then we must differentiate between that which is living and that which is non-living. We may refer to substances in nature that are composed of inorganic chemicals, such as rock, air, water and parts of sand and soil as non-living. We may refer to objects fashioned by man as also being non-living. Through the years of attempting to survive and

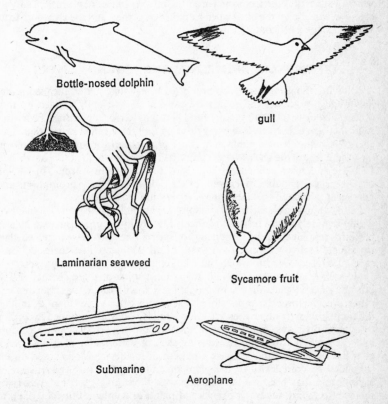

Bottle-nosed dolphin

gull

Laminarian seaweed

Sycamore fruit

Submarine

Aeroplane

Figure 3

build stable communities, scientists have studied living plants and animals to determine how they have adapted or adjusted themselves. From these studies and observations, men in many fields of the arts and manufacturing have been able to fashion non-living things that in many ways imitate living things which are well-adapted to their surroundings. See Fig. 3.

Are you able to recognize man's successful imitation of living things in his building of planes and boats? Consider the first three pictures: the streamline shape of the dolphin, the location of the fins, the dorsally placed nostril, are all natural adaptations for its life and activities in the water. The seaweed, though not actively moving through the water, is continually subjected to the tidal currents of the sea. Its elongated shape and slimy covering allow the minimum of friction over its surface. Can you see how the submarine is a pretty close copy of this animal and this plant?

Consider the second three pictures: the streamline shape of the bird, its wing shape and spread, its retractable legs, the feather-covering for warmth and weather proofing, the direction in which the feathers grow are all natural adaptations for its life and activities in the air, on land and even on water. The wings of the sycamore fruit are admirably adapted to catch wind currents which will carry it far from the parent plant to colonize new areas. Can you see how man copied the birds when he built aeroplanes, and the sycamore fruit when he made a helicopter?

DIFFERENCES BETWEEN LIVING AND NON-LIVING

All living things are made up of a greyish, jelly-like material called **protoplasm** which possesses the quality we call life. It is usually divided up into units called cells. They all require food and thus perform **nutrition.** From this food they are able to release energy during a process called **respiration.** This energy is required to manufacture more protoplasm for growth, for movement, and for all the chemical reactions (metabolism) which go on in the cell. In birds and mammals energy is needed to keep them warm. Thus living organisms are capable of **growth** by the addition of new protoplasm and **movement,** although this latter may be very limited in plants.

Living things are **sensitive** to changes or stimuli in their environment or within themselves and respond to them. Mature living organisms are able to perform **reproduction** by producing offspring like themselves and so they perpetuate their own kind. As a result of all these activities there will be a certain amount of waste which must be removed, i.e. **excretion** occurs.

Non-living objects may be able to perform some of these characteristics, but not all, and generally on investigation it will be found that man or some other outside force is responsible. Consider a car. More than a million different species of organisms are known today. They are grouped according to natural divisions. The largest of these divisions are: the Plant Kingdom and the Animal Kingdom. In studying each of these major divisions, biologists have been able to recognise a pattern of further divisions based on the simplicity or complexity of the plant or animal form. For convenience, a classification has been made beginning with the simplest form and carrying through to the most complex species of plants and animal life known, up to and including man.

Names (mostly Latin in origin) are given which give a clue to the outstanding characteristics of the plant or animal and its relationship to a group or family with similar characteristics. (See Appendix A.)

Although all living forms have a very basic sameness, there are certain characteristics that distinguish plants from animals. Most of us think we can tell by merely looking at the living thing whether it be plant or animal. For example, which of these pictures are of plants and which are of animals?

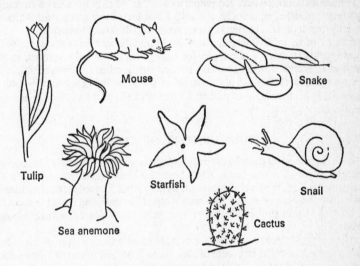

Figure 4   Living things

There are forms of life, however, which exist in water, many microscopic forms, which can be grouped only after careful and detailed study, as either plants or animals. Perhaps you have seen coral growing in the warm southern waters, or highly coloured sea anemones, sea urchins, or hydra, or even sponges. Have you remarked about the beauty of these underwater flowers? Actually they are forms of animal life much lower in the animal kingdom than fish or birds.

DO PLANTS DIFFER FROM ANIMALS?

Perhaps you have examined a drop of water under the microscope and have seen single-celled animated forms of life and wondered—are these plants or animals?

The outstanding characteristics which distinguish plants from animals are:

The green plant has the ability to manufacture food within itself using the substances in the environment in this process. This activity or process is known as **photosynthesis.** All animals, including man, get their food either directly from plants, or indirectly by eating animals which have eaten plants.

Plants generally are stationary, fixed to a spot. Movements of the plant are usually in response to a stimulus in the immediate environment. Plants do not have the power of locomotion. Animals on the other hand, can usually move about—have the power of locomotion to seek food and shelter.

In external appearance, plants are usually green. They grow, mainly at their extremities, throughout their lives in a branching fashion. Animals are very diverse in outward appearance. They have a time-limit to their growth, which occurs throughout the length of the animal, and results in a comparatively definite size and shape.

The basic difference between plants and animals lies in the unit of structure and function of each, namely, the cell. Plant cells have a cell wall which is actually non-living in chemical nature. Animal cells do not have this.

In spite of these differences, plants and animals both have the same basic requirements of food and oxygen for energy. Both show movement, grow, reproduce, excrete and are sensitive to their surroundings. However simple or complex they are, they are all made up of the same living substance—**protoplasm.** This is chemically similar in all forms of life and its activities are also identical.

BRIEF HISTORY OF CELLS

With the advent of the microscope, biologists were able to study the physical characteristics of protoplasm. Just about the time LEEUWENHOEK made his early microscope, the English scientist, ROBERT HOOKE, studied the structure of cork from the bark of an oak tree with a strong magnifying lens. He found it to be made up of tiny empty boxes with thick walls. He named these boxes **cells.**

After the microscope was made available to all scientists, further investigations were made of the structure of tiny water forms, of pieces of human skin, blood, of parts of leaves, roots and stems of plants and even of parts of insects. They were all found to contain a substance that FELIX DUJARDIN, a French scientist, described as living stuff, jelly-like, greyish matter with granules scattered in it.

At the same time (1835–40) in other countries, scientists began to study the basic structure of all living things. In Czechoslovakia, a scientist named EVANGELISTA PURKINJE saw the living stuff and gave it the name **protoplasm** (proto—first; plasm—form). He based his conclusions on the study of embryos of certain animals.

Several years later, HUGO VON MOHL in Germany, studied the living material in plant cells and applied the name protoplasm, recognizing the similarity between plant and animal cells. He also observed that the protoplasm was in constant motion and that there appeared to be green particles in the plant cells. These he called **chloroplasts** (chloro—colour; plasts—particles).

Some fifteen years later, two German biologists, SCHLEIDEN and SCHWANN, working independently, published books on the cellular nature of all plants and animals.

ROBERT BROWN, a botanist and surgeon's mate in the British army, made an intensive study of orchids. He recognized the cellular structure of each flower part. With the use of stains, he was able to find a slightly thicker particle which appeared in every cell. This particle seemed to control certain activities of the cells, especially that of reproduction. He named this the **nucleus** of the cell.

Scientists in many countries, with the aid of microscopes, working independently and in groups, established what is known as the Cell Theory:

Cells are the units of structure of all living things. (All plants and animals are made up of cells.)

Cells are, therefore, the units of function of all living things. (It is within the cells that our life activities occur.)

All living cells come only from other living cells.

CELL STRUCTURE

There are certain basic structures which appear in every cell. There are certain structures which differentiate a plant and animal cell, which make the basic differences between the plant and the animal. For convenience of study, let us look at typical plant and animal cells.

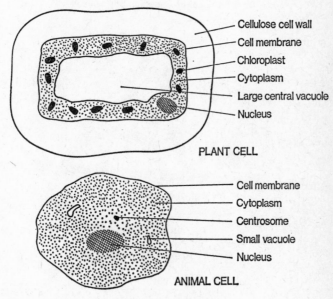

Cellulose cell wall
Cell membrane
Chloroplast
Cytoplasm
Large central vacuole
Nucleus

PLANT CELL

Cell membrane
Cytoplasm
Centrosome
Small vacuole
Nucleus

ANIMAL CELL

Figure 5

Structures both kinds of cells have in common (each structure has a definite job to do in the cell):

Cell membrane or plasma membrane—the outer surface of the cell protoplasm or cytoplasm. Its job or function is to regulate the passage of liquids and gases into and out of the cell.

Cytoplasm—the protoplasm (other than the nucleus) that is in all plant and animal cells. Its function is to carry on all the activities of metabolism (the building up and breaking down of protoplasm).

Nucleus—a definite structure within the cytoplasm of every cell. Its function is to control the activities of the cell, especially the function of cell division—either to make a group of like cells or tissues, or to reproduce the species.

Chromosomes—are thread-like bodies within the nucleus. Their function is extremely vital. They determine the inheritance or heredity of characteristics from one generation to another.

Vacuoles—spaces within the cytoplasm which store water and necessary

Plant cells

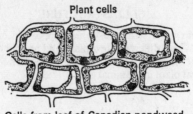

Cells from leaf of Canadian pondweed

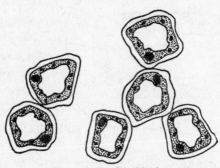

Mesophyll cells of leaf

Animal cells

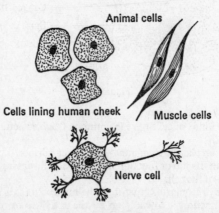

Cells lining human cheek   Muscle cells

Nerve cell

Figure 6

materials dissolved in water. In plants this forms cell sap. In animals the vacuoles tend to have a temporary structure and may be excretory in function.

Structures found only in plant cells:

Cell wall—a hard outer substance called **cellulose** which surrounds the soft cell. Its function is to protect the cell and give it stiffening and support.

Chloroplasts—the green colour-bearing bodies or particles in the cytoplasm. The green colour is known as **chlorophyll**. It plays a vital role within the green plant, in the manufacture of food.

Structures found only in animal cells:

Centrosome—a tiny structure found in the cytoplasm just outside the nucleus. Its function seems to be to aid in the process of cell division.

In Fig. 6 are diagrams of various plant and animal cells. Do you recognize the structures common to both? And those typical of only the plant cell or only the animal cell?

VOCABULARY

adaptation	cell	vacuoles
environment	protoplasm	chlorophyll
photosynthesis	cytoplasm	microscope
stimuli	nucleus	cellulose
sensitivity	chromosome	centrosome

Exercise No. 1

Which is the correct answer to each of the following?

For example:

1 Biology is the study of: (a) the human body; (b) all living things; (c) the chemistry of the blood; (d) the method of digestion in animals.
Answer: (b).

2 The science which explains the phenomena of heredity is: (a) Histology; (b) Physiology; (c) Embryology; (d) Genetics.

3 The science which deals with the relationship between living things and their environment is: (a) Endocrinology; (b) Pharmacy; (c) Ecology; (d) Agriculture.

4 Jean Henri Fabre was a famous: (a) Entomologist; (b) Bacteriologist; (c) Physiologist; (d) Cytologist.

5 A scientific experiment is inaccurate unless it includes: (a) the use of a microscope; (b) a control; (c) reference; (d) more than one factor.

Exercise No. 2

Which *one* term in each of the following includes the other three?

For example:

1 water, natural habitat, woods, environment.

Answer: environment.

2 seal, animal kingdom, sponges, man.
3 cellulose, chlorophyll, plant cell, vacuole.
4 protoplasm, cytoplasm, nucleus, cell membrane.
5 glass, sand, water, inorganic.

Exercise No. 3

Match a number in Column *A* with a letter in Column *B*.
For example: 1b.

A	B
1 Hooke	a green colour in plants
2 Purkinje	b cells in cork
3 Brown	c controls the cell
4 chlorophyll	d named protoplasm
5 cell wall	e plant cell
6 nucleus	f building up and breaking down of protoplasm
7 chromosomes	g named nucleus
8 Leeuwenhoek	h carry hereditary characteristics
9 Von Mohl	i early microscope
10 metabolism	j saw protoplasm in motion

Exercise No. 4

Complete the following statements:

For example:

1 The part of a cell which regulates the passage of liquids in and out is called the ——.

Answer: cell membrane.

2 —— are the spaces in a plant cell that store the cell sap.
3 The unit of protoplasmic structure and function is the ——.
4 The study of the structure of living organisms is called ——.
5 The function of the cell wall is to ——.
6 The instrument used to study one-celled forms of life is called a ——.

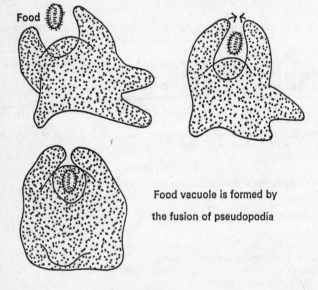

Food

Food vacuole is formed by
the fusion of pseudopodia

Figure 7   Amoeba ingesting food

Since protoplasm is basically the same, physically and chemically, both plants and animals carry on the same activities for living.

FOOD-GETTING

In order to provide the necessary energy for growth and to carry on life's activities, we must take in food or eat. This process is known as **ingestion.**

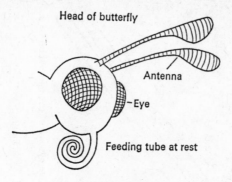

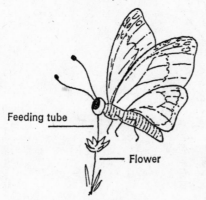

Figure 8

In the discussion of the adaptations of plant cells it was noted that the cells are provided with structures called chloroplasts which help in the manufacture of food within the green plant. It is only in the green parts of the plant, the leaves and stems, that this food-making takes place.

Green plants in presence of light are able to take in the gas, carbon dioxide, from the air and combine it chemically with water to produce their carbohydrates.

$$\text{Carbon Dioxide} + \text{Water} \longrightarrow \text{Sugar} + \text{Oxygen}$$

This food manufacturing process is known as photosynthesis. By combining the sugars and starches made in this way with dissolved mineral salts from the soil, green plants are also able to manufacture their own proteins.

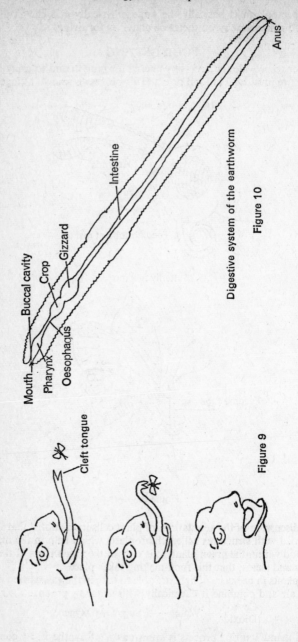

Cleft tongue

Figure 9

Mouth
Pharynx
Oesophagus
Buccal cavity
Crop
Gizzard
Intestine
Anus

Digestive system of the earthworm

Figure 10

Animals are unable to do this. They secure their food either directly or indirectly from plant sources. Animals are adapted by nature to ingest food either directly into the cell, as in the case of very simple forms, or into parts of the body which prepare the food for all the cells to use.

For example, one of the simplest, one-celled animals, Amoeba, actually surrounds its food with its flowing, ever-changing protoplasmic structure. See Fig. 7.

The starfish has an unusual manner of ingesting food. It clamps down with its five arms on an oyster until the muscles of the **bivalve** (sea animal with two shells) tire from the force. The oyster, unable to keep itself tense, relaxes. As soon as the starfish feels this, it allows the oyster shells to open, projects its own stomach into the soft tissues of the oyster and proceeds to devour it chemically.

The butterfly takes in food by uncoiling a long tube-like structure (**proboscis**) inserting it into the nectar container of a flower and sipping gently as through a straw. See Fig. 8.

The frog is an example of another type of food-getting. It sits quietly on a leaf or log and waits for a flying insect to approach. When the unwary insect is within reach, the frog's long, cleft tongue darts out, catches the prey and directs it into his mouth. See Fig. 9.

Animals higher in the scale of life are well adapted to move around to choose, secure and to bring food to the mouth or part of the body which first takes in food.

DIGESTION

In both plants and animals food must be broken down into its simplest forms and made soluble. Only in soluble form are cells able to use food to provide energy for all life processes and to build new protoplasm and repair old. The process of simplifying food and making it soluble is called **digestion.** Water is an essential substance in this process.

The change from insoluble starch, protein and fats to soluble forms is brought about by the action of chemicals called **enzymes** which exist in both plants and animals. These enzymes bring about changes in the composition of foods without being in any way changed themselves or used up in the process. The chemist calls them **activating agents** or **catalysts.**

In plant cells, during the process of digestion, the starch that is manufactured in the green leaves is changed into simple sugars which can be dissolved in water and carried to all other parts of the plant.

In animal cells, much the same is true. Foods containing insoluble starch, proteins and fats must be digested before they can be made available to all cells. Simple animal forms digest foods within each individual cell. Enzymes provide the necessary stimulus for this process.

More complex animals are especially fitted or adapted for digestion. In the earthworm the digestive system (series of body parts adapted solely for digestion) is extremely simple, a slightly modified single tube extending the length of the body. See Fig. 10.

Higher in the animal kingdom this tube becomes divided into specialized parts each with a specific function in the process of digestion. In man and other highly developed **vertebrates** (animals with backbones) the digestive system is most specialized. Enzymes produced by glands serve as catalysts in animals as well as in plants.

ABSORPTION

Digested food must reach every cell in the living plant and animal. The cell walls of plants are porous so as to allow soluble food to pass through. The cell membranes are actively selective or semi-permeable: that is, constructed so that only required soluble substances can pass directly through into the cell protoplasm. This process whereby digested or soluble food passes through the cell membrane is called **absorption.**

One-celled and other extremely simple animals contain food vacuoles in which digestion takes place. Digested food diffuses directly into the rest of the cell protoplasm. See Fig. 7.

In higher animal forms, including man, absorption takes place in specialized parts of the body. For example: in man, the small intestine is adapted to absorb digested food into the blood stream which carries it to all parts of the body.

TRANSPORT

Soluble food and oxygen are distributed to all parts of plant and animal bodies, heat is distributed and waste removed.

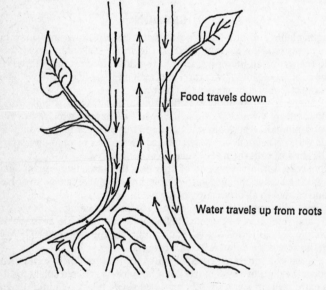

Food travels down

Water travels up from roots

Figure 11

The ever-moving protoplasm distributes digested food to all parts of the single-celled plant and animal.

In more highly developed plants there are tubes in the leaves and stems through which food and oxygen are circulated. Water containing dissolved minerals is transported from the roots up to other plant parts through similar tubes. This is called the sap. See Fig. 11.

Cut a stem of a growing plant, especially during the active food-making summer season—the stem will bleed. This is the sap escaping from the severed tubes. Tapping maple trees for their syrup (sap) requires cutting into the tubes through which the maple sap circulates.

In higher types of animals, there is also a specialized series of tubes through which digested food and oxygen are distributed to all parts of the body and waste removed. In man, circulation is performed by a blood stream which flows in blood vessels (**arteries, capillaries** and **veins**) to every cell.

ASSIMILATION

When digested food reaches the cells in all plants and animals, part of it is chemically combined with oxygen, actually burned, in the process of **oxidation,** to produce energy. The rest of it is changed into more protoplasm for growth and repair of cells. This process of changing digested food into protoplasm is called **assimilation.**

RESPIRATION

Another substance which all living things require is oxygen. This gaseous element exists in air and also dissolves in water. The process of taking oxygen

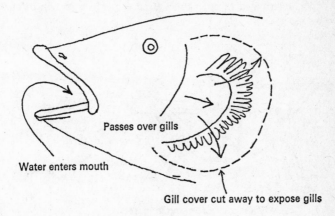

Passes over gills

Water enters mouth

Gill cover cut away to expose gills

Figure 12

into the cells, using it for the release of energy from food materials and the elimination of the subsequent waste products (carbon dioxide and water) is known as **respiration.**

Land-living plants and animals naturally secure the necessary oxygen from the air. Plants are provided with small openings on the under surface of leaves, **stomata,** through which air enters. Within the leaf, oxygen diffuses in from the air, dissolves in the plant sap and circulates to all cells. Oxygen enters the cell membranes and is used by the cytoplasm to combine with digested food (oxidation) to produce the energy with which to carry on all life processes.

Characteristic of green plants is their ability to return oxygen, a by-product of photosynthesis, to the atmosphere. This replenishes the supply of oxygen in the air.

Plants that live in water select oxygen from the water via cell membranes. This is true of one-celled water-living animals as well.

Other animals are variously adapted for respiration. Fish are equipped with delicate, well-protected structures, gills, on each side of the head for this process. Water enters the mouth of the fish, passes back over the gills and comes out from under the scaly gill-coverings. As water passes over the gills, oxygen is absorbed from the air dissolved in the water. It is carried by the blood stream to all parts of the body. See Fig. 12.

The earthworm, a land-living animal, absorbs oxygen through its skin, which must be kept moist and is well supplied with blood vessels. Thus the earthworm always seeks damp earth into which to burrow. If the soil around it should become dry and the skin of the animal should dry up, the animal will die from its inability to carry on respiration.

After a heavy rain you will probably see many earthworms on top of the soil in the country or park and on the pavement in the city. Contrary to popular belief they do not drown when immersed in aerated water.

Land-living animals breathe in air containing oxygen. **Invertebrates** (animals without backbones) have varied adaptations for breathing.

Insects take in air through **spiracles** which are holes on each side of the body. Air is distributed through tubes **(tracheae)** which branch throughout the body.

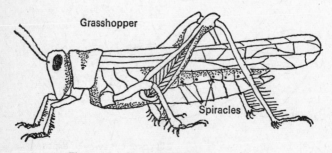

Figure 13   Breathing in insects

Most land-living vertebrates (including man) take in air through nose and mouth into lungs. The linings of these organs are kept moist, like the earthworm's skin, by the secretion of mucus. The blood of these animals selects oxygen from air in the lungs and carries it to all cells where oxidation of food takes place. The blood carries a waste gas (carbon dioxide) and excess water back to the lungs from which they are passed out of the body through the nose and mouth of the animal.

EXCRETION

After plants and animals have oxidized digested food and carried out their natural functions, waste products result. Some are common to both plants and animals because of the nature of all protoplasm. These wastes are given off in the process of excretion.

Inability of the organism to rid itself of waste materials produces a toxic or poisonous condition within the cells. Such a condition leads to inadequate and abnormal performance of all life processes and may eventually be fatal.

The waste gas, carbon dioxide, and excess water vapour are excreted from plant cells through the stomata in the leaves of green plants. It is believed that other organic wastes accumulated in the leaves during the summer are eliminated when leaves fall in autumn.

Animals are adapted for the process of excretion. In one-celled animals (as well as plants) carbon dioxide and liquid wastes collect in vacuoles and are excreted directly through the cell membranes.

Many-celled animals, of greater specialization, produce solid wastes to be voided in addition to carbon dioxide and liquid organic wastes.

Lung-breathers eliminate carbon dioxide and some excess water through mouth and nose after these wastes have been brought by the blood to the lungs. The kidneys and the skin are specialized organs in man which collect and expel liquid wastes and **urea**.

GROWTH AND REPRODUCTION

Early in the history of biology, experimental work proved that all cells come from other cells of the same kind and that all living things come only from other living things of the same kind. The life process known as reproduction ensures the continuity of all forms of life; that is, it provides other individuals of the same species or kind. There are two basic methods:

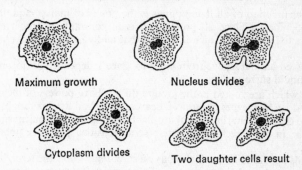

Maximum growth   Nucleus divides

Cytoplasm divides   Two daughter cells result

Figure 14   Binary fission in Amoeba

Simple forms of plants and animals reproduce themselves in the most primitive manner, without any special adaptation for the process. Single-celled plants and animals grow to capacity and then split into equal parts, each part becoming an individual. This method of reproduction is called **binary fission**.

Multicellular (many-celled) plants are adapted in several ways for the vital function of reproduction. Mosses and ferns produce numerous spores which, when growing conditions are favourable, develop into new moss and fern plants. This splitting off of a part of the parent to produce a new individual is **asexual** reproduction. **Sexual** reproduction is a more complex process.

Flowering plants are adapted to produce seeds. In this highly specialized form of reproduction the flower is the important part of the plant. Within separate parts of the same flower or within two separate flowers, male and female elements are developed. The combination of male and female cells (fertilization) results in the formation of seeds. A seed contains the embryo (the infant plant) which, when conditions are favourable, will develop into the new plant.

In order for most animals to reproduce their kind, male and female cells are necessary. The female reproductive cell is referred to as the **ovum** or **egg cell.** The male reproductive cell is referred to as the **sperm cell.** The union of a sperm cell with an ovum results in a fertilized egg which develops into the new infant animal. Since the new animal is a combination of both parent cells it inherits the characteristics of both parents. (Recall that ROBERT BROWN discovered that the nucleus of the reproductive cells contains chromosomes which carry these hereditary characteristics.)

Insects, fish, frogs, reptiles and birds produce eggs from which their young develop. Where there is little or no parental care—in the case of most fish, frogs and reptiles—large quantities of eggs are produced to ensure the survival of a species.

Where there is some parental care (as in the case of birds) in providing food, shelter and protection against natural enemies, fewer eggs are produced.

Animals classified as **mammals** (vertebrates that possess hair or fur and suckle their young) produce their young alive from eggs fertilized within the body of the female or mother. Man is a member of this group of animals.

MOTION AND LOCOMOTION

Another function of all living things is the power of motion and, in some cases, locomotion. Since all protoplasm is in constant streaming motion, under normal conditions, then it follows that all living things move in some fashion.

One-celled animals move from place to place independently (locomotion) in their liquid surroundings.

Plants which are rooted in the ground do not have powers of locomotion but they do exhibit types of motion. Leaves, stems and flowers turn in the direction of the sun; tendrils of climbing plants wind about convenient supports; roots turn in the direction of water; some sensitive plants respond when touched.

Animals appear to be more alive, as we commonly know the term, because, with few exceptions they have powers of locomotion. Sponges and corals grow in a fixed place at one stage of their lives, and in this way they resemble plants.

SENSITIVITY AND BEHAVIOUR

Sensitivity or irritability is another life function common to all protoplasm. This refers to the response of protoplasm to stimuli or changing conditions in the environment.

All plants and animals react or respond in some way to light, heat, need for food, physical contact and other external and internal stimuli.

SUMMARY

Biology is the study of all plants and animals, including man. All plants and animals are composed of protoplasm, the smallest unit of which is a cell. The discovery of the microscope gave us the key to the basis of life.

Since all protoplasm is basically the same, plants and animals carry on the same activities to keep alive. They feed, respire, excrete, grow, reproduce, are sensitive and capable of movement. The greater the specialization and the more complex the adaptations to perform all life functions, the higher (more advanced) is the plant or animal in the kingdoms of life.

VOCABULARY

function	oxidation	sperm
ingestion	soluble	binary fission
carbon dioxide	enzyme	sap
photosynthesis	catalyst	stomata
Amoeba	vertebrates	gills
bivalve	semi-permeable	spiracles
proboscis	oxidize	trachea
embryo	ovum	fertilized egg
	spore	

Exercise No. 5

Complete the following statements:

1 The life process by which food is taken into an animal body is ——.
2 Plants combine —— from the air and —— from the soil to make food.
3 The process of carbohydrate manufacture in plants is called ——.
4 The process in which food is made soluble for all cells is ——.
5 The life process whereby digested or soluble food passes through the cell membranes is called ——.
6 In single-celled plants and animals digestion takes place in the ——.
7 A chemical which activates digestion but is in itself unchanged is called an ——.
8 Digested food is carried to all parts of an animal body by the process of ——.

Exercise No. 6

Which *one* term in each of the following includes the other three?

1 Oxygen, food, waste, oxidation.
2 Circulation, life process, absorption, excretion.
3 Soluble, simple sugar, digested food, water.
4 Carbon dioxide, water vapour, urea, waste products.
5 Blood vessels, cell sap, circulation, water.

Exercise No. 7

1 How is energy produced for the work of living cells? What is its ultimate source?
2 How is the exchange of gases effected in a green plant?
3 Define excretion.
4 What do you understand by binary fission?
5 What functions do plants and animals have in common?
6 What is the fundamental difference between plants and animals?

Exercise No. 8

Match a number in Column *A* with a letter in Column *B*.

A	B
1 carbon dioxide	a unborn plant or animal
2 kidney	b controls cell activities
3 embryo	c contain hereditary characters
4 reproduction	d collects liquid wastes
5 fertilized egg	e independent moving from place to place
6 nucleus	f develops into embryo
7 locomotion	g ensures continuity of species
8 chromosomes	h waste gas
9 irritability	i response of protoplasm to stimuli

CHAPTER III

THE ROLE OF ENVIRONMENT

Living things which exist all over the earth are numerous and extremely varied. Where conditions are favourable, plants and animals are most abundant and successful. Scientists are exploring the deepest oceans and the rarefied atmosphere above the earth's surface and have found evidence of some life. There are relatively few places where no forms of life can exist.

ENVIRONMENT

The nature and success of living things depend upon environmental conditions. By environment, we mean the immediate surroundings of an individual plant or animal. The environment furnishes the basic needs for all living things to carry on their life functions.

These essentials are food, air, water and sunlight. Food is necessary to provide the energy to grow and perform life's processes. Air is necessary because it contains oxygen with which food must be oxidized to release energy. Water is essential, as protoplasm contains between 60–99% water and is thus essential for growth. It is also required for the removal of waste so that substances can be made soluble for entrance into all cells through cell membranes.

Since plants need sunlight to supply energy for the manufacture of food (photosynthesis) and animal food consists directly or indirectly of plants, sunlight is necessary for animals. The heat as well as the light is essential for life to exist.

In addition, the environment includes such factors as other living organisms, temperature, gravity, wind, electricity and air or water pressure.

Throughout the years of man's residence on earth, he has learned to improve his environment. To some extent, he has learned to conquer the forces that change his environment and threaten his ability to survive.

HABITAT

The same kinds of plants and animals do not live everywhere on earth. For example, polar bears live in the arctic regions. Crabs are found among the rocks in salt water, whereas carp live in fresh streams and lakes. On the other hand, salmon spend their lives partly in fresh water and partly in salt. The eagle builds its nest and rears its young on a craggy mountain ledge, whereas the sparrow and robin nest in apple trees.

Plants, too, can be found growing in specific areas. Palm trees grow naturally in moist, hot regions, whereas pines and other evergreens are more successful in drier and more northern areas. Orchids are flowers characteristic of tropical climates, whereas dandelions grow rampant on lawns in the temperate zones.

The specific environment in which a particular plant or animal or group of plants and animals is found is called its natural habitat. All living things are adapted to live in their natural habitats. If they are inadequately adapted, they either die or move to another area for which they are better fitted. If change in habitat occurs gradually, some plants and animals can gradually adapt themselves to the changes and live successfully.

Natural habitats vary greatly, thus the flora and fauna characteristics vary. **Flora** refers to the sum of plant life in a zone or habitat within a given length of time. **Fauna** refers to the sum of animal life of a given region and time period.

Natural habitats are distinguished from one another as follows:

Aquatic—referring to water-dwelling plants and animals. Not all types of aquatic forms live in the same kind of water. The type of indigenous (native) life depends upon whether the water is fresh or salt, still or flowing, shallow or deep, of hot, cold or moderate temperature, smooth or rocky bottomed—or a combination of these factors.

Examples of **fresh water** life, that is those living organisms whose natural habitat is ponds, lakes, streams, and rivers are: plants include algae, water cress, pondweeds and water lilies, whilst some fish, snakes, snails, crayfish and leeches are among the animals.

Salt water plants and animals may be divided into three groups:

Those which live on the beach or in shallow shore regions only, such as, sand-eels, oysters, crabs and starfish, barnacles and seaweed.

Those which live near the surface of the ocean, such as, most sea fish, jellyfish, sea turtles, sharks, seals, porpoises; diatom plants.

Those which live in the ocean's depths where it is dark and very cold and where food is limited, such as colourless plants (diatoms and some bacteria), a few fish, some barnacles.

Terrestrial—this refers to land-living plants and animals. Although these flora and fauna live either on the surface of the ground or burrow underground they all need water to carry on their life processes. Terrestrial plants with few exceptions live on the surface of the ground, most of them anchored to the ground by roots or some sort of processes (stem-like growths). Trees and ferns are examples. Most terrestrial animals live on the surface of the ground. There are a few species that live part of their lives beneath the ground, for example, moles, rabbits, earthworms and some insects.

Arboreal—this refers to animals whose existence is confined mostly to trees. Examples are some monkeys, sloths, opossums, and some lizards and insects.

Aerial—refers to animals who spend a good part of their lives in the air. Examples are birds, some bats and most insects. Aerial or epiphytic may be used to describe some plants which live on trees mainly in tropical and subtropical regions.

CLIMATE CONDITIONS

Climatic conditions determine in great part the distribution of plants and animals over the world.

In arctic regions where there is flat, frozen iceland, the flora is limited to low-growing plants such as mosses and lichens, tough grasses, a few hardy species of dwarf poppies and even forget-me-nots. The fauna is usually confined to penguins, polar bears, seals, walruses and whales, some fish, birds and insects.

Plants and animals are greatly varied in temperate regions where there is variety in temperatures, and there are four annual seasons.

In tropical climates, where there is abundant rain and concentrated sunlight, plant life is luxuriant, always green and varied. Among the plant life are such trees as ebony, mahogany, rubber, date palms, bamboo, banana and thick-stemmed hardy vines; such flowers as orchids, gardenias and other heavily scented, superbly coloured ones. Animals such as monkeys, apes, lemurs, sloths, elephants, parrots, birds of paradise, huge beautifully coloured butter-flies and innumerable insects are indigenous to this region.

In mountainous climates, because of characteristic high altitudes where the oxygen content of the air is less concentrated and there are strong, cold winds, both flora and fauna are relatively limited. Up to a certain line of demarcation, called the timber-line, we find hardy oaks and evergreen trees, some poppies, gentians, onion-type grasses, mosses and lichens. This vegetation is low growing and extremely tenacious. Among the animals native to this region are huge spiders, eagles, bears, mountain goats and sheep.

Desert climates provide few factors favourable for most types of plants and animals. Because of the scarcity of water, the sand, and the steady intense light and heat of the sun only hardy plants like cactus, yuccas, sagebrush and tough grasses can exist. These are able to store water for long periods, have extensive roots and are tough enough to withstand the sun's burning intensity and the sharp drops in temperature at night. Such animals as rattlesnakes, horned toads, some lizards, a few more hardy rabbits, in addition to some un-attractive birds, buzzards and vultures (scavengers) and a few species of in-sects, can exist in the desert where food is scarce and water even scarcer.

NATURAL BARRIERS

There are natural barriers which prevent the indefinite distribution of successful growing plants and animals. These are large mountain ranges, widespread oceans, and large rivers, far-reaching deserts, soils lacking or overabundant in a certain chemical, and the indestructible presence of natural enemies.

Earthquakes, the disappearance of small islands as a result of tumultuous internal earth upheavals, volcanic eruptions and large-scale glacial movements are also factors which produce natural barriers.

COMMUNITY LIVING

Within a given area or community, groups of plants and animals live to-gether in natural co-existence. These living things are adapted or adapt themselves to all the factors in the immediate environment. In a community there always appear to be one or several dominant forms of plant and animal life which are more successful than the other plants and animals which share the community.

An example of community living can be found in a local park. There are trees which grow successfully in that particular climate and type of soil. There are birds which inhabit the trees, build nests and rear their young, feeding on the trees and other plants, and insects that live in the area. There are insects adapted to live in the air, in the trees, on flowering plants and even in the ground.

Some insects serve as food for other animals, some help to propagate new generations of the local flora. Other animals live on the seeds, roots, stems and other parts of plants in the community. Some animals contribute their share in community living by destroying harmful animal pests.

If the environmental factors remain relatively stable, then a balance of living may be achieved and all forms of flora and fauna in the area will live successfully.

PROTECTIVE ADAPTATIONS

All living things are adapted to secure the necessities of life from their immediate environment.

There appears to be a constant struggle among plants and animals to secure food and living space. Those plants and animals which are best adapted for

Figure 15   Praying Mantis

these activities will be most successful. Those which are weakly adapted will be forced either to fight constantly for survival, withdraw to another community, or eventually perish.

Since every form of life has a natural enemy which will seek to destroy it, either to use it as food or in self-protection, all forms of life are adapted to protect themselves. These adaptations are called protective adaptations.

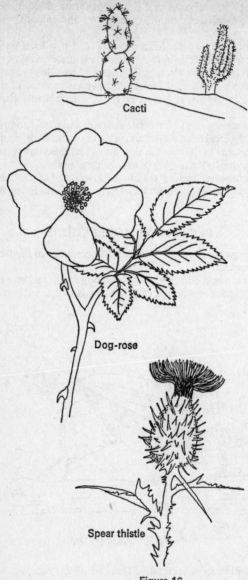

Cacti

Dog-rose

Spear thistle

Figure 16

Among plants, the rose is a fine example of protective adaptation. Thorns on the stems discourage animals bent on destruction. Another example is the thistle with its needle-like flower cup, stems and leaves. The cactus has horny spines which are most painful to the touch. See Fig. 16.

The necessity for protective adaptation is great among animals because of their ability to move about.

Most animals have some natural colour protection from their enemies: that is, they resemble in colour their natural surroundings, or are camouflaged, and may have other special adaptations for protection.

Insects, which are so numerous and varied, show interesting and successful adaptations. For example, the green-brown praying mantis with its formidable front claws and its wary stance, appears most menacing to a potential attacker. See Fig. 15.

The stick insect, a gentle animal, is protected by its resemblance to the twig on which it crawls.

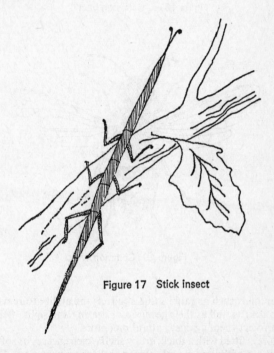

Figure 17   Stick insect

The tiny leaf insect looks like a spring green leaf on which it alights in its relatively short life on earth.

Beetles have claws and fierce-looking **mandibles** (chewing mouth parts) for protection as well as for food-getting. See Fig. 18.

Bees and wasps have warning coloration and painful stinging apparatus for protection against their enemies. See Fig. 19.

Plaice are able to intensify their colour in patches in order to resemble their stony background.

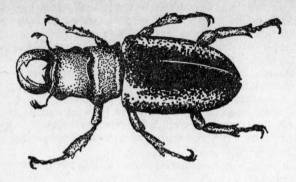

Figure 18   Male stag beetle

Figure 19   Common wasp

Among animals such as rabbits and squirrels the ability to remain breath-lessly motionless as well as their keenness of hearing and sight, their alertness and speed protect them against natural predators.

The tortoise is fitted with a thick, horny shell which encases its soft body and into which it can withdraw completely for shelter and protection. See Fig. 20.

PLANT AND ANIMAL INTERDEPENDENCE

It is obvious that in any environment one plant or one animal cannot survive by itself. All animals depend upon green plants for food and oxygen whilst all life depends upon the decaying activities of bacteria and fungi to return substances to the environment for future generations to use. Man depends

Figure 20   Tortoise

upon other animals and plants for his success on earth. This mutual inter-dependence is what provides the balance in Nature.

Most plants and animals live in groups. Some trees, for example, are adapted to a specific climate and type of soil. Beech and holly trees grow together in a temperate region where there are dry ridges. Elm, willow and birch will be found growing together in more moist areas. Evergreens (firs and pines) are usually found in more northerly climates but can grow elsewhere.

Ferns and mosses flourish together in moist shady places.

Most animals live gregariously in communities or herds. Man is such an animal.

Some insects, bees and ants especially, live in communities and actually share in the many activities of food-getting, shelter-building, care of the young and protection against natural enemies.

In a warm sea-water community certain fish, coral, sponges, lobsters, crabs and jellyfish live together.

Local ponds provide community living for water-insects, frogs, snails, eels and other fish.

Such animals as buffalo, elephants, cows and other cattle live in herds for mutual benefits. Wolves and baboons travel in packs for maximum mutual strength and protection.

Relatively few animals prefer to live alone. The advantages of solitary living are few. Escape from natural enemies is perhaps easier for a swift, lonely animal; less disturbance and interference in rearing the young; less competition for mating and securing food are sometimes possible advantages.

Generally speaking there is safety in numbers, therefore group living is usually the most successful type of living.

SYMBIOSIS

The close living together of organisms for mutual benefits is called **symbiosis** and the plants and animals involved are known as **symbionts.** An example of symbiosis among animals is the relationship between common ants and greenfly or **aphids.** The aphids suck the sap from roses or other plants. With this plant fluid they produce a sweet substance within their bodies. Ants milk the aphids and feed their queen and also the young. (The greenfly are known as ant cows.) In return for this service, the ant cows are protected by their mutual benefactors against natural enemies and are also given shelter in ant hills during the winter.

Another example of mutual give and take is found in the termite. This wood-eating insect provides food and shelter for a protozoan animal that lives in its intestines. The protozoan rewards its host by producing chemicals which digest the wood fibre for the termite.

Another interesting form of symbiosis between animals exists in the relationship of the hermit crab and the sea-anemone (a member of the jellyfish family). The hermit crab lives in a discarded snail shell which covers the soft part of the crab. The anemone lives on top of the snail-shell house, and has stinging apparatus which protects it and the crab from natural enemies and captures food. It also gives protective coloration for the crab which in turn,

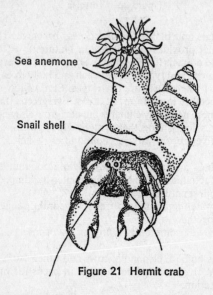

Sea anemone

Snail shell

Figure 21 Hermit crab

provides the anemone with transportation and food bits that escape its own mouth.

A classic example of plant symbiotic relationship is the lichen which is found growing on rocks and tree trunks. This is not a single plant but a mutually beneficial combination of a non-green fungus and a group of one-celled green plants of the algae group. The fungus cannot make its own food. It provides shelter, anchorage, protection, water and carbon dioxide for its algae companions. These simple green plants use the water and carbon dioxide to manufacture food and supply oxygen for the fungus. Because of this association, lichens can survive under the most difficult conditions such as occur on bare rock faces. See Fig. 22.

PARASITISM

Some plants and animals feed on other living organisms without giving anything in return. This relationship is known as **parasitism**; the offender is called a **parasite**, and the victim, the **host**. In most cases the parasite is structurally degenerate and entirely dependent upon the host. The host may either gradually lose its vitality, become abnormal and diseased and then die, or it may develop a natural protection against the parasite. It may adapt itself to live with, and in spite of, its burden. In some cases, the host produces a substance which either renders harmless or kills the parasite.

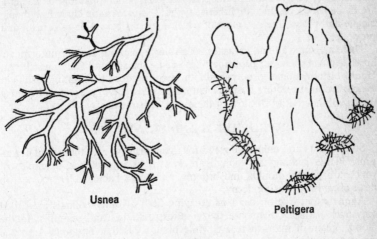

Usnea

Peltigera

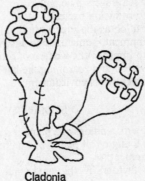

Cladonia

Figure 22 Lichen forms

The mistletoe plant, which conjures up romantic notions, is actually a parasite as it relies on another plant for its water. Its host, usually an apple or poplar, may eventually perish from malnutrition.

Other plant parasites which depend on and slowly devitalize their hosts, causing great economic loss to man, are wheat rust, Dutch elm disease, corn smut and chestnut blight. In each case the plant mentioned in the name is the losing host to the destructive parasite plant.

There are some parasitic plants which do damage directly to man's person. These offenders are members of the **fungus** group of plants, that is, a group having no chlorophyll. The unpleasant ringworm and athlete's foot ailments are examples.

The most numerous and destructive of all plant parasites are among the **bacteria** (a type of single-celled plant). Some species cause blights on apples, pears, cabbage, cucumbers and other plants. Other species cause diseases in man and are referred to as **pathogenic** bacteria. Among pathogenic bacteria are those which produce diphtheria, typhoid fever, Asiatic cholera, bubonic plague and other illnesses, most of which man has been able to control and prevent.

There are some animal parasites which single man out as their unfortunate hosts. Among them are protozoa which cause malaria and sleeping sickness. Hookworm and tapeworm, parasitic in man, produce devastating results in their often unsuspecting hosts. Scientists have learned to prevent and control the harmful activities of most of these animal parasites.

SAPROPHYTES AND SCAVENGERS

Some plants and animals depend for their existence on other, dead organisms. Plants lacking chlorophyll are known as **saprophytes,** examples of which are yeasts, moulds, mushrooms, and some bacteria. These feed on dead organisms causing decay.

Animals that live on dead or decaying flesh of other animals are called scavengers. Among them are the vultures, buzzards and sea-gulls. In the blood stream of man, there are white blood cells that resemble Amoebae which act as tiny scavengers by engulfing and eating foreign particles including some disease-producing bacteria.

Man, in his position as the superior animal of our universe, has learned to change his environment, sometimes to his misfortune but generally to his advantage, and to improve the welfare of other living things. Because of his powers of observation and reasoning, he has been able, to a great extent, to control many factors of his environment.

SUMMARY

The immediate surroundings of a plant or animal are its environment.

The successful living of all plants and animals depends on proper adaptation to the environment.

The essential factors in the environment are food, air, water and sunlight.

Green plants manufacture their own food in a process known as photosynthesis.

The specific environment in which a particular group of plants and animals is found is known as the natural habitat.

Climate conditions determine in great part the distribution of plants and animals.

Natural barriers prevent indefinite distribution of plants and animals.

Plants and animals have protective adaptations against their natural enemies.

Group living appears to be more successful, with greater mutual benefits, than living individually.

Man has learned to modify, control and somewhat change his environment to his advantage.

VOCABULARY

natural habitat	arboreal	symbiosis
flora	aerial	parasite
fauna	scavenger	saprophyte
aquatic	fungus	pathogenic
terrestrial	lichen	aphid
	symbiont	

Exercise No. 9

Name 5 animals and 5 plants that live in each of the following habitats: ocean, pond, desert, polar regions.

For example: ocean-whale, etc., diatom, etc.

Exercise No. 10

Match the number in Column *A* with the letter in Column *B*.

A	*B*
1 habitat	a tree-living animals
2 fauna	b sum total of animals in an area
3 flora	c immediate surroundings
4 arboreal	d sum total of plants in an area
5 environment	e specific environment of groups of plants and animals

Exercise No. 11

Which *one* term in each of the following includes the others?

1 environment, sunlight, fauna, air.
2 food, air, aquatic, water, environment.
3 thorns on rose plant, protective adaptation, swift flight, camouflage.
4 mountains, oceans, barriers, deserts.
5 green leaf, water, carbon dioxide, photosynthesis.

Exercise No. 12

Complete the following sentences:

1 The hard shell of the tortoise is an example of —— adaptation.
2 The living together of organisms for mutual benefit is known as ——.
3 A —— is a plant or animal which takes its livelihood from another plant or animal, giving nothing in return.
4 The —— is an example of a parasitic plant.
5 The relationship between the protozoa in the intestines of termites and the termites is an example of ——.
6 The lichen is an example of ——.
7 The vulture is an example of a —— because it lives on dead or decaying flesh.
8 Bacteria which cause disease in man are known as ——.
9 White blood cells sometimes perform the function of —— because they feed on foreign particles in the human blood.

CHAPTER IV

ORGANIZATION AND CLASSIFICATION

All living things are made of protoplasm. The smallest unit of structure and function of protoplasm is the cell. All plants and animals are made up of either a single cell or many cells.

SINGLE-CELLED LIFE: PLANTS

The simplest form of plant life exists as a single cell which is able to carry on all the necessary life processes. Most one-celled plants belong to the algae group which live in water. There are some which live in symbiotic relationship with other plants (lichens) and with animals in a moist environment but out of the water.

A common example of a single-celled plant is the **pleurococcus** which is usually found growing on the north side of moist tree trunks and rocks in the woods. These tiny green plants are legendary Indian Friend or Woodsman's Compasses because they indicate the direction North.

They contain chlorophyll with which to combine carbon dioxide from the air and water to manufacture food. Under the microscope they appear singly or in colonies, each cell living independently within its colony. See Fig. 23.

A drop of pond water will reveal a variety of single-celled plants. What is commonly known as pond scum is a group of green thread-like colonies called **Spirogyra.** They reproduce prolifically and form the greenish scum that appears on the surface of sluggish streams, small ponds and pools. See Fig. 24.

Among the independent single-celled forms which can be viewed under a microscope are the **diatoms** and **desmids.** These plants are curiously symmetrical, each kind having a specific design on its shell-like outer covering which encloses and protects the soft protoplasmic cells.

Diatoms seem to have existed in abundance centuries ago. Large deposits of their empty shells have been discovered in salt as well as fresh water and on land that shows evidence of once having been under water. These deposits, called **diatomaceous earth,** are used commercially as the basis of polishing materials and also for filtering purposes in sugar refineries.

Another common group of single-celled plant life is found in ocean water, as part of **plankton.** These are tiny green plants that provide much of the food for fish and other sea-living animals.

Many other algae of varied colours inhabit the oceans and shore lines. When they occur in concentration they actually give colour to their surroundings, for example, the Red Sea.

Perhaps the most abundant and varied single-celled plants are the bacteria. Among this group are many most helpful to man and others, most harmful.

One single-celled form of life, **Euglena,** has created dissension among biologists. Botanists consider it a simple plant because it contains chlorophyll bodies with which it manufactures its own food. See Fig. 25.

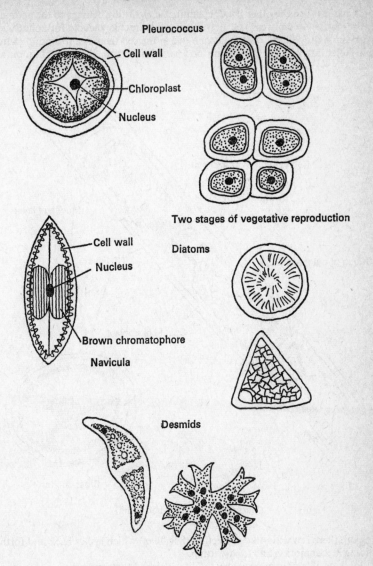

Figure 23 Single-celled plants

Zoologists, on the other hand, claim that it rightfully belongs to the animal kingdom for several reasons. It contains a contractile vacuole for collecting and eliminating liquid wastes. At one end of the cell there is a form of mouth and gullet into which it takes some food particles from the water. At the mouth

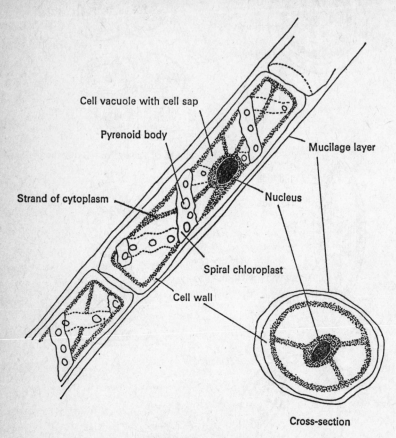

Figure 24   Spirogyra (common pond scum)

region, there is a whip-like projection (**flagellum**) which lashes back and forth aiding in locomotion and food-getting.

Perhaps this controversial bit of life is proof that one-celled plants and animals have a common ancestor.

SINGLE-CELLED LIFE: ANIMALS

This leads us to the fascinating group of true one-celled animals called **protozoa** (proto—first; zoa—animals). A drop of pond water reveals a variety of tiny animals, some darting about and others moving lazily.

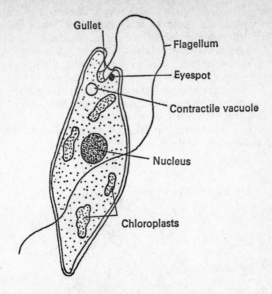

Figure 25 Euglena (plant or animal?)

Among these may be Paramecia and Amoebae. Each of these animals is well-equipped within its protoplasm to carry on all the life functions.

The simplest of all animals is Amoeba. It has no definite or constant form. The protoplasm within the cell membrane flows into projections known as **pseudopodia** or false feet. The presence of food particles in the water seems to stimulate the formation of these false feet which carry the rest of the cell in the direction of the food; thus the animal moves from place to place.

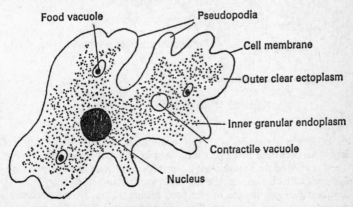

Figure 26 Amoeba

Food is engulfed and digested within vacuoles and is absorbed directly into the surrounding cell protoplasm. Oxygen dissolved in the water is absorbed directly through any part of the cell membrane. Solid wastes are left behind as Amoeba flows sluggishly on. A contractile vacuole regulates the water content of the animal expelling water to the outside from time to time through a temporarily thin spot in the cell membrane.

The centrally located nucleus of Amoeba controls all cell activities. It splits in half to produce two Amoebae in the process of reproduction. This simple type of reproduction is known as **binary fission.**

Paramecium, a more complex type of one-celled protozoa, is slipper-shaped and constant in form.

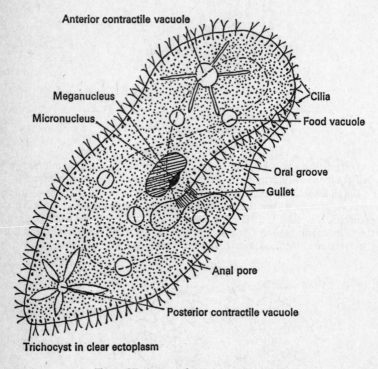

Anterior contractile vacuole

Meganucleus

Micronucleus

Cilia

Food vacuole

Oral groove

Gullet

Anal pore

Posterior contractile vacuole

Trichocyst in clear ectoplasm

Figure 27 Paramecium

Its cell body is covered with tiny projections of protoplasm called **cilia** which wave back and forth providing means of rapid locomotion in water. Other cilia around the mouth region direct food particles into the gullet which is also lined with cilia to push the food into food vacuoles.

Constant flowing motion of the protoplasm within the paramecium cell body distributes each food vacuole to all parts of the cell. Digestion of food takes place in the vacuole, and the digested food is absorbed directly into the surrounding protoplasm.

Oxygen dissolved in the water is absorbed directly through the cell membrane into the cell protoplasm.

Solid food wastes are expelled through a weakened area in the cell membrane called an anal pore. Excess water is forced through the cell membrane by the contracting action of the contractile vacuoles located one at each end of the tiny animal.

Minute threads of protoplasm called **trichocysts** are embedded just inside the cell membrane. These provide means of anchorage.

Two nuclei, one larger than the other, control all life activities and provide the means for reproduction. Paramecium divides by binary fission, similarly to Amoeba, and also by a simple type of sexual reproduction called **conjugation**. In this type of reproduction two Paramecia fuse temporarily, exchange nuclear material, separate, and then each proceeds to divide by binary fission. This process seems to revitalise the species.

There are other types of protozoa which exist individually and still others which live in colonies.

Vorticella attaches itself by a long stalk at one end to a stationary object.

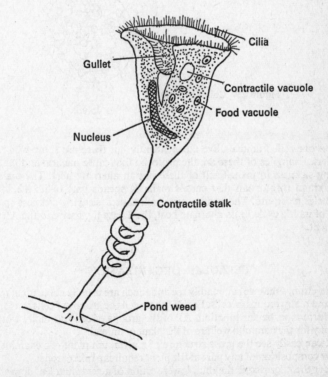

Figure 28 Vorticella

Colonial protozoa live in groups, each animal in the colony functioning independently. Some colonies have a thick, gelatinous substance encasing them while others have glass-like coverings. The famous white cliffs of Dover are composed of countless chalk-like shells which have accumulated through the years after the soft protoplasm of each protozoan animal has ceased to exist.

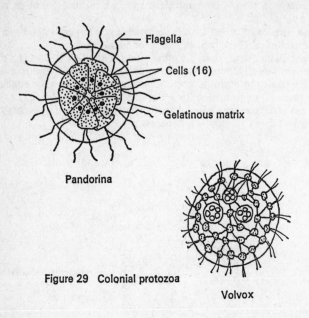

Flagella

Cells (16)

Gelatinous matrix

Pandorina

Figure 29 Colonial protozoa

Volvox

Most one-celled animals live independently but there are some which are parasites. Examples of these are the protozoa that cause malaria and African sleeping sickness in man. Each of these has an alternate host. The malarial Plasmodium (protozoan that causes malaria) spends part of its life in the Anopheles mosquito. The protozoan which causes sleeping sickness spends much of its life cycle in its alternate host, the Tsetse fly, native to the African continent.

CELLULAR ORGANIZATION

Living things that we can readily see and touch are usually made up of many cells, and many groups of cells. Each of these cells or groups of cells is adapted to perform a particular function. All of the groups of cells normally work in harmony for the common welfare of the plant or animal.

One can easily see the gross structure of a geranium plant. To examine the cellular composition of any part of the plant requires a microscope.

Under the microscope the thin, lower section of a geranium leaf appears to be made up of many cells similar in size and shape, fitted together like a series of bricks in a brick wall. At intervals there are openings guarded by two kidney-shaped cells. The surface view of the lower epidermis of the leaf appears to be a pattern of well fitted flagstones among which are guarded openings.

30 30

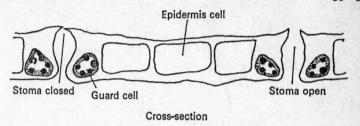

Epidermis cell

Stoma closed   Guard cell   Stoma open

Cross-section

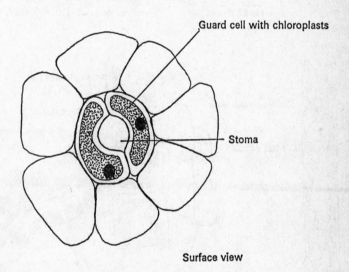

Guard cell with chloroplasts

Stoma

Surface view

Figure 30   Under surface of leaf

The continuous layer of cells is adapted to protect the under surface of the leaf. The openings or **stomata** with their guard cells control inward and outward passage of gases. Oxygen is taken into the leaf and carbon dioxide is released. During the process of photosynthesis carbon dioxide is taken in through these stomata and oxygen is released. Other cells (containing chloroplasts) in the leaf are adapted to combine carbon dioxide and water to produce food for the plant.

In a later discussion of the flowering plants, plant cells and their specialized functions in groups or tissues will be considered in detail. Note a few more examples in Fig. 31.

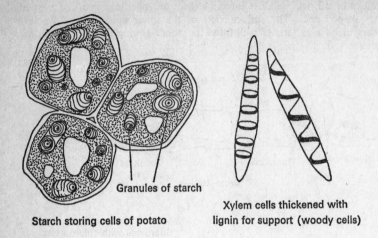

Granules of starch

Starch storing cells of potato

Xylem cells thickened with
lignin for support (woody cells)

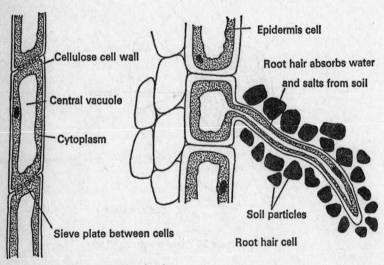

Cellulose cell wall

Central vacuole

Cytoplasm

Sieve plate between cells

Phloem cells for transporting food

Epidermis cell

Root hair absorbs water
and salts from soil

Soil particles

Root hair cell

Figure 31 Plant tissue cells

Among many-celled animals, there are also groups of cells similar in structure with a similar common function.

For example, examine Fig. 32 showing cells from the cheek lining of man. If a microscope is available to you, prepare a slide of cheek lining cells. Scrape the inner surface of your cheek with the dull edge of a knife and mount this in a drop of water on a glass slide. These cells are adapted for their job of protecting the softer, inner cells of the mouth.

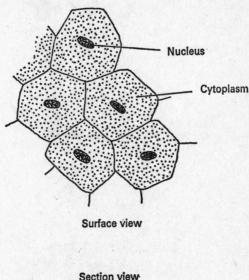

Nucleus

Cytoplasm

Surface view

Section view

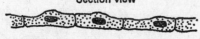

Figure 32   Human cheek cells

In Figs. 33 and 34 there are surface views of several types of cells found in the human body. Note how they vary in size and shape, also in function.

Groups of cells similar in size, shape and function make up **tissues**: thus nerve cells working together form nerve tissue; muscle cells grouped together form muscle tissue; and cartilage cells form cartilage tissue.

There are other types of cells in the human body (as well as in all other animals and in plants) that, because of structural and functional similarities, form tissues. See Fig. 35.

Groups of different kinds of tissues working together to perform a particular function for the plant or animal are called **organs**.

Examples of plant organs are leaf, stem, roots, flowers, fruits, and seeds. See Fig. 36.

Examples of organs found in the human body are larynx, trachea or windpipe and lungs. See Fig. 37.

Cells of human tissues

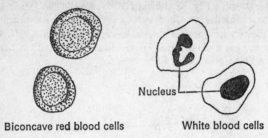

Biconcave red blood cells   Nucleus   White blood cells

Nerve cell

Figure 33

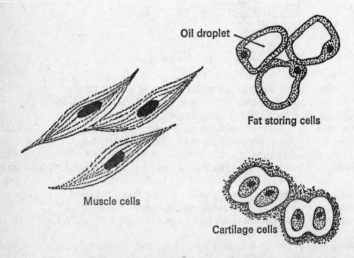

Oil droplet

Fat storing cells

Muscle cells

Cartilage cells

Figure 34 More cells of human tissue

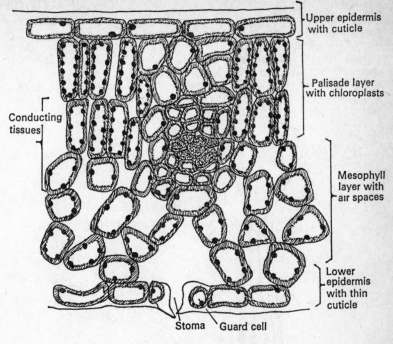

Figure 35 Cross-section of a leaf

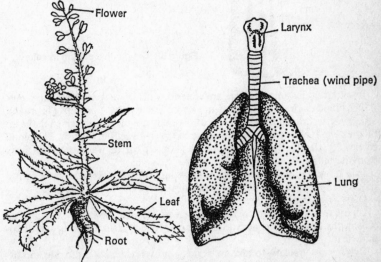

Figure 36 Plant organs   Figure 37 Organs of human respiration

A group of organs working together to perform a specific function is called a **system.**

A simple experiment which can be performed at home will illustrate the **conductive** system in plants. Place a stalk of celery (leaves included) in a solution of red ink and water for several hours. Observe the red colour which appears in tubes or veins in the stalk and leaves. Cut across a piece of the stalk and observe the row of red dots in Fig. 38.

This experiment indicates the conductive system through which water containing dissolved minerals from the soil rises up through the stem to all other parts of the plant.

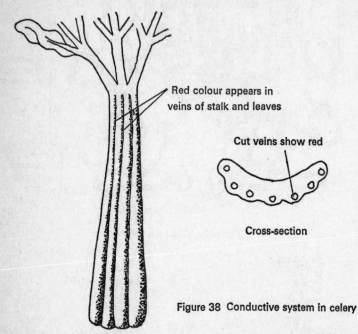

Red colour appears in
veins of stalk and leaves

Cut veins show red

Cross-section

Figure 38 Conductive system in celery

In multicellular animals there are systems which have specialized functions.

The blood or **circulatory system** in fish is one example. A primitive heart and blood vessels branching to all parts of the body are the organs which make up this system. Its function is to distribute blood to all cells in the fish. The blood carries digested food and oxygen to the cells and carries waste products away from the cells to be eliminated.

In a more complex animal there are many different systems, each with a specialized job. We shall mention some of them briefly at this point:

Digestive system—to digest food.

Circulatory system—to circulate or deliver digested food and oxygen to all cells in the body and to carry away gas and liquid waste products and distribute heat.

Respiratory system—to take in oxygen and release carbon dioxide and excess water vapour from the body.

Excretory system—to rid the body of wastes.
Reproductive system—to produce another generation of animals.
Nervous system—to control activities of the body.

Let us analyse the human digestive system to show the organs of which it is composed: the mouth, gullet or oesophagus, stomach and intestines. There are glands that produce chemicals (**catalysts**) which aid the digestive organs in their function.

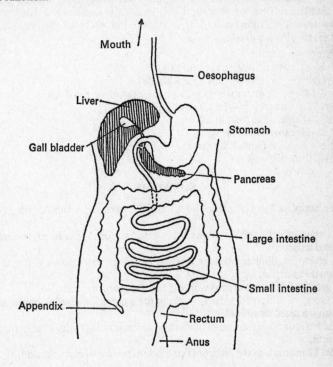

Mouth

Oesophagus

Liver

Stomach

Gall bladder

Pancreas

Large intestine

Small intestine

Appendix

Rectum

Anus

Figure 39 Human digestive system

The sum total of a group of systems working together results in a complete **organism,** otherwise called a plant or animal.

Over a million varieties of living things have been discovered on our earth. In order that they may be studied and recognized they must be grouped in some orderly fashion, or in other words, classified.

For example, books in a library are not just placed on shelves in any haphazard fashion. They are divided first into large general groups, that is, fiction and non-fiction. Each of these groups is divided further into subdivisions. For example, non-fiction are grouped according to their main topics: biography, history, science, art, etc. Each of these divisions is further subdivided; for example, science books are classified according to their specialities: astronomy, biology, chemistry, physiology, etc. Subdivisions finally narrow down to the title of the individual book, such as *Biology Made Simple.*

Our modern system of classification or taxonomy of all living things was devised by LINNAEUS (Carl von Linné) in the latter part of the eighteenth century. He used Latin names because Latin was the universal language of scholars. He gave names to plants and animals that are short and often descriptive in nature.

The largest groups of living things are the Plant and Animal Kingdoms. Each of the kingdoms is divided and subdivided depending first on general and then more detailed structural and functional similarities. The smallest subdivision is the individual plant or animal. For example: the classification of Man. (See Appendix A.)

Kingdom—Animal
Phylum—Chordate (with a skeletal axis)
Sub-phylum—Vertebrate (having backbone)
Class—Mammal (mammary glands, young born alive, have hair)
Order—Primate (primo—first; opposable thumb)
Family—Hominidae (mankind)
Genus—Homo (human being)
Species—Sapiens (wise, discerning)
Man—Homo sapiens

SUMMARY

The simplest form of plant and animal life exists as a single, independent cell.

A group of cells similar in size and shape, performing a function together is called a tissue.

A group of different tissues working together to perform a function is known as an organ.

A group of different organs working together form a system.

A group of different systems working for a common good is called an organism—a plant or animal.

The basis of classification of plants and animals is similarity of structure and function.

Carl Linnaeus was the father of our modern system of classification.

VOCABULARY

specialization	diatom	pseudopodium
tissue	desmid	flagellum
organ	Spirogyra	anal pore
system	Vorticella	conjugation
organism	diatomaceous	stomata
algae	earth	Pleurococcus
plankton	trichocysts	

Exercise No. 13

Complete the following statements:

1 The unit of structure and function of protoplasm is the ——.
2 A single-celled animal that has an ever-changing shape is ——.
3 The —— in one-celled animals collects and eliminates excess water.
4 The white cliffs of Dover were formed from the —— of protozoa.

5 Paramecium reproduces by ——.
6 All one-celled animals belong to the group called ——.
7 —— is a one-celled organism that has characteristics of both plants and animals.
8 Amoeba surrounds food particles with its ——.

Exercise No. 14

Match a number in Column *A* with a letter in Column *B*.

A	B
1 tissue	a father of classification
2 multicellular	b lungs
3 Linnaeus	c cheek lining
4 cell theory	d study of classification of plants and animals
5 organ	e cells are the units of structure and function in all living organisms
6 stomata	f lobster
7 organism	g many-celled
8 Taxonomy	h openings on under surface of leaf

CHAPTER V

CYCLES OF LIFE

In previous chapters we have learned that all living substances are made of a substance called protoplasm. Scientists have discovered that protoplasm is composed of many different substances which originate in the non-living environment.

MATTER

Many ancient Greek scientists believed that everything in the world was made up of one or more of four substances: air, water, earth and fire. PLATO gave these four the name elements. He also declared that everything that existed was **matter.** Subsequent Greek scientists defined matter as that which occupies space and has a definite weight.

Subsequently, DEMOCRITUS advanced the introduction to modern work on the **atom.** His theory stated that the smallest unit of all matter is a tiny, invisible and indivisible particle which he called an atom (*atomos* means 'indivisible' in the Greek language).

In the early nineteenth century, an Englishman, JOHN DALTON, revised and enlarged on the Atomic Theory of Matter.

We are now living in what is commonly referred to as the Atomic Age. With the aid of special tools, the atom-smashing machine or cyclotron, it has been established that an atom can be divided (contrary to early Greek theory) or split into smaller units. When atoms split and when they link up with other atoms, energy is released.

ELEMENTS, MIXTURES AND COMPOUNDS

Atoms are rarely found existing singly in nature. Usually two or more atoms are linked together into a structure called a **molecule.** Two or more atoms of the same kind form a molecule of an **element.**

Chemists use H as the symbol of one atom of the gas element hydrogen. However, a stable molecule of hydrogen contains two atoms, thus the symbol for a molecule of hydrogen is H_2. The symbol for a molecule of oxygen is O_2, for nitrogen it is N_2.

Sometimes atoms of different kinds, of two or more elements, become linked together; this results in a molecule of a **compound**. For example, when two atoms of hydrogen (H_2) link up with one atom of oxygen (O) the result is a molecule of H_2O which is water. Water is therefore a compound of two elements.

The particular nature of an atom is determined by the number and arrangement of its electrical charges. At present, it is known that there are 104 different kinds of atoms. A substance, all of whose atoms are alike is called an element. There are 104 elements known to man.

Among the more commonly known elements are:

Element	Natural Form
Hydrogen	Gas
Oxygen	Gas
Nitrogen	Gas
Helium	Gas
Mercury	Liquid
Carbon	Solid
Iron	Solid

All matter is composed of one or more elements. Matter exists in three different states or forms, namely, gas, liquid and solid. Matter includes non-living and living substances. Scientists refer to non-living matter (that which has never been alive) as **inorganic** and to living substances and that which comes from living substances as **organic**. All plants and animals and their products are thus organic.

EXAMPLES OF MATTER

Organic	Inorganic
Blood	Iron
Leather	Glass
Wood	Copper
Meat	Salt
Fur	Phosphorus
Eggs	Rock
Milk	Sand
Coal	

Living things can take inorganic matter from the environment and change it into organic matter. They can change the form or state of matter but never destroy it.

Certain elements form the basis of protoplasm; they are: carbon, oxygen, hydrogen and nitrogen and usually some phosphorus, sulphur and iron. Other elements may be present in small quantities depending on the function of the cells containing these elements. For example, bone cells contain calcium to furnish strength to bone tissue.

Plants and animals get essential elements from the air, from water and from other living or dead plants and animals in the form of food.

In air these elements exist either in free form or in compounds. Air is a mixture of several elements and compounds: namely, oxygen, nitrogen, carbon dioxide (a compound) and water vapour (a compound). The oxygen in air is absolutely essential for all living things and constitutes 20 per cent of the air.

A mixture is the result of the combination of two or more elements or of elements and compounds in such a way that each substance retains its own identity. A compound, on the other hand, is the result of a combination of two or more elements which lose their identity to form a third, new substance. The formation of a compound is a chemical change.

Water, a compound resulting from the chemical union of hydrogen and oxygen, is an essential part of all protoplasm. It exists, within our everyday

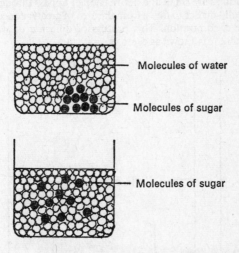

Figure 40   Diffusion—sugar in water

experience, in all three states or forms of matter: as a gas it is water vapour; as a liquid it is water; and as a solid it is ice.

Carbon dioxide, a compound which exists in gas form, is a waste gas given off by both plants and animals during the process of oxidation.

Protoplasm contains other compounds such as proteins, sugars, starches and fats. These compounds contain carbon, hydrogen and oxygen in different proportions. Proteins contain the element nitrogen, the basic element in the formation of protoplasm, in addition to the other three.

Because molecules of matter are always in motion, changes are constantly taking place in all living things and in the environment around them. Some of these changes are physical and others are chemical.

DIFFUSION AND OSMOSIS

Among the physical changes that affect our life functions are the processes of **diffusion** and **osmosis**. As molecules of matter move about (their speed depending on the form of the matter and the temperature surrounding it), they collide with one another constantly. As they move, they tend to spread from an area where they are more concentrated to an area of less concentration. This phenomenon is known as diffusion.

For example, the fragrance of perfume will spread through the air in a room from a drop applied to the hand. The liquid perfume changes to a gas, the molecules of which move away from the concentrated drop and diffuse through the air.

Another example: drop a lump of sugar in a glass of water and note how it seems to disappear after a while. See Fig. 40.

The molecules of sugar move from the concentrated area (the lump) and diffuse through the water. Stirring and heating hasten diffusion.

Water molecules are small and active enough to pass through an extremely thin layer of solid matter to move from the area of greater concentration to the area of lesser concentration. This process of diffusion of water through a selective membrane is known as osmosis.

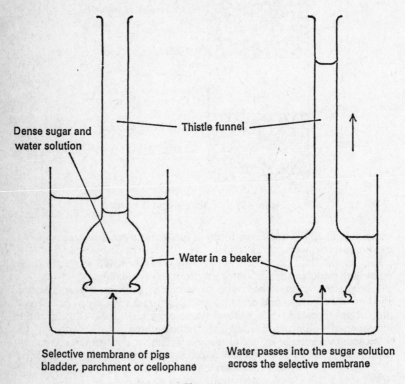

Dense sugar and water solution

Thistle funnel

Water in a beaker

Selective membrane of pigs bladder, parchment or cellophane

Water passes into the sugar solution across the selective membrane

Figure 41

By the combined processes of diffusion and osmosis, cells are able to take in through their thin cell membrane the materials needed for living. By this same method they are able to rid themselves of waste matter which accumulates within the cells. Cell membranes are naturally selective. Only molecules of matter dissolved in water are permitted to pass through.

Just as molecules of sugar move from greater to less concentration, so water on either side of a cell membrane seeks to find a balance of concentration of its molecules. If the concentration of water is less outside the cell than inside, molecules of water pass through the cell membrane to the outside. This may result in the drying out, shrivelling and eventual killing of a cell or tissue.

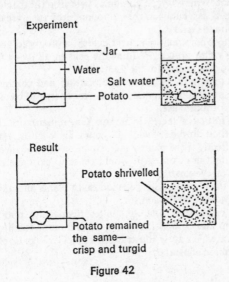

Figure 42

Try this experiment: place one slice of apple or potato in a glass of plain water and another in a glass of water in which a tablespoonful of salt has been dissolved. Let this stand for several hours and then observe the results.

OXIDATION AND ENERGY

Living things can be distinguished from non-living things because the former can carry on certain essential activities within themselves. Protoplasm has the ability, by its very composition, to move about, to take in food, grow, and to reproduce more of its own kind. Non-living things cannot do any of these things without the activating force provided by man. A machine will function only if it is fed fuel by man or some mechanical device provided by man.

Elements and compounds used by living things undergo changes within the plant and animal cells. These essential substances contain stored or potential energy which can be changed into active energy within the cells.

Let us define active energy as the ability to do work. In plants and animals that work is keeping alive. Keeping alive necessitates carrying on all of the life processes successfully.

Chemical changes occur within cell protoplasm that produce the necessary energy to keep alive. The most vital chemical change is **oxidation.**

From the word itself and from what you have learned in previous chapters you will realize that oxidation refers to some activity in which the gas oxygen is involved. In this case, it refers to the combining of oxygen with another substance to produce a compound in which the original substances have lost their original characteristics.

When oxygen combines with the element carbon, the gas compound resulting is carbon dioxide. When oxygen combines with hydrogen, the result is the compound water. When oxygen combines with iron (in the presence of water vapour which acts as a catalyst) the compound iron rust results. We call these resultant compounds oxides.

In each of these combinations, heat energy is produced because oxidation is actually a burning process. Within the cells of all living things oxidation occurs to provide the energy for life's activities.

Animal cells take in oxygen during respiration and combine it with food elements in the process of oxidation to provide energy to be used immediately or to be stored for future use.

The original source of energy is the sun. Green plants are able to manufacture their own food during the sunlight hours. Since animals secure their food directly or indirectly from plants, the original source of their energy is also the sun. All living things on earth would cease to exist therefore, if the sun ceased to shine on the earth.

Thus we see the absolute interdependence of plants and animals, and their combined dependence on the sun.

It has been established that all matter (living and non-living) is used, changed in form and composition, re-used and never totally lost. There are cycles in Nature which aptly illustrate this theory which is referred to as the **Law of Conservation of Matter.**

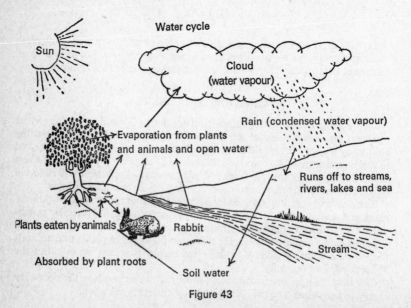

Figure 43

1 The Water Cycle

All plants and animals require water in order to carry on the activities of living. Plants secure water from the ground through their roots. Excess water that is not used by green plants in food manufacturing, is given off into the atmosphere during a process called **transpiration.**

Animals feed directly or indirectly on plants, thus taking in some water. Animals take water vapour from the air and replace it in the atmosphere during the process of breathing. Water is also put back to the soil in the form of liquid waste products.

All water vapour in the atmosphere eventually condenses and finds its way back to the soil where the cycle continues. See Fig. 43.

2 The Oxygen–Carbon Cycle

Animals take in food containing the element carbon, which is oxidized, chemically combined with oxygen from the air to produce energy. The waste gas of this combination is carbon dioxide which is breathed out and returned to the atmosphere.

Green plants take in carbon dioxide from the air around them, turn it back into carbon (an element of the manufactured food) and oxygen and release the

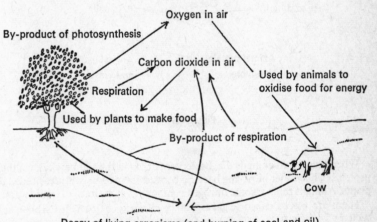

Figure 44   Oxygen—carbon cycle

oxygen into the atmosphere during the process of photosynthesis. Plants also require oxygen from the air for respiration.

Thus the cycle continues.

3 The Nitrogen Cycle

The basic element of all protein is nitrogen. However, neither plants nor animals (other than certain types of bacteria) are able to use the free nitrogen which makes up 79 per cent of the mixture–air. Plants must obtain the necessary nitrogen from compounds (nitrates) dissolved in soil water in order to make their proteins for growth and the repair of damaged tissues.

Animals get nitrogen from plant protein. Man obtains proteins from eating plants and other animals which have in their turn eaten plant proteins.

Nitrogen cycle

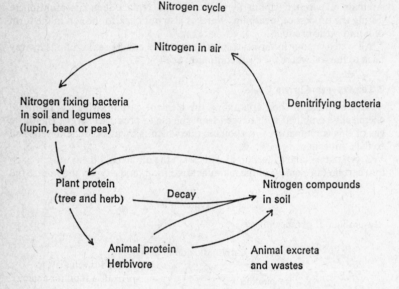

Figure 45

When plants and animals die, bacteria of decay in the soil break down their proteins, while other nitrifying bacteria convert them to the nitrates needed by plants. Animals replace some nitrogen compounds in the form of liquid wastes.

There are plants called **legumes** (lupin, clover, peas) which harbour soil bacteria in their roots (a form of symbiosis). They are the nitrogen-fixing bacteria, and have the ability to change free nitrogen from the soil air into water-soluble nitrates for plant use. There are also free-living bacteria in soil that perform the same function.

Still other denitrifying bacteria break down nitrates releasing nitrogen back into the air. This and the other chemical actions carried out by bacteria are ways in which they obtain their own energy.

BALANCE IN NATURE

One way to better understand the interdependence of plants and animals and the various cycles in nature which provide a balance of life is to build a balanced aquarium.

Get a fish tank or gallon glass jar. Fill the tank with clean pond water, clean sand and pebbles to cover the bottom. Anchor several green water plants in the sand. Add two or three goldfish and a few small snails. Cover the top of the tank with a fitted glass plate and seal it. Place the aquarium where it will get daylight, and some sun, but never in direct sunlight.

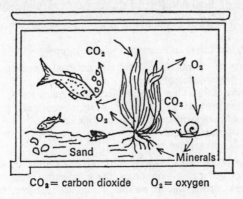

CO_2 = carbon dioxide O_2 = oxygen

Figure 46 Balanced aquarium

Both plants and animals should live and thrive successfully because:

1 The fish and snails breathe out carbon dioxide as a result of oxidation of food.

2 The green plants use this carbon dioxide (CO_2) to manufacture food (photosynthesis) and give off oxygen for the animals to breathe in.

3 The fish and snails eat the plants and give off liquid wastes containing nitrates, which the plants use to make into proteins.

4 The snails eat solid waste matter excreted by the fish (snails act as scavengers).

5 Sunlight provides the original source of energy.

The various cycles in nature provide a true balance of life which could perhaps exist for many ages—barring natural disasters such as freak weather conditions, floods, earthquakes and volcanic eruptions.

Unfortunately man, either through ignorance, carelessness, or ruthlessness has often upset the balance of life in a given area.

Examples of man's misuse of the environment:

1 Cutting down large forests, for economic motives, without adequate replanting.

2 Destruction of forests by careless fires.

3 Uncontrolled diseases or blights on trees and other plants.

4 Loss of their natural habitats (e.g. forest land) results in extinction of animal inhabitants, sometimes entire species.

5 Overworking farm and pasture lands resulting in barren and loose soil which is then subject to erosion by wind and rain.

6 Introduction of foreign insects and birds to control native insect scourges without proper control resulting in over-population of introduced animal.

7 Destruction of fish and other water animals and valuable water plants by over-fishing without planned restocking.

8 Careless contamination of waters with oil, sewage and industrial wastes resulting in unhealthy surroundings for water life.

9 Uncontrolled use of pesticides.

10 Pollution of the atmosphere by smoke, car fumes and industrial waste.

Efforts have been made in the past and are being made now to restore the balance of nature.

Among the preventative and curative measures are:

1 Education of the public by local and national agencies, and societies set up for the preservation of nature.

2 Replanting of forest lands and protection of young trees.

3 Game laws protecting wild life in forests, streams, and public parks.

4 Conservation of farmland soil by scientific farming.

5 Control of plant diseases.

6 Control of natural insect enemies.

The more the public is made aware of the causes and means of prevention of destruction of our natural resources, the greater the tendency will be to avoid the dangers. Preserving our natural wealth will help keep the balance of nature intact.

SUMMARY

Everything which exists is matter. Matter is that which occupies space and has weight.

The simplest form of matter is the element.

The smallest component part of all matter is the atom.

Compounds contain stored energy which can be released by chemical changes.

Elements combine physically to form mixtures and chemically to form compounds.

There are at present 104 known elements.

Plants and animals secure elements essential for living from the air, water, soil, and other plants and animals.

Oxidation, a burning process which occurs in organic and inorganic matter, results in the production of energy for work, heat and light.

The cycles in nature, when uninterrupted, maintain the balance of life.

The sun is the original and ultimate source of all energy.

VOCABULARY

matter	compound	inorganic
atom	oxidation	nitrates
molecule	transpiration	potential energy
element	diffusion	legume
mixture	osmosis	protein
	organic	

Exercise No. 15

Complete the following sentences:

1 Matter is characterized as anything which —— and ——.

2 The simplest form of matter is an ——.

3 The smallest part of any form of matter is the ——.
4 Diffusion is an example of a —— change.
5 A combination of two or more elements without loss of original characteristics results in a ——.
6 During a chemical change —— is released.
7 The compound water results from the chemical combination of the gases —— and ——.
8 The chemical symbol for water is ——; for carbon dioxide is ——.
9 There are —— elements known to man.
10 The three forms in which matter exists are ——, ——, and ——.

Exercise No. 16

Write paragraphs explaining:

1 The ways in which the amounts of oxygen and carbon dioxide are maintained in the atmosphere.
2 The importance of the various types of bacteria in soil.
3 The water cycle.

Exercise No. 17

Match a number in Column *A* with a letter in Column *B*.

A	B
1 sun	a protect wild life
2 carbon dioxide	b element essential to protoplasm
3 oxidation	c wearing away of top soil
4 soil erosion	d ultimate source of all energy
5 game laws	e compound necessary for building protoplasm
6 nitrogen	f release of water vapour by green plant
7 energy	g waste gas
8 legumes	h burning
9 protein	i ability to do work
10 transpiration	j nitrogen-fixing bacteria

CHAPTER VI

THE PLANT KINGDOM: NON-FLOWERING PLANTS

The plant kingdom has been divided by botanists into four major groups. The simplest of these is called **Thallophytes** (Greek: *thallos*, a young shoot, and *phyton*, a plant). Plants in this group do not have true roots, stems, leaves, flowers or seeds; they include the **algae** and **fungi**. Many of them are one-celled; some grow in chains or colonies of cells. Bacteria are difficult to classify and are often included in the plant kingdom.

CHARACTERISTICS AND DISTRIBUTION OF ALGAE

With few exceptions the algae are water-dwelling plants, found growing in seas, lakes, rivers and ponds and also on land, usually in damp places. These simple plants are entirely self-sufficient in their watery habitats. They all contain chlorophyll with which to manufacture food. Although the green colour bodies are always present, they are often masked by other pigments so

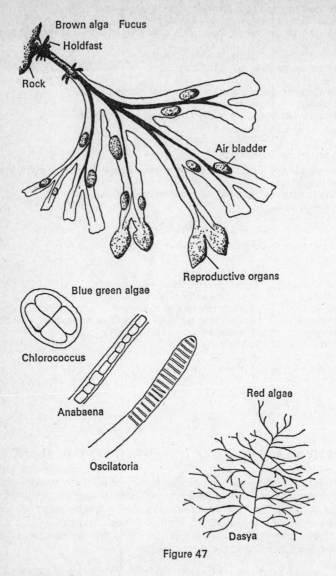

Figure 47

that some appear bluish-green, some brown and others red. Most of the blue-green algae have no visible nuclei; the nuclear material seems to be scattered evenly in the cell protoplasm. Of other types, some are single-celled, some multicellular, and both sexual and asexual methods of reproduction are of general occurrence.

The cell walls of most forms enclose the soft cell protoplasm and cell membranes to provide the characteristic shapes of most algae. Others, like the diatoms and desmids, are enclosed in chalk-like or glass-like (silica) shells.

Some algae float on the surface of water, some under water. Some attach themselves to other plants and still others are provided with independent means of locomotion. They live in enormous numbers in both fresh and salt water of every temperature and nature, providing the primary source of food for aquatic animal life. Fish in ponds, streams, rivers and lakes are nourished by algae native to their habitats.

TYPES OF ALGAE

A few types of algae grow out of water but require a great deal of moisture to exist successfully. The most common of these is the microscopic Pleurococcus. They grow in large colonies and appear as light green mossy-like growths on the damp surfaces of tree trunks, stones and walls, especially where there is much wet weather and little direct sunshine.

When you come upon such a growth, flat and tight against a rock or tree, scrape some off. If possible, examine a bit in a drop of water on a glass slide under a microscope. You will see the individual green cells or groups of cells growing independently but together.

We have already mentioned the land-living algae which make up part of the symbiotic relationship of the lichens. These provide food and oxygen for their fungus hosts and receive water, protection and anchorage in exchange.

Among the best known fresh water algae are those that are known as pond scum. These appear to be slimy masses of tangled green threads. Spirogyra is the green algae responsible for this growth. Each thread consists of a linear arrangement of cylindrical cells, each containing a spiral, ribbon-like band of chlorophyll and a definite nucleus which is held in place by bands of protoplasm. See Fig. 48.

They form masses of slimy plant growth on the surface of ponds or sluggish streams and also on tree stumps or rocks submerged under the water.

This scum is found in pools that have not been scraped or cleaned for a long period of time. Chlorine added to pools prevents the growth of Spirogyra in well-kept swimming pools.

Occasionally, towards the end of the summer, a reservoir has an unpleasant, fishy odour and taste. This may be due to decaying green and blue-green algae which have managed to get a foothold along the rocky sides or bottom of the reservoir.

Extremely hardy types of algae live in the hot spring waters in Yellowstone National Park in America.

Seaweeds are algae. Although comparatively simple in structure, they are far more complex than the one-celled or colonial types. They are many-celled, often of large dimensions and show a marked division of labour (specialized cells forming tissues to carry out individual functions). Seaweeds may be green, brown or red and are found under water, floating on the surface or growing between tide marks. The Red Sea earns its name from the myriad red algae which float on its surface. Red algae living among coral reefs in tropic waters produce lime salts that the tiny coral animals use to build their coral homes into reefs and islands.

Agar Agar, used in some medication and in laboratories as the basis of the gelatin-like food substance in which bacterial cultures are grown, comes from a species of red algae growing round the Pacific Ocean.

Some brown algae grow to considerable sizes and are extremely useful to man. Off the coasts of France and Ireland, huge fronds of kelp, reaching a

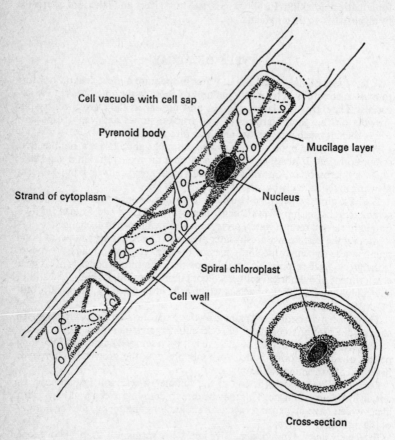

Figure 48   Spirogyra (common pond scum)

length of 50–60 feet, were at one time pulled from their rocky attachments and burned to yield potassium and iodine in the resulting ash.

Sea lettuce (Ulva) is another large, tough, branching green alga that is often washed up on beaches. One type is used as food in Japan and China.

The famous Sargasso Sea derives its name from floating brown algae, **Sargassum,** that float on the surface for hundreds of square miles. It is in this sea, near Bermuda, that eels come from their natural river habitats, thousands of miles away, to spawn (lay their eggs). The young eels then swim back to the rivers to live and mate.

One of the most interesting groups of algae is the tiny **diatoms.** Their jewel-like appearance is due to the glassy shell (silica) that encloses the soft proto-plasm cell. They are usually bi-symmetrical, the two parts of the shell fitting together like a minute box, each side appearing to be delicately carved and traced. Diatoms reproduce by simple fission: the two parts separate, each half completing its box and maturing as a separate individual diatom.

Large deposits of diatom shells (now diatomaceous earth) have been found along the coast of California. They have been mined and used as a basis for polishing and scouring powders, as filters in bacteriological studies and in special kinds of glass and porcelain.

Diatoms serve as an important source of food for oysters. They also form a large part of the organic material called plankton which floats near the sur-face of oceans. Plankton is a conglomerate of diatoms, other algae, protozoa, fish eggs and even small jellyfish. Indirectly, plankton is of great value to man, for it serves as the main source of nourishment for fish and other sea-living animals.

Jules Verne, in his story *Twenty Thousand Leagues Under the Sea*, predicted that men could live on the microscopic life of the sea. The brave adventurers on the now famous *Kon-Tiki* strained plankton from the rich surrounding waters and made a nourishing meal. In Japan, scientists have been studying methods of securing large enough quantities of plankton, studying methods of separating, preparing and preserving it for use in the Japanese daily diet. The sea would yield a rich source of food for the world's growing population.

MOSSES AND LIVERWORTS

A more advanced form of division of labour appears among the mosses and liverworts. These plants are many-celled, the cells divided into groups with specialized functions. In this group appear simple stems and leaves. Roots serve only for anchorage; they are not true roots because they lack conducting tubes through which water is conducted to the rest of the plant.

Mosses and liverworts are a step closer to the most advanced type of plants known as the true flowering plants. They grow mostly on moist, shaded ground, on tree trunks in thick forests, in crevices of rocks and on old de-cayed pieces of wood.

There are at least 14,000 varieties of mosses known at present. They grow successfully in every type of habitat where there is moisture. Mosses have been found growing abundantly on high mountains, in the Arctic regions, and some even in fresh water. One variety has been discovered covering the bottom of a two-hundred-foot-deep lake in Switzerland.

Moss plants grow low and thick on moist ground forming a soft, spongy carpet. The plant has a short stem, small green leaves and roots that are called **rhizoids.** The stem differs from more advanced plants in that it does not con-tain any woody tissue and contains only a little chlorophyll. Since the leaves contain the chlorophyll they act as the food manufacturing centre for the entire plant.

Pigeon Wheat, one of the more common leafy mosses, is given that name because the upright spore cases resemble miniature wheat spears. See Fig. 49.

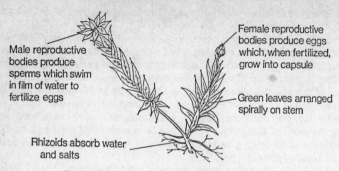

Male reproductive
bodies produce
sperms which swim
in film of water to
fertilize eggs

Female reproductive
bodies produce eggs
which, when fertilized,
grow into capsule

Green leaves arranged
spirally on stem

Rhizoids absorb water
and salts

Figure 49   Life cycle of moss (sexual stage)

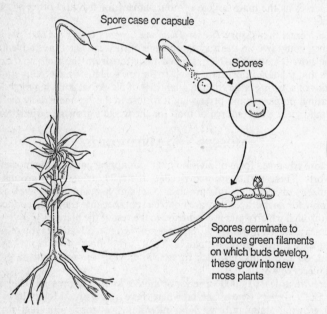

Spore case or capsule

Spores

Spores germinate to
produce green filaments
on which buds develop,
these grow into new
moss plants

Figure 50   Life cycle of moss (asexual stage)

Liverworts, dark green in colour, are similar in nature to the mosses, but they are liver-shaped and grow mat-like on moist shady ground, on old tree trunks and, like lichens, on rocks that are constantly wet. They have no true roots, nor woody stem tissues, but a thallus-like body which may be divided into leaf-like lobes.

In the life history of mosses and liverworts we find a considerable advancement over the algae. Algae and related single-celled plants reproduce mostly by simple fission. In some forms spores are produced. In others, Spirogyra and some seaweeds, there is an exchange of nuclear material between male and female cells resulting in sexual reproduction.

The process of reproduction in mosses and liverworts begins to take on complexity due to specialization of cells. There are two periods in the life cycle. During the asexual stage, spores that develop into new plants are produced in spore cases. During the sexual stage the male reproductive body produces male cells which combine with the female cells (eggs) to form fertilized eggs. The fertilized egg grows into the spore-bearing structure that produces spores which grow into new plants. This sequence of asexual and sexual methods of reproduction is known as alternation of generations. See Fig. 50.

Mosses serve mankind well. They prevent erosion or wearing away of soil by the thick close-knit carpet they form. In this way they also prevent great evaporation of moisture from the ground. Because their root-like structures grow into rocks little pieces of rock break off and form particles of soil, thus aiding in soil formation. Dead and decaying moss plants add to soil fertility and richness.

Peat mosses that grow so profusely in swampy areas, eventually fill up swamps and result in more land surface. Layers of peat are formed, after long periods of time, that can be used in place of coal as fuel. There are extensive peat bogs in Ireland and in the northern part of America. Gardeners use peat moss to retain the moisture in the soil and to improve it.

You can build a terrarium for amusement in a former fish tank or in a large glass jar. Collect clumps of different varieties of mosses from a moist, local wooded area and place them on stones in the bottom of the glass enclosure. Keep your moss garden well watered, covered with a glass plate, to prevent drying, and in the shade. Observe the life histories of these delicate plants.

FERNS

Modern ferns and their relatives show a further advance in development of plants from the mosses and liverworts. In addition to leaves and stems, they have true roots and a conductive system through which water rises from the ground and is distributed to the rest of the plant. The most noticeable part of ferns are the leaves or fronds—most of the stems (called **rhizomes**) grow underground in the form of horizontal runners from which fibre-like roots extend farther into the soil.

Ferns and related plants also grow best in moist soil with little direct sunshine. In tropical countries, ferns grow to huge sizes and sometimes dominate a habitat.

Horsetails alone seem to be renegades from their moisture and shade-loving relatives. They may be found growing successfully along railway lines in a sandy open area. Their roots grow down deep in the soil until they find water. See Fig. 51.

The life history of the fern is very similar to that of the moss family, with characteristic alternation of sexual and asexual generations. In ferns, however, the asexual generation is the more prominent growth (the frond), the sexual generation being a small leaf-like growth, next to the ground, which bears both male and female reproductive bodies.

Examine the back of a fern frond and notice small reddish or brown spots.

These spots are spore cases which contain thousands of tiny spores, each of which is a potential fern plant.

At one time, horsetails, because of their glass-like outer covering, were used as scouring materials. At present, ferns are used by florists, and club moss is used for making decorative wreaths. The spores of some club mosses are sometimes used to coat pills to prevent moisture from dissolving the medication and to prevent them from sticking together.

The fern family has a history that dates back to prehistoric ages. The study of old rock formations of fossils and coal beds shows us that ferns grew large and lush as tropical trees.

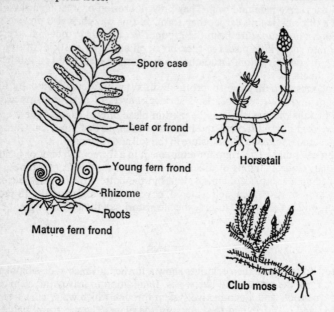

Figure 51 Ferns and their relatives

When our earth was in its infancy, the climate was very hot and humid. As the earth grew older, the climate changed and the huge fern forests died. Aeons of time, extreme heat and the pressure of dead and decaying vegetation and massive animals (dinosaurs and other gigantic reptiles) plus the weight of rock and soil caused decay and deterioration. The final disintegration of organic matter resulted in our rich coal beds, petroleum veins and pockets of natural gas.

BACTERIA

Bacteria are an abundant, widespread and prolific family of one-celled plants. They live everywhere—in air, water, milk, even in the human body.

Bacteria are commonly despised because they are best known as causes of disease. However, there are many which are directly and indirectly useful to man, and some actually necessary for life's activities.

Since they are visible under the microscope, bacteria have been seen to have various and distinct shapes. Some have no powers of locomotion, and are carried from place to place by air, by water and other liquids, and by plants and animals. Others have, like protozoa, projections of protoplasm called **cilia** and **flagella** with which they move about in a liquid medium.

Here are diagrams of three common shapes (with variations) of bacteria:

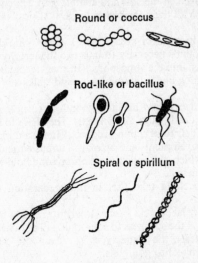

Round or coccus

Rod-like or bacillus

Spiral or spirillum

Figure 52 Types of bacteria

Bacteria, being living cells, must carry on all life processes. Characteristically, as plant cells they have a cell wall which surrounds a cell membrane. Their basic internal structure is difficult to study even under the microscope, because the nuclear material is scattered in, and looks like part of, the cytoplasm of the cell.

Under favourable conditions, they reproduce by binary fission (splitting in half after maximum growth). Most get their food from other plants and animals; a few are autotrophic (can synthesise their own carbohydrates).

Conditions favourable to growth and reproduction of bacteria are:

1 Moisture
2 Oxygen in some form
3 Suitable temperature
4 Lack of direct sunlight
5 Prepared food
6 Proper chemical environment

Opposite conditions are unfavourable for the growth of bacteria.

There are some hardy forms of bacteria which adapt themselves to withstand unfavourable conditions, some times temporarily and sometimes for many years. Their cell walls become very hard, developing into spore cases or cysts. The protoplasm of the cell within the spore case is quiescent until conditions are favourable again. In some measure, it resembles the bear, who hibernates during the long, cold, unfavourable winter.

USEFUL BACTERIA

Let us consider first in detail the useful bacteria—useful to man directly or indirectly.

Some bacteria nourish and replenish the soil. In the previous chapter, we mentioned nitrogen-fixing bacteria, which specialize in transforming the air's free nitrogen in the soil into soluble nitrogen compounds (nitrates) for plants to use. With them the plants make first proteins and later, protoplasm.

There are also bacteria of decay, useful in breaking down dead organic matter into compounds necessary to improve the fertility of the soil, and to release free nitrogen into the atmosphere. Farmers recognize the work of these bacteria by ploughing under unused leaves and stalks and by adding manure to the soil.

The bacteria of decay serve also to prevent our earth from being physically overcrowded with dead plants and animals. They help to restore the balance of life in nature. Their total action produces **humus**, a dark-coloured material resulting from decayed plants and animals. Humus enriches the soil, forms a spongy top layer which can hold air and absorb and hold water, and prevents wind erosion of the soil.

Other helpful bacteria take part in the preparation of some of man's foods.

Bacteria in milk, lactic acid bacteria, when properly controlled, give the colour to butter and the sourness to sour milk. All our cheeses are ripened by the action of bacteria, the bland types of cheese and the malodorous, the flavour of which appeal to gourmets.

Other foods are prepared by bacteria: meat may be tenderized by the action of bacteria which break down the tougher muscle fibres. Vinegar is produced by acetic acid bacteria which act upon fermented fruit juices, ciders and wines. Sauerkraut is the result of bacterial action causing fermentation on shredded cabbage which has been salted and pressed tightly.

Linen fibres are produced when bacteria consume the soft parts of the flax plant, a process called retting, so that the fibres can be separated, cured, washed and made into linen threads. Natural sponges result from bacterial action on the soft animal bodies within the fibre-like colonies, leaving only the communal outer structure, the part we know as sponge. Some bacteria aid in the tanning of leather by separating the flesh from the skins. Other bacteria assist in the curing of tobacco.

Within the bodies of living animals, bacteria are also helpfully active. In the intestines of cows, sheep and other animals that chew the cud (ruminating animals) bacteria help break down the cell walls of grasses so that the animals can better digest their food.

HARMFUL BACTERIA

At one time the extremely numerous harmful bacteria were the scourge of mankind. Since the use of the microscope and the development of laboratory techniques, scientists have been able to recognize, isolate and control most of these destructive plants.

Among them are bacteria of decay, mentioned above, which have a split personality. On the one hand, they keep nature's balance by decomposing dead plants and animals and restoring elements to the atmosphere and to the earth. On the other hand, their decaying action produces toxins, or poisons, which are harmful and sometimes even fatal to man.

Proper refrigeration, canning, salting, smoking and dehydrating are methods used to prevent decay of foods by bacteria.

Decay bacteria working on food particles left in teeth, cause dental caries (cavities).

Bacteria which cause diseases in man are referred to as pathogenic. Each type of pathogenic bacteria has a specific entrance to the body, and a specific reaction in the body. The results may be the destruction of certain tissues and/or the production of toxins which affect a local organ, a specific system or the entire body.

The body has natural defences against invasion of disease-producing organisms. One such is its millions of white blood cells. Another is an army of antibodies developed in the blood after the bacteria enter the body.

Diseases caused by pathogenic bacteria are: diphtheria, tuberculosis, typhoid, pneumonia, tetanus, whooping cough, septic sore throats, skin acne boils and venereal diseases.

FUNGI

The fungi comprise the simplest sub-group or class of Thallophytes. Plants belonging to this group do not contain chlorophyll and cannot manufacture their own food. Thus they must get their food from other plants or animals. Those that get food at the expense of living things are known as **parasites;** if from dead organisms, they are called **saprophytes.**

YEAST

One form of fungus plant with which we are familiar is yeast. If a microscope is available to you, you can see the structure of yeast cells and actually watch the plant in the process of reproduction by budding.

Buy a small yeast cake, the kind used in baking, at the grocer. (One ounce of brewer's yeast contains about five billion cells.) Break off a small piece and place it in a glass of warm water in which a spoonful of sugar has been dissolved. Place this on a radiator or in some warm part of the room. After an hour, put a drop of the solution on a glass slide, and observe under low power of the microscope. You will see the structures in Fig. 53.

Yeast cells carry on all life functions except the process of locomotion. Since they have no chlorophyll, they obtain food elsewhere. They produce **enzymes** (chemical catalysts) which digest their food outside the cells. Digested food enters into the cell by the process of diffusion through the cell membrane. Yeast cells require oxygen, as do all other living cells, and give off carbon dioxide and water vapour through the cell membrane.

These simple plants reproduce by budding. The mother cell grows to capacity; then the nucleus divides in two, and a small bud (the daughter cell) appears. This may remain attached to the mother cell or split off to form an individual cell and reproduce itself by budding. Yeast cells sometimes encase themselves as spores until favourable conditions arise.

Yeast cells can also respire anaerobically without the presence of oxygen.

In this case their energy comes from the breakdown of sugars, aided by an enzyme called **zymase**, resulting in the production of carbon dioxide and alcohol. The bubbles that appear on the surface of your yeast mixture are bubbles of carbon dioxide. This process is known as fermentation and is made use of by man in the manufacture of wines, beer and bread.

Yeast causes bread or cake dough that is placed in a warm spot to rise before baking. Warmth and the presence of sugar stimulate rapid growth and

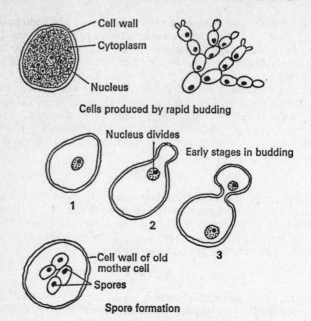

Cells produced by rapid budding

Spore formation

Figure 53 Growing and budding yeast cells

reproduction of the yeast cells. Bubbles of carbon dioxide fill the dough and make it rise, making bread or cake lighter in texture. Wine and beer industries depend on yeast to produce the necessary alcoholic content by fermentation of fruit juices, hops or barley.

RUSTS AND SMUTS

Another family of fungus plants is commonly known as organic rusts and smuts: rusts because they produce reddish spores, and smuts because their spores are black. The term organic is used here to differentiate plant rust from inorganic iron rust.

These fungi are a serious menace to farmers because they live on and damage such grain plants as corn, wheat and oats.

One reason that these plant diseases are difficult to control is that the fungi form spores which withstand unfavourable conditions for a long time. But a second reason is a more terrible one: the harmful rust fungus may have an alternate host. By that, we mean that it spends part of its life cycle on another plant; for example, the wheat rust lives part of its life on the common barberry bush.

Control of these parasitic fungi has been the object of much research. Spraying crops may be effective in some cases. Where alternate hosts are needed, these must be destroyed to deprive the fungus of one medium necessary for its life cycle. Recently, varieties of wheat have been bred which are rust-resistant.

MOULDS AND MILDEWS

Moulds and mildews affect our daily lives. These fungi are small, but visible to the naked eye. If you have never inspected carefully the common bread or fruit mould, set up the following home experiment.

Moisten a slice of bread, put it on a piece of wax paper or on a saucer, cover it with a wide-mouthed glass or jar (to keep the moisture from escaping into the air) and put it in a warm place for several days. Do the same with a piece of apple.

You will observe small black knob-like structures on top of fine stalks growing up from the bread. You will also see a thread-like mass spreading and clinging to the surface. Cut or break a piece of the bread and you will observe these thin, colourless filaments growing down into the bread.

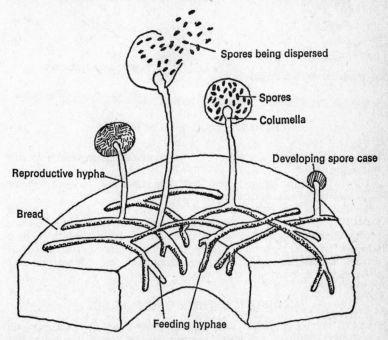

Figure 54 Bread mould

The whole tangle of threads is called a **mycelium,** and each individual thread a **hypha.** Most of these hyphae are concerned with nutrition of the fungus. They spread through the food source, producing enzymes to digest starch and other foods, thus causing gradual decay of the substratum. Digested foods are absorbed into the fungal threads. Some of the hyphae grow upwards and develop spore cases at their tips. These are the tiny black spots you can see. Each contains hundreds of minute spores which are set free and carried by currents of air. If they should land on a suitable food source, each

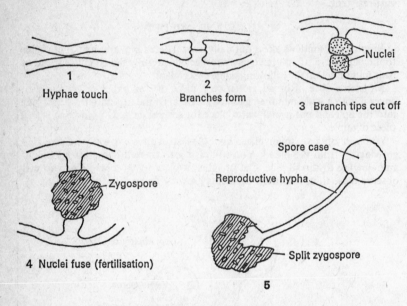

1
Hyphae touch

2
Branches form

3 Branch tips cut off
Nuclei

4 Nuclei fuse (fertilisation)
Zygospore

5
Spore case
Reproductive hypha
Split zygospore

Figure 55 Conjugation in bread mould

spore will develop into a new growth. The mould can also reproduce sexually by conjugation.

Observe the same for the piece of fruit. The mould may be green, because different types of moulds require different foods.

Moulds, as well as bacteria, are both harmful to man and useful. Harmful varieties spoil food, rot clothing (left damp over a period of time) and some cause diseases in man. Among the latter are the moulds which produce athlete's foot and ringworm. Useful varieties grow on cheeses such as Roquefort and Danish Blue, Camembert, Brie, Gorgonzola, etc., giving them their characteristic flavour.

ANTIBIOTICS: THE WONDER DRUGS

In 1929 an eminent British scientist, ALEXANDER FLEMING, was working on a laboratory culture of pathogenic bacteria. By chance the spores of a blue-green mould settled and grew on the culture. Fleming observed that the mould prevented the growth of the bacteria in the culture. He also found that certain streptococci bacteria which produce toxins in man were killed by the mould.

It was not until the Second World War that this information was brought to light again and put to practical use.

Great quantities of the drug **penicillin** made from this blue-green mould were then and are now produced and used to combat such diseases as pneumonia, boils and carbuncles, blood poisoning (septicemia), burn infections, venereal diseases, epidemic meningitis and several other diseases.

Since the success of penicillin, scientists have been discovering other antibiotics, some prepared from moulds and others from certain soil bacteria. An American called WAKSMAN produced the drug **streptomycin** which he made from soil bacteria. It has been used effectively in the control and cure of tuberculosis and other pulmonary (respiratory) diseases, whooping cough, meningitis, influenza and infections of the urinary tract (liquid waste system of the body).

Many more antibiotics are being discovered, each with the ability either to inhibit or destroy some disease-producing organism. See Chapter XIII.

In the early days of antibiotics there was a tendency for them to be used indiscriminately. In Britain, however, they can only be obtained through a doctor's prescription, and the medical profession is fully aware that over-use of antibiotics may do considerable harm and may even prove fatal. Constant use may result in the building-up of a tolerance for the drugs by the body, thus making them ineffective against the specific disease for which they may be needed at a future time.

Antibiotics have been known to produce allergic reactions such as a skin rash, or other unpleasant conditions.

MUSHROOMS

Another type of fungus, more familiar to us, is the mushroom and its relatives. Mushrooms sometimes grow to considerable size, but their structure is simple in spite of this. It consists of a mass of hyphal threads, the mycelium

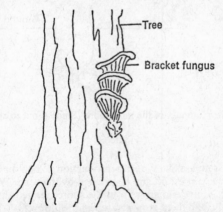

Figure 56 Shelf or bracket fungus

similar in form to that found in the moulds. This serves as an anchorage and as a means of digesting and absorbing food.

Most mushrooms are saprophytes: that is, they live on dead plants. A few, like shelf-fungi, which can be seen growing on the sides of trees, are parasitic. They get their nourishment from the living tree to which they are attached.

Moisture, shade, cool temperatures and the presence of dead organic material provide the ideal living conditions for mushrooms.

Most mushrooms are tan to brown in colour. Some species are vivid red and orange, and answer the fairy-tale descriptions in size as well as hue; others are yellow or white.

Common mushrooms have two distinct parts: an umbrella-shaped cap and a supporting stalk. On the underside of the cap are soft, slit-like tissues called gills.

Reproduction is by means of spores which are produced by special reproductive bodies called **sporangia** (singular: -ium) which develop on the surfaces

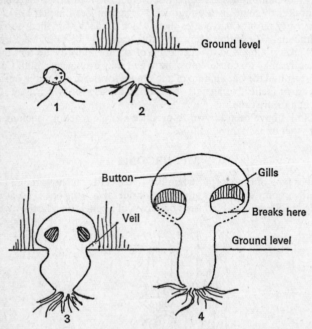

Stages in development of the mushroom (3 and 4 cut to show gills)

Figure 57

of the gills. This is an asexual type of reproduction. When the spores are fully developed, they are nipped off and distributed by the wind. When conditions are favourable, new mycelia grow from the spores, attach themselves to the future food supply, and there grow and repeat the life cycle.

Puffballs, close relatives, do not have exposed gills. They develop spores inside their ball-shaped structures, which burst when ripe and disseminate (scatter or spread abroad) small clouds of spores.

There are as many as sixty-three varieties of edible mushrooms. They produce black spores. Inedible and highly poisonous types are commonly referred to as toadstools, but this is not a scientific term. The most deadly mushroom, the **Amanita** (meaning death cup) looks a great deal like its edible

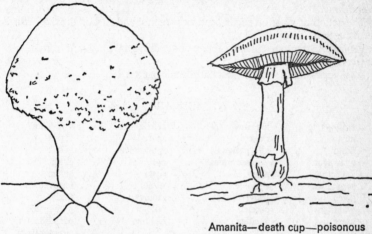

Figure 58 The puffball

Amanita—death cup—poisonous

Figure 59

cousin. Careful observation, however, shows a difference in external structure. In the poisonous one, there is a definite cup-like structure at the base of its supporting stalk and a fleshy collar or ring just below its smooth grey or smoky brown cap. The reproductive spores are always white. Another type of Amanita has a warty bright yellow-orange surface on its cap. This beautiful but fatal plant is deadly to flies as well as to human beings.

Since it is most difficult to tell growing edible and fatally poisonous mushrooms apart, it is wise not to try eating the ones you find in the field. Buy them from a reputable shop. Commercial mushrooms are isolated when grown, and therefore controlled.

SUMMARY

Thallophyte is the name given to the simplest plant group, including algae and fungi.

Algae are found in both fresh and salt water. They are independent plants containing chlorophyll with which they manufacture their own food, and may reproduce sexually or asexually. In this group we find the beginning of division of labour. Algae are the main source of food for fish and other water-living animals. Plankton is a combination of algae, protozoa, fish eggs and small jellyfish.

Mosses and liverworts are green plants which show an advance in structure over algae. They have true leaves and stems and root-like anchoring structures. Their life cycle shows alternation of generations.

Modern ferns show advance over mosses in greater specialization of tissues and functions. They also exhibit alternation of generations in their life history. Prehistoric fern trees and other similar vegetation are responsible for our present coal deposits.

Fungi do not contain chlorophyll. They include bacteria, yeasts, rusts and smuts, moulds and mushrooms.

Bacteria may be useful or harmful. Disease-producing bacteria are called pathogenic.

The action of yeast on sugar produces alcohol and carbon dioxide. This is fermentation.

Penicillin, streptomycin and other wonder drugs are produced from moulds and certain bacteria.

Antibiotics are used to combat pathogenic bacteria.

VOCABULARY

thallophyte	liverwort	spirillum	mycelium
algae	rhizoid	spore	hypha
fungi	alternation of	sporangium	gills
agar agar	generations	cyst	antibodies
sea lettuce	peat	rusts	humus
sargassum	rhizome	smuts	fermentation
silica	frond	moulds	toxins
plankton	coccus	mildew	pathogenic
moss	bacillus	budding	penicillin
			streptomycin

Exercise No. 18

Complete the following statements:

1 Brown algae are able to manufacture their own food because they contain——.
2 The Sargasso Sea gets its name from the —— which float near the surface.
3 The chief source of food of all fish is ——.
4 Lichens exhibit a —— relationship between a fungus and green ——.
5 Among the best known water algae are those commonly known as ——.
6 Large, leaf-like algae that grow in the ocean, from which iodine and potassium are abstracted, are called ——.
7 The product of red algae that is used in laboratories for raising bacteria cultures is called ——.
8 Large deposits of —— are used in special kinds of porcelain.
9 Scientists are investigating the means of preparing —— found in sea water as food for man.
10 Pond scum may be cleared out of swimming pools by the addition of ——.
11 The common green alga that has a spiral, ribbon-like chlorophyll body is ——.

Exercise No. 19

Match a number in Column *A* with a letter in Column *B*.

A	*B*
1 rhizoids	a asexual reproduction
2 moss	b pigeon wheat
3 life history	c leaf of fern
4 peat	d roots of moss
5 rhizomes	e alternation of generations
6 frond	f related to ferns

7	coal	g liver-shaped leaf structures
8	liverwort	h moss used for fuel
9	horsetail	i horizontal, underground stems
10	spores	j originally prehistoric fern forests

Exercise No. 20

Select the correct word or phrase for each of the following:

For example:
1 The disease called athlete's foot is caused by (a) fly bite; (b) perspiration; (c) a mould; (d) bacteria.
Answer: (c).
2 The poisons produced in the body by bacteria are called: (a) toxins; (b) drugs; (c) wastes; (d) chemicals.
3 A scientist associated with antibiotics is: (a) Brown; (b) Fleming; (c) Leeuwenhoek; (d) Koch.
4 The best method of preserving foods against decay is: (a) baking; (b) covering; (c) keeping them in the dark; (d) refrigeration.
5 Moulds reproduce by: (a) budding; (b) spore formation; (c) binary fission.
6 In the process of fermentation yeast produces: (a) sugar; (b) oxygen; (c) nitrogen; (d) alcohol.
7 Since mushrooms get their food from dead organic matter, they are known as: (a) saprophytes; (b) pests; (c) scavengers; (d) parasites.
8 All bacteria are: (a) pathogenic; (b) found in milk; (c) fungi; (d) without definite nuclei.
9 Bread dough rises because of the action of: (a) heat; (b) kneading; (c) bacteria; (d) yeast.

Exercise No. 21

1 What conditions are unfavourable for bacteria?
2 What is penicillin?
3 Explain how yeast makes dough rise.
4 Name three diseases of man caused by bacteria.
5 What is humus and what is its value?
6 How does bread mould: (a) feed; (b) reproduce?

CHAPTER VII

SEED-BEARERS

The most advanced plants in the Plant Kingdom are known as the true seed plants. In this group, division of labour is highly organized, each well-developed structure having its specialized function. The main parts of all such plants are roots, stems (trunks and branches in tree forms), leaves, seed-producing organs, and seeds. The conducting system, better called the **vascular system,** is highly efficient, penetrating to all parts of the plants. The plants reproduce by means of seeds.

CONIFERS

The group is divided into two subdivisions. The first embraces the conifers (pine, fir, hemlock, spruce, etc.) which are characterized by needle-like leaves and cones in which naked seeds are produced. See Fig. 60.

There are male cell-producing cones (**staminate** cones) and female egg-producing cones (**pistillate** cones). Early in the spring, when the male and female reproductive cells are mature, the cones on the conifers grow upright with

Conifers—Cone bearers

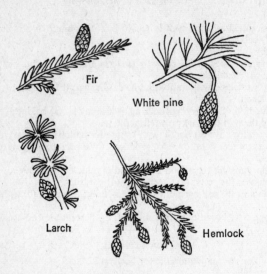

Fir

White pine

Larch

Hemlock

Figure 60

the scales open. The wind carries the male cells (pollen) to the receptive female cells (eggs) which remain in their cones, located on the inside of each individual scale on a female cone.

The union of pollen cell with egg cell (fertilization) results in a fertilized egg. After fertilization of most egg cells, the scales close up, and the cones turn down. When the cones are two years old, the fertilized eggs have developed into seeds. Then the scales open, and the seeds drop out and are scattered by the wind (dissemination). Each seed that finds favourable growing conditions will grow into a new tree.

The common cone-bearing trees, or conifers, are found in both temperate and cold climates—some even in hot swampy lands. The largest and most varied coniferous forests of the world are found in the western part of the North American continent, and in Scandinavia.

Most conifers keep their leaves all year long. Some, like the bald cypress and larch, lose their leaves in the autumn. The size and shape of the spear-like leaves vary somewhat. All pines have long, needle-like leaves, commonly called pine needles, arranged in clumps or bundles on the stems. Firs, balsam and spruce have smaller and flatter needle-like leaves growing from all parts of the stems. Cedars have small, scale-like leaves that hug the stems.

Some conifers have been found to be the oldest living things on earth. The giant redwoods in California (Sequoias) show evidence of having lived for several thousands of years, and some of the Douglas firs have been living for as long as seven or eight hundred years.

Conifers are of great economic value to man. They are used universally for building purposes, for furniture making, for masts of ships, and for telephone poles. Much of our paper comes from the wood pulp of a variety of spruce trees. Resin, turpentine and tar are products of pine trees.

FLOWERING PLANTS

The second subdivision is that of our commonly-known flowering plants and familiar trees other than conifers. A typical flowering plant depends upon its specialized parts for the processes of life. See Fig. 61.

It consists of roots, stems, leaves, flowers, fruit and seeds. The seeds produced by fruits (w... evelop from flowers) are the means of reproduction of the species.

Each main part of the flowering plant has specific functions:

PART	FUNCTIONS
Roots	To anchor plant in ground; to absorb water and mineral salts for the rest of the plant.
Stems	To support leaves, flowers, etc.; passage for vascular tubes.
Leaves	To manufacture food for plant; to give off excess water; to effect exchange of gases for the plant.
Flowers	Contain reproductive organs of plants. In some instances, attract insects to ensure pollination.
Fruit	Womb of the seeds; provides protection for seeds.
Seed	Contains unborn plant (embryo) which will develop into new plant under suitable conditions, and food store.
Vascular System	Bundles of tubes, which conduct water and salts upward from the roots and carry dissolved food from leaves to other parts of plant.

Although each major part of a flowering plant is adapted to perform a specific function, all parts work together to keep the plant and species alive.

Man is dependent on flowering plants directly and indirectly for his well-being. In addition to providing food for animals useful to man, and shelter for man and animals, plants are the main source of our food, spices, clothing and fuel.

VOCABULARY

fruit	needles	pollination
vascular	Sequoia	embryo
conifer	dissemination	seed
cone	root	leaf
staminate	resin	stem
pistillate	turpentine	flower

The most highly organized plants are among the true flowering plants. In this group we find the greatest specialization of cells and tissues into organs that perform a specific function for the plant.

Let us consider each part and its structural adaptation for its vital functions.

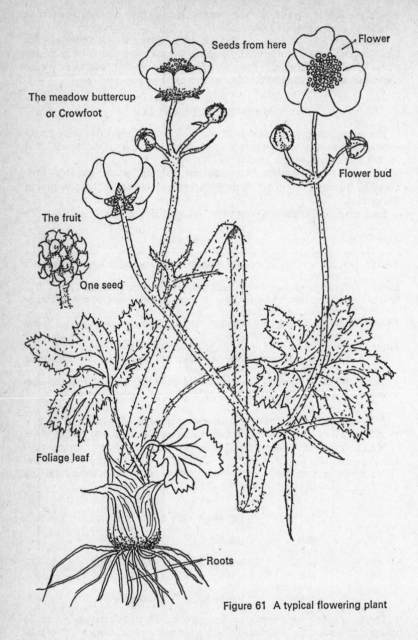

Seeds from here

Flower

The meadow buttercup or Crowfoot

Flower bud

The fruit

One seed

Foliage leaf

Roots

Figure 61 A typical flowering plant

ROOTS

The chief function of the root of a plant is to absorb water containing dissolved minerals usually found in the soil. Another important function is to anchor the plant firmly in the ground. Roots often have other functions for which they are structurally adapted.

A common taproot that is usually available and easy to study is the carrot. This is one of the fleshy taproots with an additional job to do for the carrot plant; namely, it acts as a food storage warehouse.

Select a good-sized carrot and observe its external features. Note how the broadest part from which the stems grow is at the top. It tapers to a point at the bottom—architecturally and functionally useful to the plant. The tip is the growing point which makes its way down into the soil as it increases in length and seeks mineral-laden water. Covering the very tip is a group of tough cells, the root cap, which protects the fine end of the root from injury as it pushes down into the soil.

Fibrous hair-like structures grow from scattered areas along the surface of the carrot. These are known as secondary roots, the main fleshy root being called the primary root.

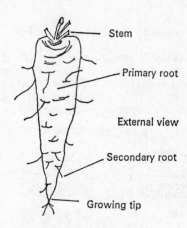

Figure 62 The carrot—a tap root

The secondary roots help to anchor the plant and are provided with specialized cells (root hairs) whose sole function is soil water absorption.

To better understand the internal structure of the root, cut the carrot across and observe the cross-sectional view. Cut the carrot lengthwise down the middle and observe the longitudinal section view. See Fig. 63.

Observe a definitely marked central core—this is known as the central cylinder. This contains tubes (vascular system): **Xylem tubes** which carry water up from the root to all parts of the plant and **phloem tubes** to carry soluble food down from the leaves to the root.

Note that the secondary roots, through which soil water plus dissolved minerals enters, lead directly into the vascular bundles in the central cylinder.

Cross-section

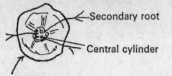

←—Secondary root

—Central cylinder

Outer protective layer
(epidermis)

Longitudinal section
(containing vascular bundles)

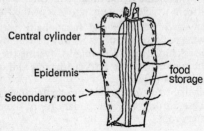

Central cylinder —————

Epidermis—————

Secondary root —————

food
storage

Figure 63 Sectional views of carrot

You can convince yourself by experiment of the important function that the root plays in the life processes of a plant. Cut off the growing tip of a carrot and place the larger part of this root in a solution of red ink and water. Allow it to stand for several hours. Cut a cross-section and a longitudinal section. Observe the red colour in the central cylinder and in the xylem leading from the secondary roots.

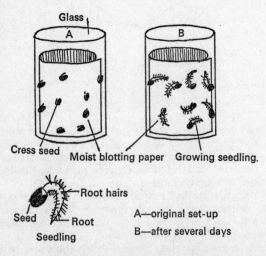

Glass

A   B

Cress seed   Moist blotting paper   Growing seedling.

—Root hairs

Seed   —Root

Seedling

A—original set-up

B—after several days

Figure 64 Experiment—pocket garden

To study in further detail the structure of the specialized cells (root hairs) that are adapted to absorb soil water by the process of osmosis, a microscope is necessary.

An interesting and satisfying home experiment is the planting of a pocket garden. A drinking glass, a piece of blotting paper, cress seeds and water are all the materials necessary. Moisten the inner surface of the glass and then scatter cress seeds over the moist surface where they will stick. Line the glass with blotting paper and then dampen the paper. Put this set-up on a shaded shelf. Remember to keep adding water enough to prevent the blotting paper from drying. See Fig. 64.

Within a few days, observe the seedlings with their white roots that are covered with tiny white fuzz. Each thread of fuzz is a root hair. If possible, place one on a slide in a drop of water and examine it under the microscope.

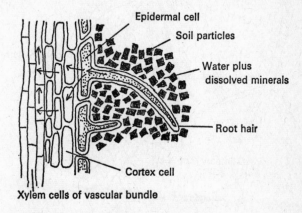

Figure 65   Root hairs—microscopic view

Root hairs are single cells which project in among the soil particles. They absorb soil water by osmosis and minerals by the process of diffusion. The water then passes from cell to cell (by osmosis) until it reaches the vascular bundles in the central cylinder of the root where it travels upward to all parts of the plant above the soil.

MODIFIED ROOTS

In some plants roots are specialized to perform functions other than absorption of water. They are known as modified roots.

Roots of plants growing in normally fertile soil vary in length. The root system of a tree is usually as large and branched as the tree itself and sometimes spreads much farther into the soil. Sometimes in towns these roots crack and destroy pavements and roads in their attempts to secure water.

Grain and other grass roots grow long, tough and fibrous. Oat and alfalfa roots may grow over twenty feet in one direction as they seek water.

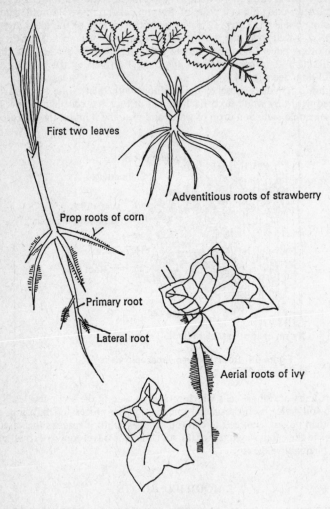

First two leaves

Adventitious roots of strawberry

Prop roots of corn

Primary root

Lateral root

Aerial roots of ivy

Figure 66   Specialized roots

Ideal soil conditions for maximum and successful growth of plant roots and therefore of the entire plant are: fairly loose and granular soil with air spaces to permit air and rain water to enter and carbon dioxide to escape; good water supply; sufficient humus and varied mineral content.

MODIFICATION	FUNCTION	EXAMPLES
Adventitious Roots	Small roots that grow from stems or leaves or from any part of the plant other than the original root system, and are all approximately the same size.	Cucumber Tomato Strawberry Grasses
Aerial Roots	Appear on the ends of stems and runners, then take root in the ground as the plant matures and function as normal roots.	Strawberry Ivy
Fleshy Roots	Store food for the plant.	Beets Carrots Turnips Parsnip Dahlia
Prop Roots	Grow from nodes in the stem just above the ground. Help to keep a heavy plant upright.	Maize
Knees	Upward growing projections usually on water-growing trees. Extend above the surface of the water to secure air for the tree.	Cypress Mangrove
Contractile	Can shorten to pull certain parts of plant underground.	Crocus corms Iris rhizomes

VOCABULARY

taproot	central cylinder	aerial
primary root	vascular system	prop roots
secondary root	root hairs	knees
	adventitious	

STEMS

The chief functions of the stem are to carry water from the roots to the leaves and to distribute manufactured food from the leaves to other parts of the plant. The stem holds the leaves up to the sunlight to manufacture food, and flowers in a suitable position to be pollinated. Some stems are modified to store food.

Every seed contains within it the embryo plant and enough stored food for the embryo to use until conditions are favourable for growth into a self-sufficient plant. The seed may contain one or two seed leaves or **cotyledons**. If one, the plant is a **monocotyledon** (e.g. corn, grasses, palms), if two, it is a **dicotyledon** (e.g. peas, beans, willow, cherry, horse-chestnut). Observe a bean or a peanut and a maize kernel—note the difference in external and internal structures.

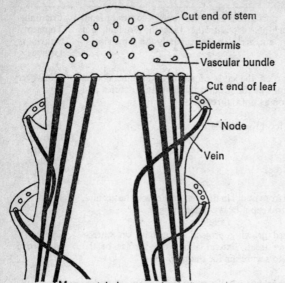

- Cut end of stem
- Epidermis
- Vascular bundle
- Cut end of leaf
- Node
- Vein

Monocotyledon stem (maize) showing the vascular bundle system

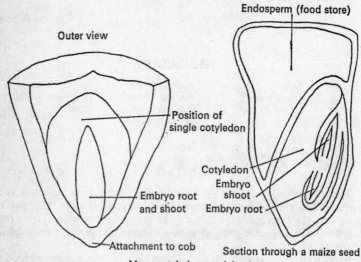

Endosperm (food store)

Outer view

- Position of single cotyledon
- Cotyledon
- Embryo shoot
- Embryo root
- Embryo root and shoot
- Attachment to cob

Section through a maize seed

Monocotyledon seed (maize)

Figure 67

Let us consider a typical monocotyledon stem—the maize stalk is a good example. Externally the stem appears to be straight and tough, uninterrupted

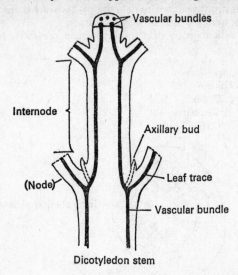

Dicotyledon stem

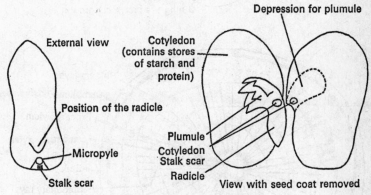

Dicotyledon seed (broadbean)

Figure 68

by branches but with nodes or joints, at regular intervals from which the leaves grow.

In cross-section, a monocotyledon stem shows three main tissue divisions: an outer protective sheath or **epidermis**; scattered vascular bundles; and a spongy tissue called pith which fills the spaces between the vascular bundles. See Fig. 67.

The epidermis gives the stem support and protection—it often contains a glass-like substance called **silica,** a compound of silicon and oxygen. The vascular bundles carry water containing dissolved minerals up from the roots to the leaves and food materials down from the leaves. Some manufactured food is stored in the pith for future use by the plant.

Dicotyledon stems are varied in external nature—such stems are found in our more common flowering plants and all woody trees.

In cross-section, a dicotyledon stem shows an outer protective layer, the

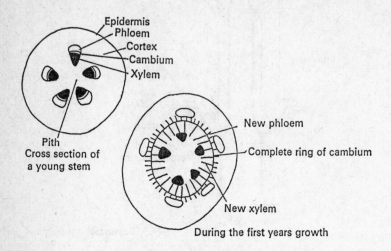

Epidermis
Phloem
Cortex
Cambium
Xylem

Pith
Cross section of
a young stem

New phloem
Complete ring of cambium
New xylem

During the first years growth

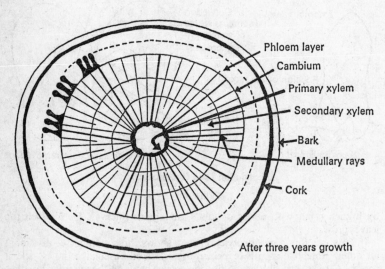

Phloem layer
Cambium
Primary xylem
Secondary xylem
Bark
Medullary rays
Cork

After three years growth

Diagram of three stages of secondary thickening in a dicotyledon stem
Figure 69

epidermis (bark develops in woody plants), a central pithy region, and an orderly arranged vascular bundle system underneath the epidermis. There are small openings, **lenticels,** in the bark through which air enters to supply oxygen to the inner growing cells.

The growing region of a dicotyledon stem, called the **cambium,** makes it possible for the stem to increase in diameter. This layer of cells is found between the xylem and the phloem, and in a woody stem forms a complete ring. As the cambium cells multiply, they form new xylem on the inside and new phloem on the outside. In woody plants this increase in stem width continues throughout their life, and is known as secondary thickening. The wood is composed entirely of xylem, the phloem forming a thin cylinder just beneath the bark. Food to the stem is conducted from here by the medullary rays composed of tube-like cells. See Fig. 68.

It is common knowledge that the age of a tree is indicated by the number of annual rings which are visible in a cross-section of the tree trunk. In autumn, when there is little moisture, the new xylem cells are small. In the spring and summer, when there is great rainfall and moisture, these cells grow large. Each successive layer of small and large woody cells forms a definite band or ring in concentric circles each year—thus, annual rings. See Fig. 69.

A simple home experiment will show the location and functions of vascular tissue in the celery stem or stalk. Place a freshly cut celery stalk in red ink and set this aside for a few hours. Observe the lines of colour in the stem and in the veins of the leaves. Cut the stalk in cross-section and lengthwise and observe results.

MODIFIED STEMS

Just as there are specialized roots, so there are specialized stems.

There are underground stems which store food. These are known as **corms** and **rhizomes.** Well known in this group are the crocus and gladiolus corms and the iris and solomon's seal rhizomes. They can be distinguished from roots by the leaf buds and scars from old leaves that appear on the surface. Adventitious roots generally grow from this type of stem. The potato is the best-known example of an underground stem. It is sometimes referred to as a **tuber** because it is enlarged with stored food. The farmer plants pieces of potatoes, each piece with an eye (young shoot) instead of potato seeds, because the new potato grows faster from the eye, and always produces the same strain of potato.

Some grasses and weeds have tough, underground stems that are far-reaching under the soil. Any piece of underground stem can grow into a new plant. Examples are couch grass, mint, enchanter's nightshade, white dead nettle, Michaelmas daisy and other garden weeds which are so difficult to get rid of because of their underground stems. See Fig. 70.

The strawberry plant, grape vine and some creeping grasses produce stems that grow along the ground. They are called **stolons** or **runners.** These send out roots at intervals at nodes along the stem into the ground and leaf shoots above, forming new plants.

Morning glory, grape vines and lima bean plants have stems which are modified to twine around some sturdy support. This also affords them greater distribution and proximity to the sunlight.

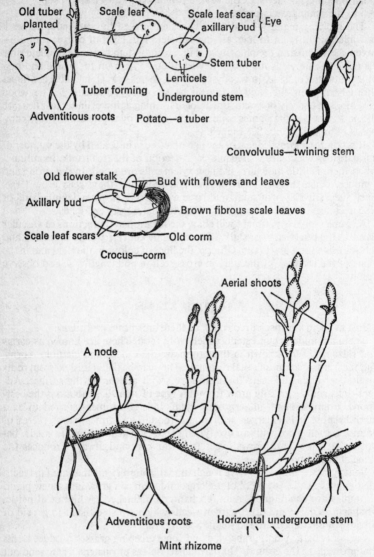

Ground level

Old tuber planted

Scale leaf

Scale leaf scar
axillary bud } Eye

Stem tuber

Lenticels

Tuber forming

Underground stem

Adventitious roots

Potato—a tuber

Convolvulus—twining stem

Old flower stalk

Bud with flowers and leaves

Axillary bud

Brown fibrous scale leaves

Scale leaf scars

Old corm

Crocus—corm

Aerial shoots

A node

Adventitious roots

Horizontal underground stem

Mint rhizome

Figure 70   Modified and specialized stems

VOCABULARY

cotyledon	pith	tuber
monocotyledon	epidermis	eye
dicotyledon	cambium	corm
	annual rings	

LEAVES

Although every part of a plant has an important job, the roots and stems seem to be the service and supply stations for the leaves. Each leaf is a factory where food for the entire plant is manufactured.

There is greater variety of shapes, sizes and arrangement of leaves on their stems than of any other part of the plant. Flowering plants and trees can be identified most easily by their leaves.

Leaves are classified into simple or single blades and compound leaves where there are several leaflets on a single leaf stem. The leaves of the elm, beech, birch, maple, oak, the fruit trees, sycamore, daisy, buttercup, all monocotyledon plants and hosts of others too numerous to list are simple. The leaves of ash, rose, clover, horse-chestnut, and many others are compound.

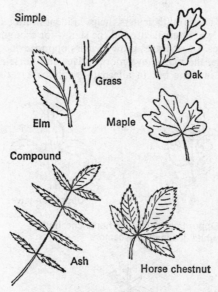

Figure 71 Simple and compound leaves

The vascular bundles rise from the root, extend up the stem into the leaf stem and branch all over the leaf, transporting water up from the roots. Other veins start in the leaves, extend into the stem and roots, and transport digested (soluble) food from the leaf to all other parts of the plant. The system of vascular bundles in the leaf is called the veins.

Monocotyledon leaf
—grass

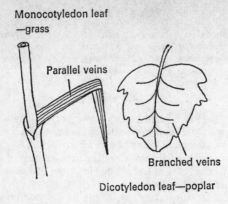

Parallel veins

Branched veins

Dicotyledon leaf—poplar

Figure 72 Venation in leaves

In monocotyledon leaves, **venation** (arrangement of veins) is generally parallel to the length of the leaf. In dicotyledon leaves, venation forms a network.

Arrangement of leaves on their stems helps in identification of plants. Some leaves grow spirally at intervals around the stem—for example, leaves of the oak and apple trees. Other leaves grow in pairs opposite one another on the stem—for example, the maple, sycamore, privet and horse-chestnut leaves. Still others grow in pairs but in alternate positions on their stems—for

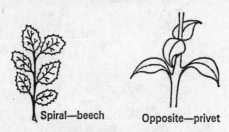

Spiral—beech   Opposite—privet

**Opposite or decussate horse chestnut,
white deadnettle, sycamore**

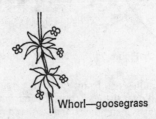

Whorl—goosegrass

Figure 73 Leaf arrangements

example, buttercup and lime. The leaves of dandelion and common plantain grow like a rosette from a node on the stem. See Fig. 73.

Whatever the arrangement of leaves on any particular plant, it is not just haphazard or chance growth. The purpose of any arrangement is to expose each leaf to the maximum amount of sunlight and air. The leaf requires energy from the sun with which to manufacture food.

MODIFIED LEAVES

There are plants with leaves that are modified to perform a function in addition to manufacturing food. A few plants have leaves that are structurally modified to catch insects from which they are able to secure the necessary nitrogen compounds in addition to the supply taken in by the roots. Among the more common of these plants are the sundew, Venus fly trap and pitcher plant. These are called insectivorous plants because of their insect-eating nature.

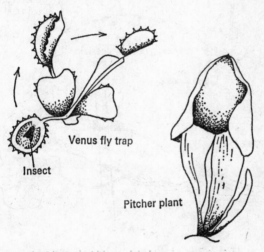

Figure 74 Insect-eating plants (Insectivorous)

The Venus fly trap is a fascinating plant. Its leaves are arranged in rosette fashion at the base of the flower stem. Each leaf has two parts which have thorn-like projections on their outer edges and hairs covering the surfaces. A sweet, sticky substance that has an odour is secreted by the leaves to attract insects. An insect will land on the leaf, the leaf snaps shut, and digestive enzymes produced by the leaf immediately start killing and digesting the insect.

There is a similar method of feeding in the sundew plant except that the leaves do not shut like a trap. In this plant, the leaves are covered with myriad short, sticky hairs which bend over, imprisoning an unwary insect.

The pitcher plant has leaves shaped like pitchers in which rain water collects. Hair-like projections grow downward from the inner surface of each pitcher.

A thirsty insect, who falls into the water, may struggle to climb out again but is prevented from doing so by the restricting hairs.

There are several other modifications among leaves. Tendrils of sweet pea and nasturtium are a specialization of leaves for climbing. Thorns of the barberry bush, hawthorn and gorse are modifications of leaves for protection against animals that would otherwise feed on these plants.

In bulbs, food is stored in thick fleshy leaves below the ground. Peel an onion and see how you can strip off these leaves one by one.

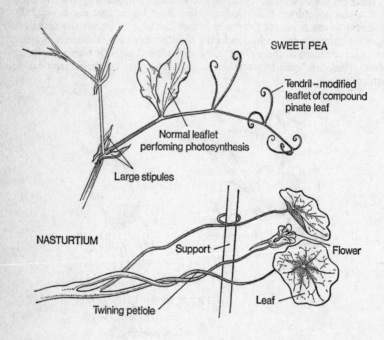

Figure 75   Leaf specialisations for climbing

THE LEAF AS A FOOD FACTORY

Throughout earlier portions of the book we have made constant mention of the importance of the leaf as a food factory. In the discussion on cells we have described cellular adaptations for this vital function. Let us consider in greater detail the microscopic structure of a typical green leaf that makes this function possible. A section across the thin blade of the leaf will reveal, under the microscope, its cellular nature.

Each specific layer of cells (tissues) has a decided function in the leaf for which it is well adapted. (See Chart, p. 96).

Peel off a small piece of the lower epidermis of a geranium leaf. Place it in a, drop of water on a glass slide and view it under the low power of the microscope.

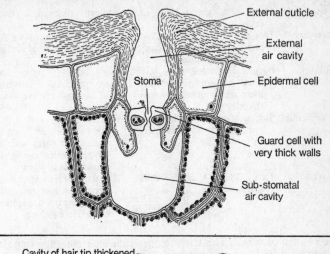

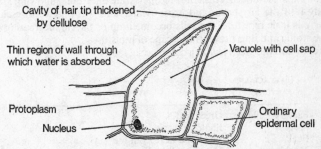

Figure 76   Leaf modifications: section of stomata from Hakea (top) ;
water absorbing hair from a molinia leaf (bottom)

The stomata are usually on the under surface of the leaf to prevent too great loss of water from evaporation and to avoid clogging by dust and insects. There are as many as half a million stomata on the average size leaf.

Leaves which grow upright have stomata distributed on both upper and lower surfaces. In leaves, like water-lily pads, that float on the surface of water, stomata are on the upper surface.

Stomata of cacti and other desert-living plants are few and imbedded deep in the thickened leaves and stems or are covered with hair-like projections or a waxy secretion to prevent loss of water. See Fig. 76.

The action of the two guard cells in regulating the size of the stoma is an interesting phenomenon. Unlike other epidermal cells, they contain chlorophyll and are able to manufacture sugar which creates an osmotic pressure so that water enters these cells. When the two cells are full of moisture they

TISSUE	ADAPTATION	FUNCTION
Cutin	Waxy substance on leaves	Prevents loss of water by evaporation
Upper epidermis	Continuous, single layer of cells	Protects inner leaf tissues
Palisade layer	Elongated cells closely packed and containing many chlorophyll bodies	Manufactures most of food in the presence of sunlight
Spongy layer	Irregularly shaped cells with some chlorophyll bodies; there are air spaces between the cells	Manufactures some food; air spaces allow movement of air and carbon dioxide
Lower epidermis	Single layer of cells with openings, stomata, at intervals	Protects inner leaf tissues; allows air and carbon dioxide to enter leaf, and oxygen, water vapour and waste gases to leave
Guard cells	Two kidney-shaped cells surrounding each stoma	Regulate size of stomata by expanding and contracting depending upon the amount of moisture present

become swollen or turgid. This tends to open wide the stoma, allowing air to pass freely into the air spaces and excess water and waste gases to escape. When there is little moisture, the cells become limp or flaccid, decreasing the size of the stoma and thus preventing escape of moisture.

Let us compare the green leaf to a commercial factory:

COMMERCIAL FACTORY	THE LEAF
Factory building	Green leaf
Process	Photosynthesis
Fuel	Light and heat from the sun
Machinery	Chlorophyll bodies
Raw materials	Carbon dioxide and water
Finished product	Food in the form of carbohydrates (starches and sugars)
By-products	Oxygen and some excess water vapour
Conveyor belts	Conducting or vascular tubes in the veins

The basic foods produced by plants are carbohydrates, sugars and starches. Plants are able to change some of these carbohydrates into fat and oil compounds which are stored in special cells. Plants are also able to combine the carbohydrates with minerals, particularly nitrogen, dissolved in soil water to form the necessary proteins which they use in building new tissues and repairing old.

HOME EXPERIMENTS

Experiments with leaves can be done at home with simple equipment. With the first experiment we will demonstrate the standard method of recording.

EXPERIMENT NO. 1

To show that sunlight is needed for photosynthesis.

Materials: Assemble these materials. [Remember that an experiment does not prove anything without a **control** (see Chapter I)]: a young geranium plant, aluminium foil or black paper, double boiler saucepans (pyrex glass is preferable), heat (Bunsen burner or gas stove burner) iodine, alcohol and water.

Method and Observation of Results:

1. Secure with a clip a piece of aluminium foil to the front and back of a part of a geranium leaf. Set plant in sunlight for several days.

The control, in this case, will be the covered part of the leaf.

2. Remove the leaf from the plant and the foil from the leaf and immediately plunge into boiling water to kill and soften the tissues. Boil out chlorophyll from the leaf in a double boiler. Fill bottom of saucepan with boiling water and put a half inch of alcohol in the top half. Place the leaf in alcohol, which will boil. *Caution:* never boil alcohol directly over a flame; the fumes will catch fire and explode. The alcohol turns green and the leaf goes pale. Wash the leaf in warm water.

3. Drop iodine on the leaf from which the chlorophyll has been abstracted. Starch turns blue-black when tested with iodine.

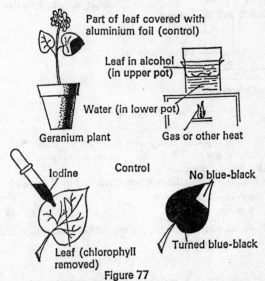

Leaf exposed

Part of leaf covered with aluminium foil (control)

Leaf in alcohol (in upper pot)

Water (in lower pot)

Geranium plant

Gas or other heat

Iodine

Control

No blue-black

Leaf (chlorophyll removed)

Turned blue-black

Figure 77

Observe that the part of the leaf exposed to the sunlight turned blue-black, whereas the part that was covered (the control) did not.

Conclusion: We conclude that sunlight is necessary in the process of photosynthesis. Sugar is formed first and immediately converted to starch, which we test for.

EXPERIMENT No. 2

To show that a green plant needs carbon dioxide to combine with water to produce starch.

Materials: Assemble the following materials: two green seedlings (a seedling is a young plant sprouting from a seed), two large-mouthed jars, two large one-holed stoppers (or cardboard to fit over mouths of jars), two glass funnels and soda-lime chips. Soda lime absorbs carbon dioxide from the air.

Place seedlings in the dark for 48 hours to remove all the starch from the leaves.

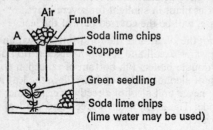

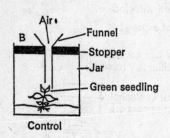

Place both A and B jars on a window sill in direct sunlight for a day

Figure 78

Refer to Fig. 78 and set up equipment accordingly. Place both jars in the sunlight for a day. At the end of the day, remove a leaf from seedling in jar A. Test with iodine for the presence of starch.

Result: No starch—carbon dioxide was absorbed by the soda-lime chips.

Test a leaf from seedling in jar B.

Result: Starch present.

Conclusion: We may conclude that carbon dioxide in the air is necessary for photosynthesis in green leaves.

EXPERIMENT No. 3

To show that chlorophyll is necessary for photosynthesis.

Material: Select a plant whose leaves are partly white and partly green (variegated). The Tradescantia or silver geranium are two types. Keep the plant in the sunlight for several hours.

Remove a leaf and dissolve out the chlorophyll (see Experiment No 1). The white part of the leaf will be the control of this experiment. See Fig. 79.

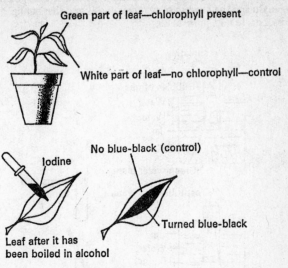

Figure 79

Test the leaf with iodine for the presence of starch.

Result: The part of the leaf that was green (contained chlorophyll) turned blue-black, showing that starch was present. The part of the leaf that was white (without chlorophyll) did not turn blue-black, showing that there was no starch present.

Conclusion: Chlorophyll is necessary for photosynthesis.

EXPERIMENT No. 4

To show that sunlight is necessary for photosynthesis and that oxygen is given off as a by-product during this process.

Materials: Two small water plants (**Elodea** from a fish tank) can be used. Place each in a jar of water. Invert a glass funnel over each plant. Invert a test tube filled with water over the stem of each funnel. Place one jar in the sunlight and the other in a dark cupboard for several hours. The latter is the control. See Fig. 80.

The test tube in jar A appears to be empty. The other test tube (in jar B) appears still to be mostly filled with water. Remove each test tube carefully by placing your thumb over the mouth of the tube before removing it entirely from the water.

Place a glowing splint in test tube A.

Result: It will burst into flame. Oxygen is the gas that is necessary to support burning of a fuel, therefore the gas in test tube A is oxygen.

Place the glowing splint in test tube B.

Result: It will not burst into flame, therefore oxygen is not present.

Conclusion: We can conclude from this experiment that green plants give off oxygen during the process of photosynthesis and that sunlight is necessary for the process to take place at all.

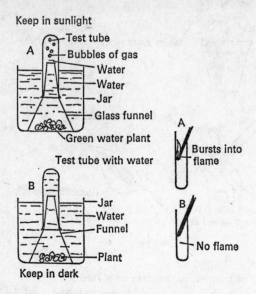

Figure 80

We are aware of the importance of water in green plants. Some of it is used in photosynthesis and some of it carries minerals and food in solution throughout the plant.

Excess water that is not used in either of these two processes escapes from the plant through the stomata and becomes part of the atmosphere. This loss of water is called transpiration.

LEAF FALL

How does the biologist account for the changes of colour of leaves in the autumn? The appearance of red, yellow and orange leaves is possible because those colour pigments are always present in some leaves even in the summer but are masked by the more numerous and active chlorophyll bodies. After a summer of manufacturing food, the chlorophyll bodies disintegrate and the other pigment which is in the leaf becomes predominant.

The leaves of elm, ash, beech and some maple trees become yellow and brilliant orange. Oak, sugar or red maple and sumac leaves become purplish-red and vivid scarlet. After a while the cells of the leaf die, the other colour pigments disintegrate, and the leaf turns a dull, dry brown. Its vital function of food manufacturing is done for the year. It has supplied the plants that live through the winter without leaves with stored food to keep them until the new leaves grow the following spring.

The leaves of most trees except evergreens fall off in the late autumn. During the steady, hot sunlight of the spring and summer months, when there is usually frequent rainfall, the leaves carry on the processes of photosynthesis and transpiration.

The falling of leaves from the tree in the autumn helps the tree prepare itself for the long winter months. At this time very little water enters the roots so that any loss of water by transpiration would be disastrous. Freezing weather and snow would freeze the water in the veins of the leaves and kill them.

To prevent bleeding of the branches of the tree, at the point at which the leaf is attached, a layer of scar tissue forms which seals the ends of the vascular tubes.

Evergreen leaves are protected against excess transpiration during the winter by a waterproof, waxy covering. The slimness and small size of pine-needles prevent them from being weighed down by snow.

VOCABULARY

simple	veins	guard cell
compound	venation	turgid
alternate	insectivorous	flaccid
opposite	cutin	soda lime
rosette	palisade	transpiration
	stoma	

Exercise No. 22

Complete each of the following statements:

1 Needle-like leaves are characteristic of —— trees.
2 Naked seeds are produced in the —— of the pine tree.
3 The system of tubes that conducts liquids in a plant is known as the —— system.
4 Balsam, spruce and fir are all well-known —— trees.
5 The seed contains the —— plant.
6 The —— trees of California are the oldest living organisms known to man.
7 Douglas —— trees have been known to live 800 years.
8 The seed bearing structure of conifers is the ——.
9 The fruit of the sweet pea plant is the —— and of the tomato plant is the ——.

Exercise No. 23

Match a number in Column *A* with a letter in Column *B*.

A		*B*
1	monocotyledon	a seed with two seed leaves
2	soil water	b fleshy tap root
3	carrot	c woody epidermis
4	dicotyledon	d potato
5	bark	e tip of root
6	growing point	f indicate age of tree
7	cambium	g horizontal stem above ground
8	root hairs	h seed with one cotyledon
9	annual rings	i root of plant
10	tuber	j tulip
11	anchors plant	k absorb soil water
12	bulb	l contains dissolved minerals
13	stolon	m growing tissue of plants

Exercise No. 24

Complete the following sentences:

1 The main function of green leaves is to —— for the plant.
2 Leaves can be identified readily by their —— on stems.
3 A single leaf blade on a leaf stem is called a —— leaf.
4 Many leaflets on a single leaf stem form a —— leaf.
5 The type of leaf arrangement of the dandelion is known as ——.
6 The venation in monocotyledon leaves is generally ——.
7 Bundles of vascular tubes branching through a leaf are called ——.
8 An insect-eating plant is called ——.
9 The process of food manufacture in the green leaf is known as ——.
10 The products and by-products of food manufacture in the plant are ——.
11 The green plant gets its energy for the manufacture of food from the ——.
12 The gas —— is necessary for the manufacture of food in the green plant.
13 Excess water escapes through the openings called —— which are on the under surface of most leaves.
14 The process by which excess water leaves the green leaf is known as ——.
15 Cells called —— control the openings on the under surface of the leaf.

THE FLOWER

The flower is the part of the plant which houses the reproductive organs. There are several parts to a typical flower, each of which has a specific function.

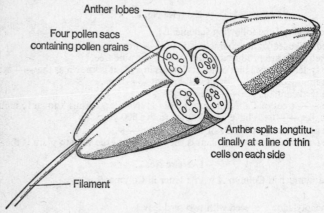

Anther lobes

Four pollen sacs containing pollen grains

Anther splits longtitudinally at a line of thin cells on each side

Filament

Figure 81   Diagram of an anther

The **receptacle**, at the base of the flower, supports the other parts.

The green **calyx**, made up of leaf-like **sepals**, protects the flower when it is in the bud stage.

The **corolla**, the ring of colourful **petals**, serves to protect the inner reproductive organs and to attract insects.

The **stamens** are the male reproductive bodies that surround the **pistil**. A stamen has two parts: (a) the **filament** which supports the (b) **anther**, in which develop the grains of **pollen**. Each pollen grain contains two male nuclei or gametes.

The pistil, the female reproductive organ in the centre of the flower, has three parts: (a) the **stigma**, sticky upper end to which pollen grains adhere; (b) the **style**, passageway for pollen tubes, and (c) the **ovary**, at the base of the pistil, which contain **ovules**, in which are female nuclei or eggs.

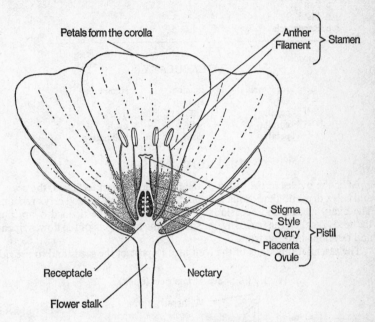

Petals form the corolla

Anther
Filament
Stamen

Stigma
Style
Ovary
Placenta
Ovule
Pistil

Receptacle

Nectary

Flower stalk

Figure 82   Half a generalised flower

In order for seeds to be produced, pollination must take place. In cross-pollination, the pollen from the stamen of one flower is transferred to the pistil of another flower of the same species. This is accomplished by insects and other animals, and, in some cases, by the wind. In self-pollination the pollen from a flower falls on the pistil of the same flower.

After the pollen reaches the stigma of the pistil, it grows a tube down the style, and enters the ovary. Here the male nucleus combines with the female nucleus and results in a fertilized egg. The fertilized cell develops into the embryo plant and the ovule into the seed.

After fertilization is complete, the sepals, petals and stamens dry up, the petals and stamens fall off, and the ovary, now containing seeds, develops into the fruit.

There are countless wild flowers of varied colours which grow in open spaces, in fields, in the woods, on sand dunes and in ponds. Some are short-lived (a week or two), others live through a season and some the whole year round.

Exercise No. 25

Complete the following chart:

PART OF FLOWER	PRIMARY FUNCTION
a Calyx	
b Corolla	
c Anther	
d Pistil	
e Receptacle	

VOCABULARY

receptacle	filament	stigma
calyx	stamen	style
sepal	anther	ovary
corolla	pollen	ovule
petal	pistil	pollination

THE FRUIT AND SEED

After the ovules in the ovary of the flower have been fertilized, the corolla and calyx dry, and the corolla falls off. Sometimes the withered calyx remains. The ovary ripens, and occasionally becomes fleshy. The ripened ovary plus the seeds is called the fruit. In some plants, the receptacle of the flower ripens, and develops into the fruit.

The essential functions of the fruit are: to protect the seeds and to provide

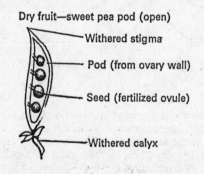

Dry fruit—sweet pea pod (open)

— Withered stigma
— Pod (from ovary wall)
— Seed (fertilized ovule)
— Withered calyx

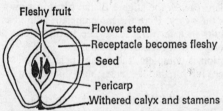

Fleshy fruit

— Flower stem
— Receptacle becomes fleshy
— Seed
— Pericarp
— Withered calyx and stamens

Figure 83 Typical fruits

means of distributing them (seed dispersal) after the seeds have become mature.

There are two types of fruits. The dry fruits are those that have a dry outer covering protecting the seeds. Thus, grains, nuts, buttercup, sweet pea, maple and dandelion are examples of dry fruits. The fleshy fruits are those whose seeds are encased in a juicy, fleshy pulp. Examples are apple, grape, cherry, tomato, peach and various berries.

Fruits are further classified into **true fruits** and **false fruits.** True fruits are those which develop directly from the ovary; false fruits develop from other parts of the flower as well as from the ovary—e.g. the receptacle; the top of the flower stem, etc.

There are many kinds of true fruits:

A **berry**—a fruit with fleshy ovary enveloping the hard seeds. Examples: grape, orange, tomato.

Drupes, or stone fruits—hard, stony-covered seeds surrounded by fleshy, edible ovary walls. Examples: cherries, plums, peaches, apricots.

Grain or **kernel**—extremely thin fruit coat that has become one with the protective seed coat.

Nuts—hard shell is former ovary wall. Softer nut is seed. Examples: walnut, hazel, acorn and chestnut.

Pod or **legume**—the ovary wall forms the pod, to which the seeds are attached, and from which they receive nourishment. Examples: peas, beans, peanuts, lupin.

Key fruits—have a wing-like projection that extends from the thin ovary wall, covering a single fleshy seed. Examples: maple, sycamore, elm and ash.

Examples of false fruits are: strawberries, apples, quince, pears. These develop from the ovary, which becomes brittle and encases the seeds. The receptacle develops into the fleshy edible part of the fruit.

Figs are an example of a false fruit developing from the receptacle and the flower stem end.

Each of the types of fruits mentioned is specifically adapted for dispersal of its seeds. Sometimes the adaptation is in the fruit itself; sometimes in the seed. The main purpose for specialized dispersal adaptations is for the seeds to find suitable environmental conditions for growth into new plants. There must be adequate food supply, moisture and sunlight for the seeds to develop successfully.

Seed dispersal adaptations determine the agent for dispersal. The wind scatters seeds that are light weight or have wings, or soft plumes and tufts. Examples are ash, sycamore, maple, elm, dandelion, willow herb, thistle, and clematis.

Some fruits and seeds are adapted for distribution by animals. The seeds of edible fruits are distributed after the fleshy part of the fruit is consumed and the seeds are dropped, or eliminated as undigested material. All the fleshy fruits are examples of this type.

Other animal-dispersed seeds have hook-like barbs, which catch on to the fur or hides (or clothing) of animals, and are distributed when they are brushed off or fall off. Examples are burdock and goosegrass.

Seeds of the snapdragon, beans, peas and wild cucumber are dispersed when their dry pods split open suddenly, forcibly expelling their seed contents for some distance away from the parent plant.

The seeds of a plant are nature's insurance for the continuation of the plant species. When the dispersed seed finds adequate conditions for growth (ogygen, warmth, moisture and sunlight) it develops into a new plant with all the characteristics of the parent plant.

Earlier in the chapter we discussed the fact that there are two kinds of seeds: monocotyledonous and dicotyledonous. See Figs. 67 and 68. Monocotyledon seeds have one cotyledon; dicotyledon seeds two.

Observe a bean or pea or peanut seed at home, in order to study the parts of the dicotyledon seeds and their functions. See Fig. 68.

The outer coat or **testa** surrounds and protects the embryo within. Externally, there are two scar-like marks near the inner curve of the seed. The larger

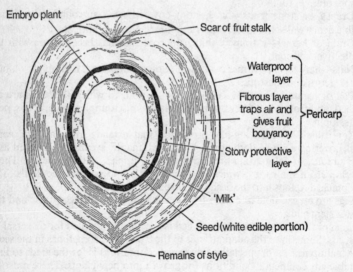

Figure 84   Diagram of half a coconut: scattered by water

of the two is the **hilum,** the point at which the seed was attached to the pod, and through which it received nourishment.

The **micropyle** is a small opening, through which the pollen tube, carrying the male cell, entered the ovule during fertilization, and through which water is absorbed for the young embyro. Gently squeeze a soaked broad bean seed and observe a small drop of water coming out through the micropyle.

Internally, we find the **radicle,** which will develop into the root of the young plant; the **plumule,** which becomes the first leaves; and the **cotyledons,** which in these seeds nourish the new plant until its leaves become green and it is able to manufacture its own food.

Observe a monocotyledon corn seed (see Fig. 67) and note the single cotyledon, the **endosperm** (food storage containing protein as well as starch), the

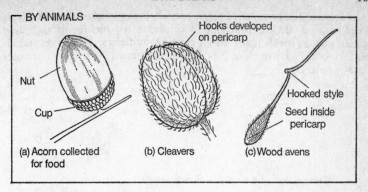

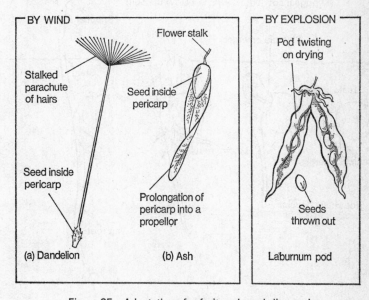

Figure 85   Adaptations for fruit and seed dispersal

radicle and plumule, all protected by the seed coat. Prop roots characteristic of corn (see Fig. 66) grow from the top of the radicle, whereas the true water-absorbing roots grow from the lower part.

Plant pocket gardens of a monocotyledon and a dicotyledon seed, and observe the stages of germination (development from seed to young plant) in each. Figs. 86 and 87. In some dicotyledon plants, the cotyledons, instead of remaining below ground as a food store, come above ground, turn green, and manufacture food until the leaves are able to take over this function.

The economic importance of plants to man, both directly and indirectly, is almost limitless. Besides providing food, shelter and fuel for us and other animals, plants provide materials for clothing, medicines, drugs, dyes and industrial products. Let us classify a few of them according to the economic uses of parts of plants.

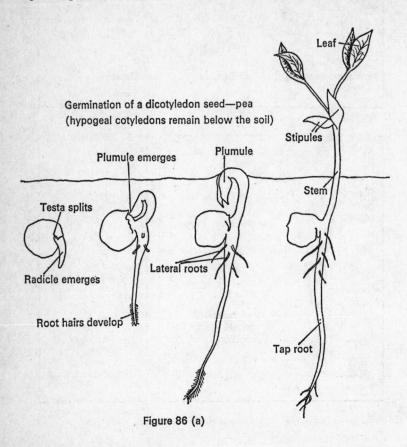

Germination of a dicotyledon seed—pea
(hypogeal cotyledons remain below the soil)

Leaf

Stipules

Plumule emerges

Plumule

Stem

Testa splits

Lateral roots

Radicle emerges

Root hairs develop

Tap root

Figure 86 (a)

Plants that provide root products:
Food: carrot, radish, beet, sugar beet, parsnip, turnip, sweet potato, cassava (for tapioca).
Flavouring: liquorice.
Medicines or drugs: ipecac, rhubarb, aconite, dandelion.

Plants that provide stem products:
Food: asparagus, celery, potato, sugar cane, arrowroot, sago palm.
Building materials: timber from conifers and other common trees; furniture is included; rubber.
Paper: spruce, pine, poplar, fir.

Fibres: flax, jute, hemp; many trees for synthetic fibres.

Tanning: chestnut, hemlock, willow, oak.

Medicines or drugs: camphor, quinine (cinchona bark), turpentine and resin from conifers; sandalwood, cascara, saponin.

Plants that provide leaf products:

Food: lettuce, cabbage, kale, parsley, spinach. Food for cattle: clover, alfalfa.

Fibres: sisal, manilla fibre.

Medicines or drugs: nicotine (from tobacco), cocaine (from coca), caffeine (from tea), digitalis (from foxglove), belladonna (from nightshade).

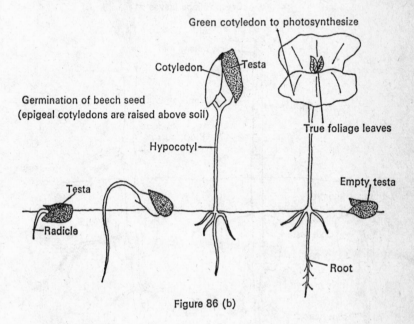

Green cotyledon to photosynthesize

Cotyledon — Testa

Germination of beech seed
(epigeal cotyledons are raised above soil)

True foliage leaves

Hypocotyl

Testa

Empty testa

Radicle

Root

Figure 86 (b)

Plants that provide flower products:

Scents for floral perfumes: violet, rose, lily-of-the-valley, jasmine, lilac, lavender, etc.

Drugs: hashish.

Spices: cloves, capers, clove oil.

Plants that provide seed products:

Food: grains (corn, rice, barley, wheat, rye, oats); nuts (chestnut, almond, Brazil, cashew, pecan, etc.).

Spices: celery, anise, caraway, mustard, pepper, nutmeg, mace, etc.

Oils: cotton, flax, cocoa, coconut, sunflower.

Medicines or drugs: castor oil, strychnine, opium (poppy).

Fibres: synthetics from the peanut.

Industrial: paints, dyes (peanut skins, pumpkin seeds).

Some plants are a nuisance to man, because they prevent the proper growth of useful plants. These are called weeds. They are usually tough, rapid-growing, and fast reproducing. They drain the soil of moisture and minerals, crowd

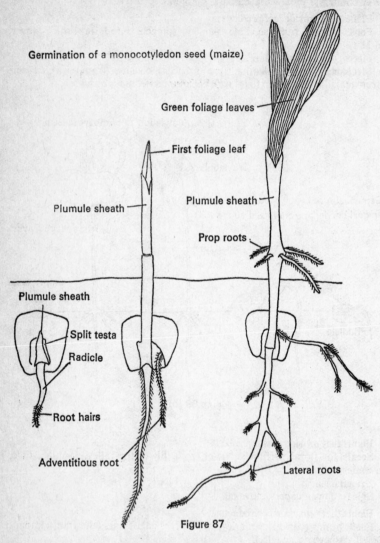

Germination of a monocotyledon seed (maize)

Green foliage leaves

First foliage leaf

Plumule sheath

Plumule sheath

Prop roots

Plumule sheath

Split testa

Radicle

Root hairs

Adventitious root

Lateral roots

Figure 87

other plants, and obscure the sunlight. Familiar weeds are couch grass, dandelion, plantain, mullein, thistle and ragweed.

Some day one of the weeds may be found to have great economic importance; then it will be shifted to the category of useful plants.

Some plants are harmful to man because they are poisonous. Examples of these are sheep laurel, deadly nightshade, bryony berries and laburnum seeds.

Other plants are harmful in that their pollen causes respiratory allergies. Examples of these are ragweed, goldenrod and hay.

The benefits man receives from plants all over the world far outweigh the harm some of them do.

It should be obvious that without plant life no other life can exist on earth.

SUMMARY

The most advanced plants in the Plant Kingdom are known as the flowering plants.

All flowering plants consist of roots, stems, leaves, flowers, fruits and seeds, and a well-developed vascular system.

The flowers of plants contain the male and female reproductive organs.

The fruit of a plant is the seed-bearing organ.

Conifers are characterized by their needle-like leaves and cones in which naked seeds are produced.

Man is dependent on flowering plants directly and indirectly for his well-being.

Flowering plants are of great economic importance to man.

VOCABULARY

Fruit and Seeds

berry	hilum
drupe	micropyle
grain	radicle
kernel	plumule
nut	testa
pod	endosperm
legume	cotyledon
key	seed dispersal

Exercise No. 26

What is the correct term for each of the following:

1 The part of the flower in which the seeds develop. ——
2 Mass distribution of seeds. ——
3 A fruit with a fleshy covering over the seeds. ——
4 A fruit with a hard, stony covered seed. ——
5 A fruit with a hard shell that is the former ovary wall. ——
6 Fruits with wing-like projections. ——
7 A young plant within the seed. ——
8 Adaptation of a seed for sticking to the fur of animals for dispersal. ——
9 The development of a seed into a new plant. ——
10 A seed with two cotyledons. ——
11 The potential root of the plant, part of a seed. ——
12 The seed leaf in a seed. ——
13 The potential leaf shoot of the plant, part of the seed. ——
14 The fruit of a sweet pea. ——
15 The outer protective covering of seeds. ——

CHAPTER VIII

THE ANIMAL KINGDOM: THE INVERTEBRATES

Throughout the first part of the book we dealt with plants and their relationship and importance to man. In the following chapters we shall consider the other half of life, the Animal Kingdom.

Just as there are countless thousands of varieties of plants growing in every known area of the earth, so there are thousands of species of animals living on the surface of the earth and in the waters.

There are extremely simple animals of a single cell only, and animals composed of many cells; some with simple life processes and others with highly organized systems and organs which perform the same life functions characteristic of all protoplasm.

All animals may be divided into two main groups: **Invertebrates** and **Vertebrates.** The former group consists of animals which have no backbones. Examples are Amoeba, earthworm and fly. The latter includes all animals which have some kind of backbone and internal skeleton. For example, fish, birds, man.

We shall consider first the simplest forms of animals, their adaptations for life, and their relation to human beings—the most specialized group of animals known to exist.

INVERTEBRATES: PROTOZOA

Protozoa may be compared in simplicity of structure and function to the simplest plants, the algae and their relatives.

Protozoa are **acellular** animals that live independently in water. (See Chapter IV.) They may be found in ponds, lakes, rivers, in fresh or stagnant pools, even in reservoirs and moist soil as well as in the oceans and seas, and as parasites in other animals.

Collect a jar of water from a still pond. Include some of the plant matter found there. If a microscope is available, examine a drop of this water on a glass slide. (Use the low power magnification.) After your eye has become trained to the area, you will be astonished to see tiny forms of life that either dart back and forth across your field of vision or swim lazily, or sluggishly, in that single drop of water.

In order to be able to observe these elusive creatures more closely, place a few strands of absorbent cotton in a drop of the water (from the jar) on a glass slide. Cover with a thin cover glass.

The threads serve as traps to ensnare the ever-moving protozoa. Study the varieties of single-celled animals that you have trapped. If the drop of water dries, the tiny animals will dry up and die. Avoid this by adding a bit of the pond water with a pipette (medicine dropper) held at the edge of the cover glass.

If the light focused on the field of vision is cut down to a minimum (experiment with various amounts of light by shifting the mirror under the stage of the microscope), you will see more clearly. This is so because most protozoa are naked bits of translucent, greyish protoplasm held within the bounds of their cell membranes.

One of the simplest protozoans you may find is Amoeba. Although its structure is simple, it nonetheless carries on every vital life process. (See Chapter IV, for descriptions.)

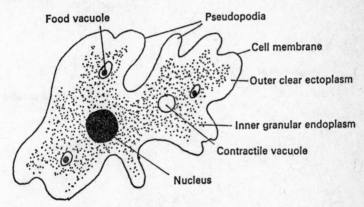

Food vacuole   Pseudopodia

Cell membrane

Outer clear ectoplasm

Inner granular endoplasm

Contractile vacuole

Nucleus

Figure 88   Amoeba

This tiny animal is irregular in outline, changing its shape constantly as it flows along in the water. It moves from place to place slowly by extending projections of protoplasm (pseudopodia or false feet) and flowing into them.

Let us chart the adaptations for all life functions of Amoeba.

FUNCTION	ADAPTATION
Locomotion	Pseudopodia.
Food-getting	Pseudopodia surround food and form food vacuole. (See Fig. 88.)
Digestion	In food vacuole by enzymes secreted by cell protoplasm.
Absorption	Directly into all parts of cell.
Assimilation	By cell protoplasm.
Respiration	Oxygen taken out of water by diffusion through cell membrane and carbon dioxide removed from cell.
Excretion	Simple diffusion through cell membrane.
Reproduction	Simple fission.
Protection	Can resist dessication by spore formation.

Water from a fish tank often contains protozoa. Observe a drop of this water from the surface under the microscope, using cotton strands on the glass slide.

You will observe many types of protozoa, among them a darting, slipper-shaped animal called Paramecium. It differs from its relative Amoeba, in many respects. It appears to show decided advance in its adaptations for the life processes.

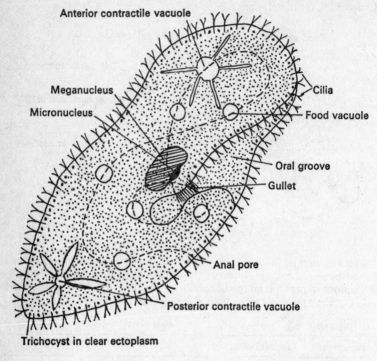

Figure 89   Paramecium

Its shape is constant. There are thread-like projections of protoplasm (cilia) covering the outer surface of the cell membrane that wave back and forth rapidly propelling the animal in the water. Directly under the cell membrane is a series of dart-like projections called **trichocysts** which are organs of adhesion by which the animal anchors itself.

Food particles (smaller protozoa and algae) are ingested through a groove in the protoplasm (oral groove), directed by cilia lining the groove, into a small depression called the gullet. Here a food vacuole is formed which is circulated through the cell protoplasm by its natural flowing motion. Digestion occurs in the food vacuole. Digested food is absorbed into the rest of the cell.

Excess water is collected in the contractile vacuoles (one at each end of Paramecium) by small canals which radiate from the vacuoles, They are eliminated through the cell membrane by contraction of the vacuoles. Undigested solids are expelled through a weak spot in the cell membrane called the anal pore.

Oxygen passes through the cell membrane from the water and the waste gas (carbon dioxide) escapes by diffusion during the process of respiration.

Paramecium reproduces by simple fission. In addition, a strain of Paramecium is strengthened just before fission takes place, when there is an exchange of nuclear material between two individuals in the process of conjugation. (A similar process takes place in the green alga, Spirogyra.)

Although neither Amoeba nor Paramecium has nerve cells, they make definite responses to external stimuli such as food, contact, light, heat and their enemies.

Most protozoa live singly, but there are colonial forms as well. In these colonies, each cell lives independently of the others.

Protozoa are of extreme importance to the welfare of man. Since they are so numerous and live in water, they provide food for other water-living animals useful to man as food. Some protozoa are helpful because they destroy bacteria in water that may be harmful to man; others are helpful in the decomposition of dead plants and animals, thus enriching the soil and avoiding over congestion of the earth.

The White Cliffs of Dover which provide important material for the manufacture of cement and mortar, were formed from the accumulation of countless limestone shells, over many hundreds of years, from a species of protozoa.

Some protozoa are harmful because they cause:

  decay of foods;
  tooth and gum decay and disease (pyorrhoea);
  diseases of the intestinal tract (dysentery and diarrhoea);
  malaria and African sleeping sickness.

VOCABULARY

invertebrate	pseudopodium	gullet
vertebrate	cilia	oral groove
	trichocysts	

Animals with increasing specialization and complexity included in the invertebrate group are further divided into sub-groups, namely: sponges, jellyfish and corals, flatworms, roundworms, segmented worms, shellfish, anthropods and starfish.

JELLYFISH AND RELATED ANIMALS

Jellyfish and coral are very simple, many-celled animals that live in salt and fresh water. Their bodies consist of two layers of cells surrounding a hollow interior which is the digestive cavity. The mouth, an opening into the digestive cavity, is surrounded by tentacles which are projections of the two-layered body. The function of the tentacles is to direct food into the mouth. Many of these animals expel stinging cells that paralyse smaller animals which they eat. See Fig. 90.

These animals reproduce both asexually and sexually. They reproduce by budding, that is, the parent animal forms an outer growth or bud which breaks off and forms a new individual (similar to yeast plants). In sexual reproduction male sperm cells and a female egg cell are produced. The sperm cells swim to the egg cell, fuse with it to form a fertilized egg which divides into the new many-celled individual.

These animals are also able to reproduce by regeneration, that is, the growth of a new individual from a piece of another that has been broken off or torn off by other animals or by forces of waves or currents.

The adult forms of some of these animals are free-swimming (jellyfish, Portuguese man-of-war); and others grow attached to rocks (Hydra and coral).

Sea anemones grow large and vivid in colour, appearing like under-sea flowers with ever-waving arm-like petals, the tentacles.

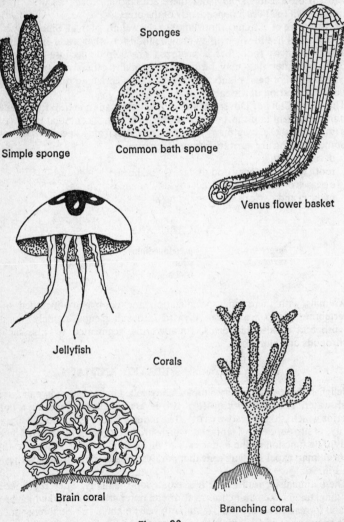

Sponges

Simple sponge

Common bath sponge

Venus flower basket

Jellyfish

Corals

Brain coral

Branching coral

Figure 90

Sponges are a group of unusual colonial animals related both to the protozoa and the jellyfish. Zoologists place them in a group of their own. Sponges secrete three different kinds of material with which they build their colonial dwellings. Lime sponges secrete little **spicules**, which are small pointed pieces of limestone. The **Venus flower basket**, found deep in the sea off the Philippine Islands, gets its name from the delicate grass-like basket which results from the use of the protective silica got by the sponge animals from the sand they grow in. The common bath sponge animal secretes a soft, buoyant material called **spongin** with which it makes its outer protective home.

Commercial bath sponges are dredged from their attachments from the waters off the coast of Cuba and from the Mediterranean Sea. They are scattered on the sandy beaches. The soft animal bodies die, leaving spongin skeletons for man to use commercially.

CORAL

The tiny coral animals live in large colonies. Many colonies grow together, side by side, attached to each other and then layer upon layer. The soft animal bodies, similar in structure to sponge animals, die, leaving delicately coloured beautifully carved outer skeletons that sometimes form coral reefs. Atolls are circular reefs enclosing a lagoon. Bermuda, the Bahamas and some of the Hawaiian Islands are made mostly of coral, as are many islands off the coast of Australia.

Some coral is extremely valuable, because of its colour and consistency, for jewellery making.

VOCABULARY

tentacles	spongin	coral reef
regeneration	Venus flower basket	atoll
spicule	Portuguese man-of-war	

FLATWORMS

The flatworms, a group of primitive animals, show an increase of specialization of structures and functions over sponges, corals, jellyfish and their relatives; they have three layers of cells.

Flatworms are not numerous. Some may be found in fresh water. Those best known to man are parasites which produce serious maladies in man and his domestic animals. Examples are tapeworm and liver fluke.

These animals are not as advanced in structural adaptations as the true segmented worms. They have no respiratory or circulatory systems, and some, the tapeworms have no digestive system, relying on food and oxygen absorbed directly through the outer layer. Liver flukes have a much-branched digestive system and a number of suckers to attach themselves to their hosts. Both groups have complicated hermaphrodite reproductive systems capable of producing large numbers of new individuals. See Fig. 91.

Flatworms reproduce by sexual means, the union of male and female cells resulting in fertilized eggs. They also reproduce by regeneration.

The tapeworm requires two hosts to complete its life history. The adult worm lives in the intestines of a mammal, e.g. man (the primary host). Segments containing fertilized eggs are passed out of the body and find their way into the secondary host, a pig. Here they develop into 6-hooked embryos

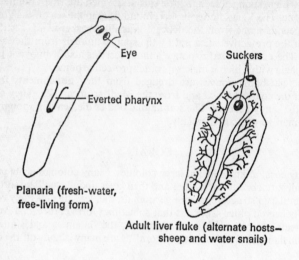

Planaria (fresh-water,
free-living form)

Adult liver fluke (alternate hosts—
sheep and water snails)

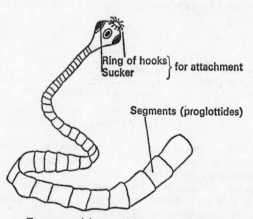

Tapeworm (alternate hosts—man and pig)

Figure 91   Flatworms—mostly parasites

which bore their way into the host's muscle and further develop into bladderworms. If man eats undercooked, infected pork, the parasites enter his intestine and complete their life cycle to become adult worms. See Fig. 92.

Tapeworms grow to considerable lengths, sometimes filling the entire intestinal tract. They sap the strength of the human host by devouring much of

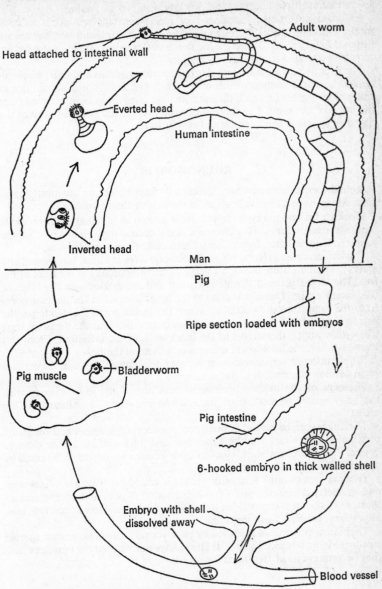

Figure 92 Life history of tapeworm

his nourishment. If the parasite offender is not discovered, the results are severe malnutrition, anaemia and possibly death by starvation.

Enforced government inspection of meat, constant reminders to cook meats (especially pork) thoroughly before consumption and efficient sewage disposal have tended to curb the incidence of tapeworm. Tapeworm infection can also be treated successfully by doctors.

The liver fluke is a parasite on sheep (sometimes rabbits and deer) whose alternate host is a common fresh water snail. The four-footed animal drinks water or eats grass in which the parasite lives after it has been excreted from the body of the snail. The fluke enters the liver of the sheep by way of the digestive system where it grows and creates havoc.

ROUNDWORMS

Roundworms, more advanced structurally than flatworms, are mostly parasites. Many have alternate hosts as in the case of the flatworms.

Hookworms and porkworms (otherwise known as **trichina**) are formidable parasitic roundworms. Hookworm disease occurs most frequently in the southern United States, India, South China and other warm climates.

The immature stage (larva) of the hookworm lives in moist, hot ground and enters the human being through a break in the skin, usually in the soles of the feet. The larvae get into the blood stream and are carried into the lungs of the human victim. Damage is done to the lung tissue when the parasite bores from the lungs into the windpipe. When the larvae reach the windpipe, the person coughs them up and then swallows them down into the digestive tract where they attach themselves to the inner walls of the intestines. From this vantage point, the hookworm matures and lives on the host.

People infected with hookworm become debilitated, sluggish, listless and often develop tuberculosis and anaemia.

The eggs of the mature hookworm pass out of the human body with the body wastes (faeces), enter the soil and are ready to resume their life cycle.

The disease can be curbed through proper education in hygiene; through the installation of sanitary plumbing facilities; and the use of sandals or shoes to protect the feet from contact. Hookworm infection can, of course, be cured by appropriate medical treatment.

Trichina (porkworm) is another parasitic roundworm which infects man and its alternate host, the pig. Thorough cooking of pork and government inspection of the meat can prevent this devastating disease from occurring and, after it has occurred, from spreading.

Trichinosis is the disease caused by porkworm. There is no known specific treatment in its advanced stages. If larvae have not reached the muscles where they become encysted, treatment is possible.

VOCABULARY

flatworm	trichina	hookworm
roundworm	liver fluke	anaemia
	tapeworm	

TRUE SEGMENTED WORMS

The well-known earthworm is an example of a true segmented worm. Others are Nereis, a marine worm, bristle worm and the leech.

In the earthworm, the long digestive tube is divided into mouth, pharynx, gullet, crop, gizzard and intestine. The circulatory system consists of a pair of tubes, one running the length (internally) of the dorsal (back) part of the soft body and the other, the ventral (under or belly region). Five branches, called pseudo-hearts, encircle the gullet part of the intestinal tract. There appears the first evidence of nerve tissue in the form of a **ganglion,** a group of nerve cells in the head end of the animal. There is a longitudinal nerve cord and ganglia and segmental nerves in each segment of the body. See Figs. 93 and 94. There is a definite tube-like structure in each segment of the earthworm in which liquid wastes are collected and excreted.

Earthworms breathe by absorbing oxygen through their moist skins. If the skin of an earthworm remains dry, it will die from suffocation.

An earthworm forces its way through soft earth by contraction and relaxation of opposing muscle blocks. Bristle-like appendages, in pairs, on the ventral surface of every body segment are used to anchor the worm in position while it draws up the posterior part of its body. As it travels, it eats soil. The digestive system selects edible plant and animal matter from the soil and the remainder is passed out of the body in the form of castings.

Earthworms are a great boon to man. They help keep the soil porous for air and moisture; they provide fertilizing material, and in addition, they add to top soil with their castings. A biologist estimated that it would take earthworms about twenty years to convert their castings into 3 inches of top soil in an acre of ground.

In the fisherman's vocabulary the bloodworm is any of certain marine segmented worms which have very soft bodies, and bright-red blood; the sandworm is also an **annelid,** and burrows in sea-shore sand.

Leeches, fresh water worms, are commonly known as blood-suckers. They attach themselves by means of sucker-like mouth discs. They secrete a saliva-like liquid which prevents the blood of the victim from clotting until the leech has completed its meal. A leech can suck up to three times its own weight of blood. In the medicinal leech it takes about nine months for all this rich food to be digested so that these animals need not feed frequently.

VOCABULARY

segment	leech	ganglion
Nereis	dorsal	castings
bristle worm	ventral	

SNAILS AND THEIR RELATIVES

Snails, clams and oysters belong to a group of animals called **molluscs** (Latin for soft flesh). The members of this group are unique in many respects. They have soft, unsegmented, rather shapeless bodies surrounded by a single or double calcareous (made of calcium) covering called a shell.

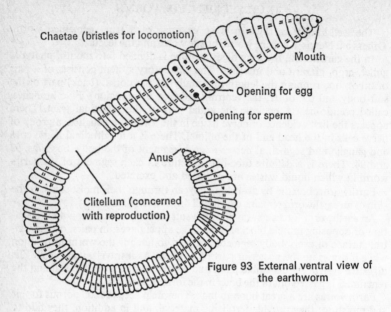

Chaetae (bristles for locomotion)

Mouth

Opening for egg

Opening for sperm

Anus

Clitellum (concerned with reproduction)

Figure 93 External ventral view of the earthworm

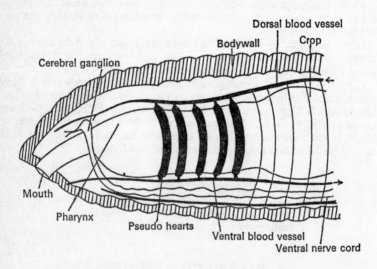

Cerebral ganglion

Bodywall

Dorsal blood vessel

Crop

Mouth

Pharynx

Pseudo hearts

Ventral blood vessel

Ventral nerve cord

Figure 94 Internal view of anterior end

There are about 80,000 known species of molluscs, some living in fresh water but the majority in salt water habitats. There are even land-living forms. Among the shells there is a wide range of variation as to size, shape and colour.

Among the better known members of this large group of animals are oysters, mussels, scallops, snails, squid, cuttlefish and octopuses.

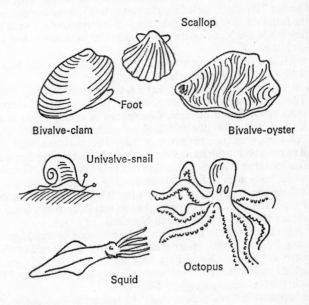

Molluscs

Figure 95

Clams, oysters, scallops and mussels are called **bivalves** because of their characteristic two shells attached at one point by a hinge of soft body muscle tissue.

They move from place to place on shore and under water in the sand by extending a muscular foot between the two shells.

These molluscs are economically important to man for the food they provide. In some regions, however, extreme caution must be taken against pollution. Oysters produce precious pearls as well.

A pearl is the oyster's method of counteracting an irritation. When a coarse grain of sand gets caught in the tender body tissue lining the oyster shell, the animal secretes a liquid called nacre or mother-of-pearl which forms smooth concentric layers as it hardens around the disturbing sand grain, resulting in a pearl. Natural pearls are formed around a sand particle or parasitic tapeworm in the oyster.

The production of cultured pearls has become a thriving industry. Grains of shell and sand are artificially introduced (by man) between the shells of oysters. These are then carefully nurtured and kept apart in water which is kept free of pollution and at a constant temperature.

Sometimes the entire inner surface of the shells of bivalves are coated with the iridescent mother-of-pearl deposit that gives them a pearl-like lustre and smoothness.

Some fish are important to the life cycle of bivalves. After the eggs have hatched, the tiny young clams or oysters make their way in the water by the opening and closing of their two little shells. Fish swallow them with food in gulps of water. The water, including the young bivalves, passes out over the gills of the fish. En route, the shellfish attach themselves to the gills of the fish where they live in symbiotic relationship until they are ready to live as independent animals.

As the soft body of a bivalve grows, a layer around the outside larger edge of each shell is added to accommodate it.

Snails are **univalves** because they have a single shell covering their soft bodies. There are many different sizes, colours and varieties of shapes even among these spiral-shelled animals. One species of snails, called slugs, has no visible shell. Just under the middle dorsal skin there is a shell-like plate which offers some protection to the rest of the soft body of the animal.

A snail moves about, with its shell-house on its back, by extending a muscular disc-like foot that clings like a suction cup to a solid object. Then it drags the rest of its body after it. Some snails develop a hardened cover over the foot that closes the animal in very firmly when it withdraws for protection to its spiral shell. The snail adds to its shell as its soft body grows larger. Some snail shells are chambered (Chambered Nautilus).

There is evidence that our prehistoric ancestors found oysters plentiful and good eating. Piles of empty oyster shells along with bones and crude stone tools known as kitchen midden, have been traced back to prehistoric man. Historians tell us that clams and oysters were party fare at Greek and Roman banquets in the first century B.C.

Mother-of-pearl buttons are cut from the iridescent-lined shells of some large clams and also from abalone shells.

In octopuses and squids the shell is internal and much reduced. The squid may reach a length of 52 feet and is the largest invertebrate animal.

Cuttlefish provide cuttle bone that is used as beak sharpeners in cages of pet birds like budgerigars and canaries.

A common destructive mollusc, a bivalve, that looks like a worm and has a narrow, elongated soft body covered by two short shells is the shipworm. It bores numerous holes in wooden ships and in the wooden pilings of wharves, eventually destroying them.

Shipworms are a menace to wooden ships and are destructive to piers and other timber under water, especially in the tropics.

VOCABULARY

bivalve	nacre	mollusc
univalve	mother-of-pearl	calcareous
cuttlefish	kitchen midden	abalone
shell	shipworm	Chambered Nautilus
	slug	

Exercise No. 27

Write paragraphs explaining:

1 How the tapeworm is adapted to its parasitic mode of life.
2 How (a) Amoeba (b) The earthworm respire and move.
3 The value of earthworms to man.

Exercise No. 28

Which one term in each of the following includes the others?

1 jellyfish, coral, flatworm, invertebrate, segmented worm.
2 tapeworm, parasite, liver fluke, hookworm.
3 budding, conjugation, fission, reproduction.
4 leeches, segmented worms, earthworms, sandworms.
5 molluscs, oysters, clams, snails.
6 clams, oysters, bivalves, scallops.
7 mother-of-pearl, nacre, oyster, pearl.

THE ARTHROPODS (JOINTED LEGS)

One of the largest and most successful groups of animals in existence today is the invertebrate **arthropod** group. They may be found all over the world, on land, in water and in the air. The most commonly known of this group are lobsters, crabs, crayfish, shrimps, centipedes, spiders and all insects. The outstanding physical characteristics of all animals of this group are:

1 Segmented bodies.
2 Paired segmented (or jointed) appendages.
3 Usually hard exoskeletons (outer skeletons or shells).

LOBSTERS, CRABS AND THEIR RELATIVES (CRUSTACEANS)

Lobsters, crabs, crayfish and shrimps are obviously related to insects. Observe a lobster or crab in a fishmonger's shop and notice the characteristics common to all members of this group. See Fig. 96.

The paired, segmented appendages of these water animals are modified either for walking, swimming or for food-getting and protection. There are usually four pairs plus a pair of large claws.

Their bodies are divided into two sections, covered by a hard skeleton, composed basically of lime which these animals abstract from the water. The hard shell serves as protection and support for the soft body parts under it. The colour of the shell is usually the colour of the native habitat, therefore a protection against natural enemies, a camouflage or protective coloration.

These animals breathe by means of gills that are usually found at the base of each walking leg.

As the soft body parts of the lobster and its relatives grow, they become too large for their rigid, brittle shells. The shell does not grow to allow for this expansion, it splits open and the soft animal crawls into a 'hide-out' where it remains until a new, larger exoskeleton has completely grown. This natural process is known as **moulting**.

All the members of this group of animals are equipped in the head region, with feelers, called antennae, that are sensitive to changes of any kind, chemical or physical, in the surrounding environment.

Lobsters, shrimps, crabs and crayfish and other smaller relatives are important for their food value for human beings as well as for larger water animals. Fresh-water crayfish are famous for their odd method of locomotion. They are able to dart backwards very rapidly.

Barnacles are related to lobsters, crabs and shrimps. They anchor themselves to ships, rocks, and docks and often become so numerous that they have to be

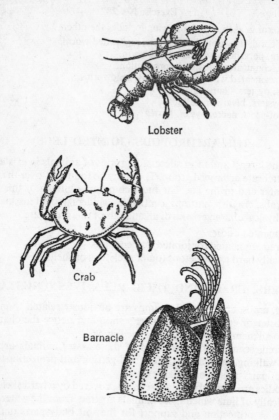

Lobster

Crab

Barnacle

Figure 96 Crustaceans

scraped off. They are hardy creatures, feeding when the ocean tide covers them and withdrawing tightly and safely into their shells when the tide is out.

CENTIPEDES AND MILLIPEDES

Another sub-group of the arthropods includes the centipedes and millipedes. The centipede has from 15 to 100 segments to its body, with one pair of leg appendages to each body segment. It is a fast-moving animal. Some species have poisonous bites which are fatal to small insects on which they feed, and may be painful to man. The natural habitat of the centipede is in dark, damp spots, under the bark of old logs and under stones.

A millipede has a black, worm-like body, with two pairs of leg appendages to each body segment. In spite of the number of legs, it is a slow-moving animal. When in danger, rather than try to exit swiftly, it curls itself up into a ball and remains still. It is plant-eating and completely harmless to man.

SPIDERS (ARACHNIDS)

Spiders are often mistakenly referred to as insects. Both animal forms are true arthropods. Spiders more closely resemble lobsters and crabs than insects.

All insects have three pairs of legs; all spiders have four pairs. Spiders have no antennae while all insects do. Insects have compound, faceted (like the surface of a cut diamond) eyes, whereas spiders have extremely simple eyes arranged in a pattern on the head, characterizing their various species. A spider's body is divided into two regions. See Fig. 97.

There are small appendages, called **spinnerets**, on the under surface of the abdomen. These are small tubes connected with glands which manufacture and secrete the substance with which the spider spins its web.

Most spiders are beneficial to man because they feed on and rid him of insect pests. There are a few, the black widow spider and tarantula (or banana spider), which are extremely poisonous. Their natural habitat is in countries with tropical climates, but a few species are found in more temperate regions.

The scorpion is a large type of spider-relative that looks very much like a crayfish. It has a sting fatal to its enemies and sometimes extremely painful to man.

The harvestman is a member of the spider family. It aids man in destroying some harmful insects.

Mites and ticks are the smallest species of spider-relatives, structurally degenerate, but are also the most important because many are harmful either indirectly or directly to man. These tiny animals are found in almost every country, on land and in the water. Some live on and destroy vegetation; some live on the flesh of animals, including man; others live on blood alone. Some cause extreme discomfort (horrible itching and burning) such as the harvest bug and southern United States chigger. Others transmit diseases such as tick fever, scrub typhus fever, scabies and mange.

Perhaps the most unlikely-looking relative of the spiders is the king or horseshoe crab. Its body is covered by a complete, dark brown, hard shell, an armour-like casing. Otherwise it answers in distinguishing features to those characteristics of the common spider.

The natural habitat of the king crab is in shallow water along the east coast of North America, where it feeds at night on bristle worms and other small sea animals.

Fossil remains indicate that ancestors of these large, strange-looking arthropods existed about 400 million years ago in the early infancy of the world of plants and animals.

INSECTS

The most advanced, structurally and functionally, the most numerous, the most successful and fascinating of all invertebrates are the insects.

The French naturalist JEAN HENRI FABRE (1823–1915) was one of the first to study the behaviour of living insects in their natural habitats. He wrote

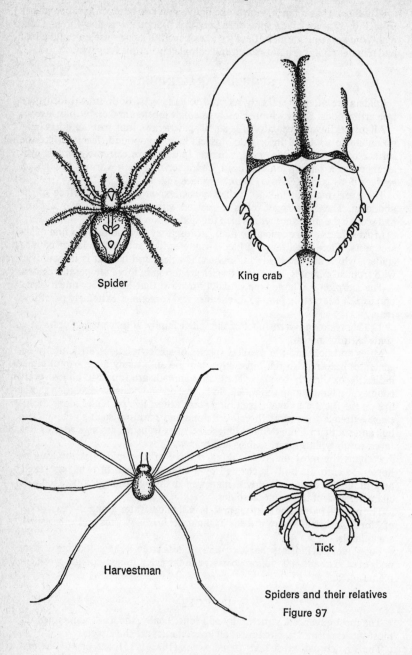

Spider

King crab

Harvestman

Tick

Spiders and their relatives
Figure 97

many books on entomology (the science of insects) that make illuminating and interesting reading.

Insects may be found in every type of habitat, in every climate, in every country on the globe. One may say that where there is life, there are insects.

If possible, observe live or preserved specimens, as we discuss the characteristics of insects, their adaptations for the life functions, their life cycles and economic importance. Visit a museum of natural history or a well-stocked zoological garden and observe the preserved and synthetic specimens in simulated natural habitats. This will enhance your understanding and appreciation of this numerous and varied group of animals.

Capture in a glass jar, a housefly, a moth or butterfly and perhaps a grasshopper from a field. Observe that all have the following characteristics which distinguish them from all other invertebrate animals:

1 Body divided into three segments: head, thorax (chest) and abdomen;
2 a pair of antennae at the top of the head;
3 a hard exoskeleton;
4 usually two pairs of wings;
5 three pairs of segmented legs;
6 breathing pores or openings on each side of body which lead into tubes that branch throughout the entire body;
7 compound, many-faceted eyes.

It is well to study the grasshopper as a typical insect because the identifying characteristics are quite visible.

A typical insect—grasshopper

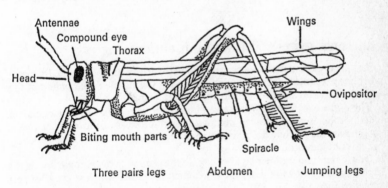

Figure 98

The body of the grasshopper is segmented (divided) into three main parts: head, thorax, abdomen. At the front of the head, near the top, are a pair of feelers or antennae which are sensitive to changes in the immediate environment of the animal. A simple nerve chain co-ordinates stimuli received and responses made.

The type of food an insect eats depends on the type of mouth parts it possesses. The mouth parts of this insect are adapted for biting. Grasshoppers eat grass and other vegetation; other insects, e.g. beetles, which have sharp jaws for piercing and biting live on other animals. Some insects have piercing and sucking mouth parts (mosquitoes and flies) and live on the fluids of plants or animals. Others have tubes for sucking the nectar of flowers (butterflies and moths).

The digestive system of the grasshopper is a single tube running the length of the body. It is divided into sections similar to those characteristic of the earthworm. It consists of an oesophagus, a crop for storing food before it reaches the stomach; a gizzard that has tough walls for crushing food; a stomach where food is digested and a small intestine which widens into a large intestine. In addition, there are digestive glands in the mouth and stomach which supply digestive juices to the crop where some food is prepared for digestion.

The three pairs of segmented legs and two pairs of wings grow from the middle body section, the thorax. The front two pairs of legs of the grasshopper are used for holding, crawling, walking and landing while the muscular hind legs are adapted for jumping.

The outer pair of wings of this insect serves as protective sheaths over the tissue-like under pair which is used in flying.

In moths and butterflies both pairs of wings are extended and locked together during flight.

Insects breathe through **spiracles**—openings in the sides of the body which lead to tubes (tracheae) that branch throughout the body. Oxygen enters the spiracles, penetrates to all parts of the body, and carbon dioxide is dissolved in the blood and then diffuses out over the whole body surface.

LIFE CYCLES AND METAMORPHOSIS OF INSECTS

The life cycle and metamorphosis of insects varies with the species. By metamorphosis we mean abrupt changes occurring during the development of the egg into the adult and the inclusion of a larval form.

There are two forms of metamorphosis, one is referred to as incomplete metamorphosis and the other, complete metamorphosis. In incomplete metamorphosis, the egg hatches into a nymph resembling the adult in some ways, but it is not identical.

The female grasshopper lays her eggs in the ground in the autumn and in the spring of the following year, the eggs hatch into tiny, wingless grasshoppers called **nymphs.** See Fig. 99.

As the nymph grows it moults several times, as the lobster does, develops wings, and finally reaches maturity. This is an example of incomplete metamorphosis.

Moths and butterflies go through complete metamorphosis in their life cycles. They pass through several entirely different forms as they grow from egg to adult stage. See Fig. 100.

The female butterfly lays eggs on a leaf or twig of a tree. The new larval form, a caterpillar, develops from the fertilized egg. This segmented, worm-

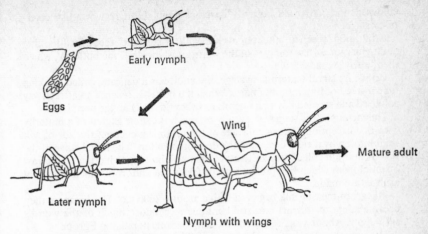

Figure 99 Incomplete metamorphosis in the grasshopper

like form has cutting and biting mouth parts with which it devours leaves, sometimes doing a great deal of damage to fruit trees and crops.

The caterpillar moults its outer skin four times as it increases in size. At the fourth moult, the caterpillar attaches itself, by a thread of self-secreted silk, head down on the twig. The result of the fourth moult is a parchment-like case that entirely surrounds the animal at this stage—the **pupa**. The pupal stage of the butterfly is called a **chrysalis**. Within the pupal case, the beautifully

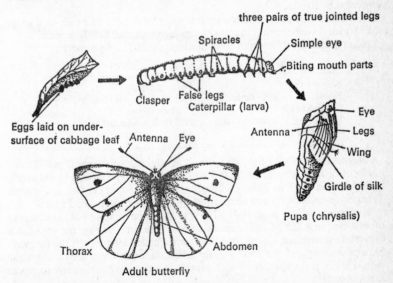

Figure 100 Complete metamorphosis of cabbage white butterfly

coloured and patterned butterfly develops from the ugly worm-like caterpillar stage.

Adulthood reached, the pupal case splits open and the wilted-looking adult emerges. A few minutes in the warm sunshine dries the butterfly, which then slowly spreads its wings.

Unlike its larval (caterpillar) stage, the adult has a delicate, coiled, sucking tube instead of biting mouth parts. When the butterfly reaches an attractively coloured and scented flower it uncoils its tube and sucks up the nectar.

The metamorphic stages of a moth are much the same as that of a butterfly with one exception. The pupal stage of the moth is a cocoon, threads of silk spun into an oval case, enclosing the developing adult. The larval stage of the silkworm moth still continues to serve man well in the production of the raw material from which fine fabrics may be fashioned and from which industrial artifices are made.

The art of making silk began in China around 2600 B.C. The Japanese then became adept at this art and still continue to produce much of the world's silk supply. About A.D. 530 the silk industry became popular in Europe.

The actual process of producing raw silk is performed by the silkworm, which is the larval or caterpillar stage of the silkworm moth. The silkworm moth's eggs develop into caterpillars, which feed on mulberry and sometimes osage orange leaves. From its silk glands, a fluid is produced which hardens when it comes into contact with the air. The caterpillar spins an oval cocoon about itself which consists of a single thread which may reach 2,400 feet in length.

It normally takes the pupal stage about two weeks to develop into adulthood within its cocoon. To avoid destruction of silk winding threads, the developing animal is killed within its cocoon and the silk strand is carefully unwound by hand.

At present machines combine several raw silk strands to result in a single silk thread. A single pound of raw silk represents about 25,000 cocoons.

Adult butterflies differ from adult moths in the following respects:

BUTTERFLY	MOTH
Flies by day	Flies by night
Holds its wings vertically when at rest	Holds its wings horizontally when at rest
Has straight antennae with clubbed tips	Has feather-like antennae

The metamorphosis of the common housefly, one of the most prolific and hardy of insect pests, is similar to that of the moth. The fly can be extremely harmful because of its habit of breeding in and feeding on filth and refuse. Typhoid fever bacteria are transferred by this insect pest. See Fig. 101.

The female fly lays from 100 to 150 eggs at a time on refuse of some sort or on manure. In a day or two, depending upon the temperature, the eggs hatch into white worm-like, legless, headless larvae, called maggots. If the temperature is high enough and the food supply adequate, each larva forms a cocoon within which it develops (in 5 to 7 days) into a mature adult, ready to repeat the life cycle.

The most successful method of preventing the spread of bacteria and dis-

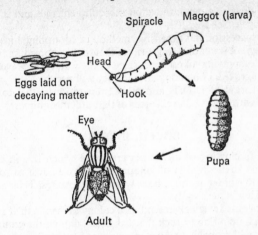

Figure 101 Complete metamorphosis of the housefly

eases carried by flies is to prevent the flies from breeding, that is, to get rid of refuse and/or to keep it covered.

Another insect pest whose life cycle exhibits complete metamorphosis is the mosquito. All female mosquitoes are adapted for piercing and sucking the blood of their victims. The mosquito secretes saliva into the pierced opening, preventing the victim's blood from clotting while the animal is sucking. Some chemical substance in the saliva of the mosquito causes itching, swelling and inflammation of an area—the mosquito bite.

There are two common species of mosquitoes: the common Culex or gnat, with which we are all familiar; and Anopheles, carrier of malaria fever.

The female mosquito lays from 200 to 400 eggs on the surface of stagnant water. The small wriggling larva hatches out of the egg after 24 hours. This larval stage is called the wriggler because it wriggles about for food in the water but comes up to the surface, with a snorkel-like projection, to breathe air. About a week later, after a series of moultings, the pupal stage (called the tumbler) develops. Unlike most other insect pupal stages, the mosquito tumbler is able to move about in the water. Like the wriggler stage, it comes to the surface of the water to breathe air.

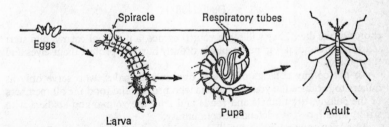

Figure 102 Complete metamorphosis of the mosquito

After two days as a pupa, the adult mosquito emerges and is ready to re-peat the life cycle. See Fig. 102.

The most successful, but expensive, method of controlling mosquitoes is to drain off stagnant water and so get rid of their natural breeding places. If this is not feasible, spraying oil on the surface of the water will prevent the larval and pupal stages from obtaining air and they will perish.

Chemical sprays of D.D.T. and other preparations lethal to insects and other animals are now used to rid areas of the adult mosquitoes.

SOCIAL INSECTS

The most fascinating of all insects are those which live in communities where there is strict division of labour. These are known as social insects. Members of this order are ants, bees, wasps and termites. Their activities and habits afford a lifetime's study.

A colony of ants amazingly resembles a colony of men in their activities and reactions. Pick up a slab or rock that has been lying on the ground for some time and you will probably find a community of ants busily going through the

Metamorphosis of the ant

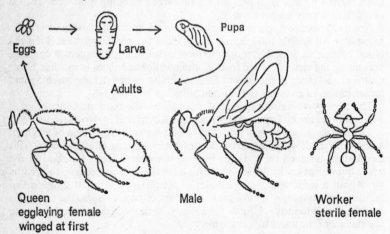

Figure 103

chores of the day. They will sense your presence, a potential enemy, and start scurrying around, not in panic, but in orderly hurry to protect themselves and their young.

An ant colony consists of several queens and males, who serve only as fathers to produce the young, workers who provide the food for all members of the colony, dig tunnels and roads and tend the young, and soldiers with strong mouth parts to defend the community.

Ants keep cows which they milk by stroking with their antennae. These ant cows are actually greenfly which give forth a sweet fluid that ants feed to the larval stage of their young. The worker ants feed and protect the greenfly during the winter season as well as in the spring and summer. See Fig. 103.

Some species of ants capture enemy young, rear them and train them to act as slaves.

A honey bee colony, the hive, consists of about 50,000 bees. A single queen reigns over a hive only in so far as she produces the eggs. Because of her specialized function, she is the best fed and cared for member of the colony.

The males or drones serve only to fertilize the eggs. The non-egg laying females are the workers. They are in the majority in the hive.

Special worker bees called nurses have but one job in the hive, and that is the feeding and caring for the larvae after they hatch from eggs. After the pupal stage is formed, it takes about 21 days for the adult bee to develop. The workers seal each wax cell with a cap during the development from pupal to adult stage.

At the completion of this final metamorphic stage, the fully grown bee eats its way out of the wax cell and assumes its special job in the hive. The job for which an adult bee is adapted depends on the type and amount of food it is fed during the larval stage.

Worker bees manufacture honey within themselves using the nectar they sip from flowers as a basis of the sweet fluid. The flavour of honey depends upon the flower from which the nectar is sipped.

The hind legs of a honey-bee worker are adapted with baskets in which pollen from flowers is collected. The tooth-like edges of the second pair of legs act as combs to remove pollen grains from the many hairs of the bee's body.

There are no soldiers in a bee colony. The queen bee and workers have barbed stings at the end of their abdomens. The sting is a modified ovipositor. When a bee stings a larger animal, it usually loses its stinging apparatus and dies.

Bees swarm, all flying out of the hive and remaining in close clusters on a branch for several hours, when a hive threatens to become overcrowded. After swarming, new colonies are formed and a queen is chosen for each.

Termites are also social insects with highly developed division of labour in their community living. They can be extremely detrimental to man's welfare because of their feeding habits. They feed on cellulose which is the organic substance found in the cell walls of woody plants.

Protozoa, which live in symbiotic relationship within the stomach of a termite, actually digest the woody material for the termite and receive food and protection in return.

A colony of termite workers can undermine the wooden foundation beams of a house in a very short time. Most termites have been found living successfully in Africa but a few species have migrated to other countries.

The use of metal and concrete instead of wood in building foundations, has done much to prevent destruction by termites.

ECONOMIC IMPORTANCE OF INSECTS

Insects are so numerous and widespread for several reasons: (1) they reproduce frequently, laying thousands of eggs in a single season; (2) they are protected by some resemblance to their immediate natural surroundings in colour and structure; and, (3) they can either fly, hop, jump or crawl (or a combination of these) quickly enough to escape capture.

Some insects are economically useful to man:

1 They help pollinate flowers and thus ensure continuation of a species (bees).

2 Some are scavengers (beetles).

3 Some produce honey (bees).

4 Some produce silk (the silkworm).

5 Some destroy harmful insects (Ichneumon fly, dragon-fly, ladybird).

Many insects are socially and economically harmful to man—they outnumber the useful insects:

1 Some transmit diseases to man (housefly, Anopheles mosquito, rat flea).

2 Some destroy woollens (clothes moth larva).

3 Some attack animals domesticated by man (animal lice).

4 The majority of harmful insects destroy many valuable crops and fruit trees annually.

INSECT	PLANT ATTACKED
Cotton boll weevil	Cotton plant
Codling moth	Apple trees
Chinch bug	Corn and wheat
Colorado potato beetle	Potatoes
Cabbage butterfly	Cabbage plant
Locust	Grasses and grains, fruit trees and other young plants
Japanese beetle	Fruit trees, shrubs and grasses

There are effective measures of controlling harmful insects and preventing total destruction of plants and crops attacked by them:

1 Rotation of crops helps rid a field of an insect blight.

2 Use of insect poisons (insecticides) that are harmless to plant hosts.

3 Burning of remains of crops to destroy breeding places.

4 Introduction of natural enemies (e.g. birds, other insects).

5 Careful inspection and quarantine of freight on planes and ships from other countries to prevent importation of insect pests.

STARFISH AND THEIR RELATIVES (ECHINODERMS)

Starfish, brightly coloured and numerous, and their relatives the sea urchins, sea cucumbers, brittle stars and sand dollars, are a group of animals found in shallow salt water and are characterized by their hard, spiny exoskeleton. Both externally and internally their body organs exhibit radial symmetry. See Fig. 104.

The water-vascular system is the first evidence of a system of tubes that circulate water and digested food through all parts of the body. There is no heart or true blood system.

These animals have a peculiar method of locomotion. Small tube-like projections extend on the under surface (ventral). They act like vacuum suction cups, as the animal attaches itself to a stationary object. It draws its body up, and then releases the cups by forcing water into each tube.

The starfish, usually five-pointed, eats in an unusual manner. (See Chapter II.) Its favourite food is the oyster which it devours by projecting its stomach

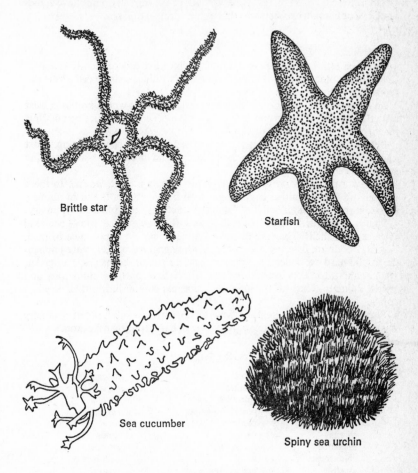

Brittle star

Starfish

Sea cucumber

Spiny sea urchin

Figure 104   Starfish and relatives

between the shells of the bivalve. It pre-digests the soft oyster body before withdrawing its stomach back into its body.

Starfish can therefore be a menace to oyster beds. At one time, oyster fishermen would catch starfish, cut them up and throw sections back into the ocean. This served only to increase the starfish population manifold because many pieces grow into whole animals by the process of regeneration. Now, starfish are hauled out of the sea and spread out far up on the beach so that they cannot possibly make their way back to the water. Here the hot sun dries them out and kills them.

In China, France and various South Sea Islands, sea cucumbers are caught, dried and sold as food for soup under the name of bêche-de-mer (in French, worm of the sea) or trepang. These relatives of the starfish do not have spines and have only small exoskeletons that appear deep in the skin.

SUMMARY

Protozoa are simple, one-celled animals which live independently in water. They are adapted to carry on all life processes within the single cell. Protozoa reproduce by fission.

Sponges, jellyfish and corals are many-celled animals whose bodies consist of two layers of cells surrounding a hollow cavity. They reproduce by budding, regeneration and also sexually.

Flatworms and roundworms show increased structural specialization. Most known flatworms are parasitic. Hookworms and porkworms are parasitic roundworms.

Earthworms, sandworms and leeches are true segmented worms. In these animals we find primitive beginnings of all body systems found in animals higher in the scale of animal life. All body structures show bilateral symmetry.

Snails, oysters and related animals have soft, unsegmented bodies enclosed in calcareous shells. They are of considerable economic importance to man.

Arthropods are invertebrate animals with segmented bodies, paired appendages and hard exoskeletons. Lobsters, crabs, shrimps, barnacles, centipedes, spiders and all insects are arthropods. Insects are the most numerous and varied animals. They go through metamorphic stages during their life histories.

Starfish and related animals are invertebrates which exhibit radial symmetry in structure. These animals are covered with a hard, spiny exoskeleton.

VOCABULARY

arthropod	facets	maggot
appendage	trachea	pupa
exoskeleton	spiracles	cocoon
moulting	protective colour	chrysalis
antennae	metamorphosis	hive
thorax	nymph	drone
abdomen	caterpillar	swarm
spinnerets	larva	cellulose
starfish	brittle star	ventral
sea urchin	exoskeleton	bêche-de-mer
sea cucumber	radial symmetry	trepang
	water-vascular system	

Exercise No. 29

Match a number in Column *A* with a letter in Column *B*.

A	*B*
1 arthropod	a larval stage of fly
2 invertebrate	b shedding of exoskeleton
3 exoskeleton	c pupal stage of moth

4 protective coloration	d ants, bees and termites
5 moulting	e hard, outer skeleton
6 spinneret	f feelers on insects
7 spiracle	g without backbone
8 metamorphosis	h jointed legs
9 maggot	i changes of form in life history
10 antennae	j larval stage of butterfly
11 cocoon	k spins spider web thread
12 tracheae	l branched breathing tubes in insects
13 caterpillar	m aphids or greenfly that provide fluid food for ants
14 hive	n breathing openings in bodies of insects
15 ant cow	o colour pattern to blend with habitat
16 social insects	p colonies of bees and wasps

Exercise No. 30

Complete the following statements:

1 Lobsters and crabs breathe by means of —— at the base of each walking leg.
2 Spiders have —— pairs of segmented legs.
3 Two poisonous spiders are —— and ——.
4 The harvestman is a member of the —— group.
5 Scabies is transmitted by a ——.
6 The horseshoe crab is really a —— relative.
7 Arthropods with three pairs of legs, usually two pairs of wings and body divided into 3 parts are ——.
8 The young grasshopper is called a ——.
9 A grasshopper exhibits —— metamorphosis in its life cycle.
10 Moths and butterflies do most damage to crops in their —— stage.
11 Moths and butterflies exhibit —— metamorphosis.
12 Moths usually fly at ——, whereas butterflies fly during the ——.
13 The common housefly is harmful because ——.
14 The most effective way to control mosquitoes is to ——.
15 The type of food an insect eats depends on its ——.
16 The wings of a butterfly are held in a —— position when the animal is at rest, and the moth, —— when at rest.
17 Honey bees —— when the hives become overcrowded.
18 Termites feed on ——.

CHAPTER IX

THE ANIMAL KINGDOM: THE VERTEBRATES

The second large division in the Animal Kingdom is the vertebrate group. Animals belonging to this group all have backbones at one stage of their lives. Most vertebrates have an internal skeleton, as compared with the shell-like exoskeleton of arthropods. Most vertebrates have two pairs of appendages in the form of fins, wings or legs.

The brain and entire nervous system, including the organs of sensation (e.g. eyes, ears, nose, etc.), are more highly developed in vertebrates than in invertebrates.

Water-living vertebrates usually breathe by means of gills whereas land-living vertebrates breathe by means of lungs. (Traces of gill areas are found even in land-living vertebrates during their embryonic development.) Characteristic of all vertebrates is a muscular heart of one or more chambers which pumps red blood through tubes (arteries, capillaries and veins) which branch throughout the body.

The main sub-groups of vertebrates are the fish, frogs, reptiles, birds and mammals.

FISH

The simplest and most numerous vertebrates are the fish. Many varieties can be found in salt and fresh water and in shallow and deep waters of every temperature.

The fish is a cold-blooded animal, that is, its body temperature is the same as the surrounding waters at all times. Warm-blooded animals maintain a constant body temperature under normal conditions. For example, the normal body temperature of the human animal is approximately 98·4°F. The normal constant body temperature of birds is a good deal higher.

Observe fish in a home-made aquarium. Watch them swim, eat, breathe, play and protect themselves. Examine a dead fish from the fishmonger and see the gills under the bony gill covering or **operculum.** Notice how well a fish is equipped to spend its life in water.

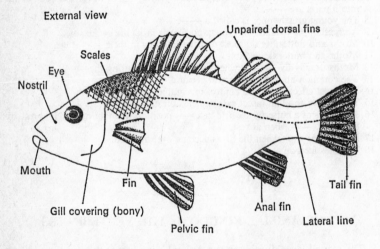

Figure 105　Vertebrate animal—a fish

The front (anterior) and back (posterior) of the fish are well-tapered to cut through the water, streamlined to meet the least resistance in swimming. There is a slimy mucous substance covering the entire outside surface of the body—another adaptation for life in the water. This is also a means of protection against natural enemies.

Notice that the scales of the fish overlap and grow outwards towards the tail—another adaptation for decreasing resistance to the water.

There are two pairs of visible appendages, fins, and several single, median fins. The chief means of locomotion is provided by the tail fin together with the muscular tail. The other fins serve for steering, balancing, stopping and reversing action. See Fig. 105.

An air bladder in the body cavity of some fishes helps the fish rise or sink and keep its balance.

The fish is well-adapted for respiration. If the gills are bright red, that is an indication that it is a freshly caught fish, that the blood in the gills still contains fresh oxygen.

Watch a goldfish in the aquarium open and close its mouth constantly. It is breathing. Water enters the mouth, passes back over the gills on each side of the head and passes out through the gill coverings. As the water passes over the gills, oxygen from the dissolved air in the water is taken into the blood in the gills by the process of diffusion. From here it is carried by the blood and circulated to all parts of the body. The waste gas carbon dioxide, a result of oxidation of food, is carried from the body cells to the gills where it passes (by diffusion) into the water.

Fish feed on tiny green plants, microscopic plants and animals, smaller fish or other water animals and some water insects. The digestive system is divided into stomach and intestine and several digestive glands (e.g. liver and pancreas) that produce juices which aid in digestion of food in all vertebrate animals.

In the fish, we find the first evidence of a true (but simple) brain and spinal cord. Nerves come to this central nervous system from the organs of sensation:

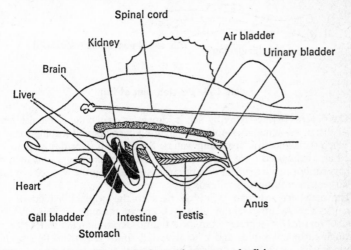

Figure 106 Internal structure of a fish

the eyes (without lids), nose apertures (openings in the head used as organs of smell not for breathing) and the lateral line. Nerves go out from the central nervous system to all parts of the body.

The lateral line consists of a series of nerve cells located along the full length of both sides of the animal about midway between the top and bottom. It is used to pick up vibrations and temperature changes in the water. Balance is maintained by a series of canals in the ear.

In the development of fish, the young develop from eggs (roe) produced in the body of the female and usually fertilized in the water by the sperm (milt) of the male. Since there are so many hazards in the waters, many hundreds of eggs are usually produced to ensure continuance of a species.

After an egg hatches, the new fish resembles the adult except that it has a reservoir of food attached to it. This food supply is yolk in the yolk sac. As the young fish grows, the yolk becomes absorbed until the fish is large enough and old enough to eat food found in its native water.

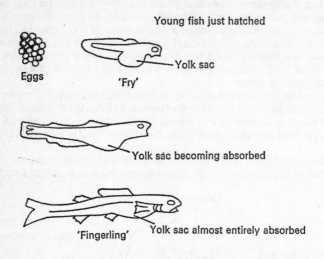

Young fish just hatched

Eggs

'Fry' — Yolk sac

Yolk sac becoming absorbed

'Fingerling' — Yolk sac almost entirely absorbed

Figure 107 Development of fish

The process of egg-laying by fish is known as spawning. Some fish travel great distances, sometimes upstream, fighting currents and leaping cataracts to reach their ancestral spawning waters. Some reach their destination, battered and exhausted from the perilous journey, lay their eggs and then die. Others cannot survive the natural hazards, succumb on the way, or are eaten by larger fish or fish-eating animals.

The new-born fish find their way back to the original habitat of their parents. The Atlantic salmon is a well-known example of this. When it reaches maturity it migrates from the Atlantic Ocean up fresh water streams, through turbulent rapids and over waterfalls until it reaches its spawning grounds which may be hundreds of miles inland. After spawning the salmon are exhausted from this extreme physical effort and from complete lack of food during the entire journey, and many die before they can reach the sea again.

The young hatch after about two months and remain in the river for several months before starting their journey back to the Atlantic Ocean where they mature and repeat the life-long journey back to the inland rivers.

Salmon native to the Pacific Ocean migrate one to two thousand miles to the Columbia river to spawn.

Some eels (snake-like fish) reverse the migratory procedure by swimming against rough odds to the cold depths of the Sargasso Sea to spawn. The young eels swim back to the fresh waters to continue their life cycle.

Since some fish are an important source of food to man, there are government laws protecting them during spawning season. There are also hatcheries where the young are reared and protected until they are old enough to fend for themselves. Then they are carefully transported to native water habitats—a procedure known as stocking a stream, lake or pond.

Besides their extreme value as food for man, some fish provide important oils (cod and halibut liver oil) which are a rich source of vitamin D. Sturgeon roe (caviare) and shad roe are considered food delicacies. The bones of some fish are powdered and used to make gelatine, also to provide fertilizer material to enrich farm soils.

VOCABULARY

backbone	cold-blooded	fins
embryonic	warm-blooded	mucous
red blood	spawn	air bladder
arteries	fry	lateral line
capillaries	fingerling	yolk sac
veins	roe	stocking
operculum	scales	

FROGS AND THEIR RELATIVES (AMPHIBIANS)

Frogs and their relatives, toads, salamanders and newts are called amphibians. These cold-blooded animals are equally at home in water and on land. They spend their early stages in water and are structurally adapted to function in both types of environments.

Observe a living frog near a pond or in an aquarium. Notice the shape and colour and how it resembles its surroundings. It is interesting to note that the colour on the upper side of the frog is green and brown or all green or perhaps a mixture of green and yellow; whereas the belly surface is very light, sometimes almost white. This serves as a source of protection for the frog when it is swimming in water. An animal underneath, looking up, does not see the frog clearly because of the reflection of the sky.

Watch the frog hop on ground and then swim in the water. Touch its skin and observe the texture. Watch it catch and devour a flying insect.

The front legs are short for landing and the hind legs are long and muscular for leaping. Note that the hind toes are webbed, an adaptation for swimming. See Fig. 108.

The body systems of the frog are more complex than those of the fish, showing a decided advance in the scale of animal life.

The young frog (or tadpole) whose developing life is spent in water, breathes by means of external and later internal gills. The adult frog, when on land takes air through the nostrils and mouth, swallows it into a trachea or wind-pipe and into a pair of sac-like lungs.

When in the water, the adult frog absorbs oxygen through its very thin, moist skin. The adult frog, then is, very well adapted to lead an amphibian life because it has two organs of respiration, lungs and skin.

The circulatory system of the frog consists of a three-chambered heart (an advance over the two-chambered heart of the fish) and branching blood vessels. Since the skin is an organ of respiration it contains many large blood vessels which carry the oxygen to all parts of the body and carbon dioxide back to the skin for excretion.

Frogs and related animals feed on living insects, some worms, snails and sometimes smaller frogs. A frog has a unique manner of capturing food. It

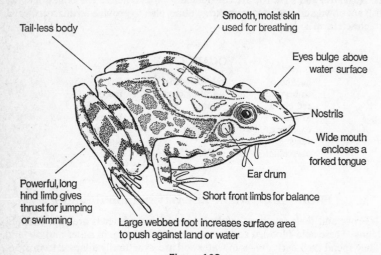

Figure 108

rests unobtrusively on a lily pad or on a stone on the edge of a pond, alert for its prey. When an unsuspecting flying insect approaches, the tongue of the frog darts out of its mouth and captures the insect on the forked, sticky end. The tongue is then pulled in to the back of the mouth and the victim is swal-lowed whole. See Fig. 109.

The digestive system of the frog shows an advance in adaptation over the digestive system of fish. The digestive tube is divided into oesophagus, gullet, stomach, small intestine, large intestine and the end of the large intestine—the cloaca. Two glands which provide digestive enzymes are the three-lobed liver and the pancreas.

As in fish, all organs of the digestive system are held in place in the abdom-inal cavity of the frog by thin membraneous tissues called **mesentery** tissues or **mesenteries.** See Fig. 110.

The frog—catching a flying insect

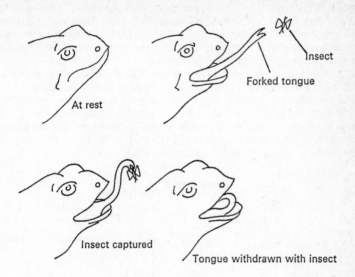

At rest

Forked tongue

Insect

Insect captured

Tongue withdrawn with insect

Figure 109

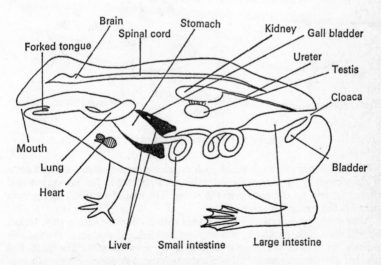

Brain

Spinal cord

Stomach

Kidney

Gall bladder

Forked tongue

Ureter

Testis

Cloaca

Mouth

Lung

Heart

Bladder

Liver

Small intestine

Large intestine

Figure 110   Internal organs of frog

Circulation of red blood is effected by a three-chambered heart. One of the upper chambers (left auricle) of the heart receives blood from the lungs, where it gets fresh oxygen. The other upper chamber (right auricle) receives blood which is depleted of oxygen from all parts of the body. The blood then enters the lower muscular chamber (ventricle) from which it is pumped by muscular contraction either to the lungs to replenish the oxygen, or to the other organs of the body to supply them with fresh oxygen.

A pair of kidneys removes liquid wastes from the blood. The wastes are collected in a bladder and excreted from the body by way of the cloaca.

The nervous system of the frog bears a decided resemblance, especially in function, to the central nervous system of mammals (including man). It includes a well-developed brain, cranial nerves, a spinal cord and ten pairs of nerves branching from the spinal cord to all parts of the body. The organs of sight, hearing, smell and touch are extremely sensitive to stimuli.

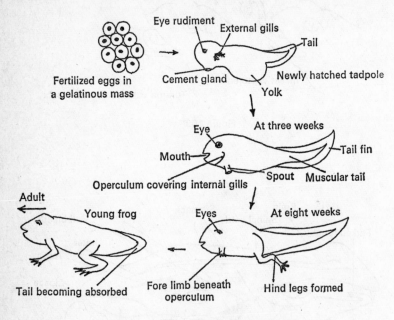

Figure 111 Metamorphosis of the frog

The life history of a frog, which includes metamorphosis, starts with a mass of eggs covered by a transparent gelatinous substance for protection and buoyancy, laid by the female in the water. The male frog fertilizes the eggs just after they enter the water.

After each egg is fertilized by a sperm cell, it develops into a tiny, legless tadpole with yolk, similar to a newly-hatched fish. At this stage the tadpole breathes by means of external and later by internal gills. The yolk and external gills become absorbed while the tadpole is developing a mouth with which to feed on vegetation.

As the tadpole grows, the hind legs appear first and the tail becomes shorter and is absorbed as food into the growing body. The lungs begin to develop at the same time as the front legs appear. The infant frog is now ready to come up on land to grow into a full-sized adult and repeat the life cycle. See Fig. 111.

Frogs hibernate in the mud throughout the winter, that is, they go into a type of sleep during which all of the body processes become extremely slow. During this time, the energy for all retarded life functions is obtained from food stored in the body during the summer months.

A toad, the closest relative of the frog, usually spends its adult life on land away from its birthplace. It skin is dark brown and rough-looking but smooth to the touch. (It does not cause growths called warts on your hand, as the old wives' tale has it.)

The development of the toad is similar to that of the frog except that the female lays her eggs in a ribbon of gelatinous material instead of a mass.

The toad is of great economic importance to man because it eats many harmful and destructive insects.

Salamanders and newts have long slender tails which they retain throughout life and two pairs of rather weak legs. They are sometimes mistakenly called lizards.

VOCABULARY

amphibian	pancreas	kidney
nostrils	spleen	bladder
lungs	wart	tadpole
oesophagus	mesentery	hibernate
cloaca	auricle	toad
	ventricle	

REPTILES

A visit to a museum of Natural History will reveal the remains of the ancient ancestors of a group of vertebrates—the reptiles. These animals are related on the one hand to amphibians and on the other to a more highly developed group in the Animal Kingdom, the birds. They are the first truly terrestrial vertebrates and have water-proof scales covering the body to stop drying up in the air.

You will see huge bony skeletons and fossil remains of dinosaurs and other related reptiles that at one time populated the air, the land and the swampy waters. They existed on earth for at least ten million years in prehistoric times as the dominant fauna along with the giant ferns and rushes which were the dominant flora of that age.

A radical change in climate, the moving of polar ice caps and huge glaciers, buried the vegetation (resulting in our current coal beds and natural gas and oil veins) and caused the extinction of these huge animals. In addition, the appearance of carnivorous (meat-eating) animals, more fleet of foot and wily than the lumbering, small-brained dinosaurs, helped rid the earth of these prehistoric creatures before they themselves were conquered by natural forces.

Tortoises, snakes, lizards, alligators and crocodiles are the common reptiles of modern times. All of these cold-blooded animals are adapted with lungs for breathing air on land. Even creatures living in water—such as water snakes, turtles, alligators and crocodiles—must come to the surface of the water to take air into their lungs.

An advance in structural adaptation is found in the appearance of a four-chambered heart (similar to the heart of man) in alligators and crocodiles.

The developmental stages of reptiles are simple. The young develop into smaller adult forms directly from the fertilized eggs which are surrounded by a waterproof shell.

The tortoise carries its home on its back. To separate the body of the animal from its shell is to kill the animal because the shell is an overgrown, elaborate fusion of backbone and ribs to which the soft body is closely attached. The tortoise can withdraw its head, two pairs of legs and tail into the shell for complete protection.

A snake is legless in its adult form. At some time in its embryonic growth (within the unhatched egg) the animal has two pairs of legs. It navigates along the ground by means of scutes which are large scales on the belly surface of the animal. A snake has a smooth, hard-scaled body covering—it is not slimy.

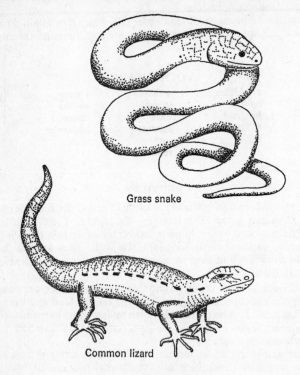

Grass snake

Common lizard

Figure 112 Reptiles

The developmental stages of the snake are, in general, similar to those of the tortoise. Some species, however, bear their young alive—that is, the young hatch out of eggs within the body of the female. As the snake grows, it moults its skin, very much like some invertebrates.

Many common snakes (grass snake, slow-worm) are entirely harmless. The red, forked tongue that darts from the mouth, when any of them is approached, can do no damage.

The cobra of India is one of the deadliest of all poisonous snakes and the most strikingly beautiful in a terrifying manner. Africa and India have a wide variety of imposing snakes. The ringhals or spitting cobra has a frightening reputation in Africa as have the mambas, the deadliest of all snakes. In the desert regions of the United States, rattlesnakes are common and dangerous. There are few places in the world without snakes both harmless and poisonous.

The two glands that secrete poison venom in poisonous snakes are usually found in the upper jaw. Tubes from the glands lead the venom into two hollow, curved teeth in the upper jaw. These are called fangs.

Huge, powerful snakes called boa constrictors and pythons, found in parts of South America, Africa and Asia, are dangerous for their ability to crush their prey to death.

Lizards, a group of reptiles covered with dry scales, are usually found in hot climates. The little chameleon (pronounced *ka me' leon*) is famous for its ability to take on the coloration of the object on which it crawls.

Most lizards have an unusual manner of self-protection. When grasped by the tail, this appendage separates from the rest of the body and the animal glides away eventually to regenerate another tail.

In the desert region of the United States, the famous horned toad that looks like an ugly, thick-skinned, horny toad with a tail, is actually a type of lizard. It is well adapted for life under the intense sun and on the burning, dry sands.

The only poisonous lizard known to exist, lives in the deserts of Arizona and New Mexico and is the Gila monster (pronounced *he' la*). The poison glands are located in the lower jaw of this orange and black, bead-like skinned lizard that sometimes reaches a length of twenty-five inches.

Many reptiles are more beneficial than harmful to man. They destroy animals such as mice, rats and insects which are pests to man and cause damage to his crops. The terrapin turtle is used in some parts of the world as food.

VOCABULARY

reptile	rattlesnake	horned toad
dinosaur	cobra	Gila monster
carnivorous	boa constrictor	scute
turtle	python	venom
tortoise	chameleon	fangs

Exercise No. 31

Match a number in Column *A* with a letter in Column *B*.

A	B
1 scutes	a meat-eating
2 fangs	b snake poison
3 dinosaurs	c scales used by snakes for locomotion
4 chameleons	d poisonous lizard
5 venom	e fusion of backbone and ribs
6 Gila monster	f hollow biting teeth of poisonous snakes
7 carnivorous	g prehistoric reptiles
8 tortoise shell	h lizards that change colour.

BIRDS

The distinguishing feature of these vertebrates is the presence of feathers covering the entire body except the beak and the hind-limbs. These latter are covered with a scale-like skin. The fore-limbs, wings, are also covered with feathers and are adapted for flying in most species of birds. All birds have feathery tails, some long and others short, which serve for balancing and steering.

Figure 113 The bird—external structure

The bird is a warm-blooded animal whose normal constant body temperature is higher than the temperature of man; it is generally 110–112°F. The soft, often brilliantly coloured feathers serve as a light-weight blanket to keep the animal dry and warm, preventing escape of body heat into the air as the bird flies.

Hollow bones make the bird light—a further adaptation for its life in the air.

Birds have a well-developed four-chambered heart (2 auricles and 2 ventricles) and breathe by means of lungs and a system of air sacs. In order to provide enough energy for their active lives, they eat frequently and breathe rapidly, taking in fresh supplies of oxygen for rapid oxidation of food.

The digestive system is much the same as that of the frog, except that a bird has a crop in which some food is stored and a tough, thick-walled gizzard. The bird swallows and stores gravel in the gizzard to help grind food before digestion takes place. Birds have no teeth.

The brain of the bird is relatively small. The sense of smell is not very well developed but the eyesight is extremely keen, as is the sense of hearing.

The base of the windpipe is enlarged into a voice box, called a syrinx, from

for seed eating

Sparrow

Parrot

for insect eating

Woodpecker

Swallow

for weed eating

for fish eating

Duck

Pelican

Eagle

for rabbit and large animal catching

Owl

for nectar eating   Humming bird

Figure 114 Beak adaptations

which the often melodic and entrancing bird calls and songs issue. Just as in the human voice box, there are vocal cords (membranes) that determine the loudness and pitch of the notes.

Since there are several thousand species of birds in every type of habitat all over the world, they are classified in many ways for ease of recognition and study.

Sometimes birds are grouped according to the structure of their beaks, thus determining the food habits and means of defence of a specific group. See Fig. 114.

For example, birds with small, strong, wedge-shaped beaks are usually seed eaters: sparrows, canaries, finches, parrots. Domesticated birds like chickens and turkeys have beaks adapted for scratching for seeds and for capturing ground-living insects.

Many birds have beaks adapted for catching insects, e.g. flycatchers, swallows, swifts and cuckoos.

Some birds have long beaks for catching live fish in the water, e.g. cranes, pelicans and storks.

The tiny, beautiful, jewel-coloured humming-bird has a long, slender beak adapted to serve as a dainty straw through which it sips nectar from honeysuckle and other sweet blossoms.

Hawks, falcons and owls have sharp, curved beaks with which they catch mice, rats, sometimes even fowl and other birds. The eagle, a powerful and large bird, has a hooked beak with which it can catch and tear apart an animal as large as a sheep.

Birds may also be classified into the following groups:

Perching Birds—Their leg muscles, clutching toes, and body-weight distribution adapt them for alighting and holding on to a branch for long periods of time without tiring. Most song birds belong to this group. Many of these birds are economically important to man because they feed on insect pests which are destructive to crops. Among the common perching birds are sparrows, larks, swallows, thrushes, crows, nuthatches, waxwings, warblers, blackbirds, starlings, kingfishers and many others.

Birds of Prey—These birds with strong curved beaks and long, sharp claws also have large strong wings that enable them to soar and glide high and long. Eagles, hawks, kites, vultures and some owls are examples. Vultures and buzzards are well-known scavengers, especially in desert regions. They feed on dead animal flesh.

Water Birds—(a) One group of water birds can actually swim. They have webbed feet for this activity and are able to dive under water for their food. Their feathers are covered with a heavy oil that prevents water from soaking through to the body. Ducks, swans, geese, gulls and terns are members of this group. (b) Another group of water birds has long bills and long, slender legs that enable them to wade in shallow water to secure water animals for food. Cranes, storks, herons and flamingoes are among them.

Non-flying Birds—The penguin's wings are modified as flippers for swimming—this bird cannot fly. The wings of the ostrich are very small compared to the size of this clumsy bird. The ostrich cannot fly but it runs very swiftly on its long legs when the need arises. This largest of all living birds has a most powerful and vicious kick.

Birds reproduce by laying eggs that are fertilized internally. The delicate, protective shell of the bird forms, just before it is laid, within the mother's body. Most birds lay their eggs in nests, some carefully made of straw, some of twigs and leaves, and some of stolen hairs or threads. A few species of birds, like the cuckoo, do not build nests of their own. The female lays the eggs in already built, and sometimes occupied nests, leaving her eggs to be hatched and cared for by the hosts.

Nature has fitted the female bird so that she can inconspicuously fetch food for and tend her young. Her plumage is generally dull and unattractive as compared with her mate's. The male bird is usually bright of plumage, first to attract the female of the species, and then to draw enemy attention away from the mothering bird after mating has taken place.

Most birds are born naked and helpless. (These are known as altricial birds.) These are tenderly fed and cared for by one or both parents until they are able to fly and secure food for themselves, two arts taught them by the parents. Robins, wrens, and eagles are among the altricial birds.

Others, like the domesticated fowl and a few wild birds, nightjars and ducks, are born with soft, downy feathers and are able to run about soon after they hatch out of the eggs and dry their feathers in the sun. These are known as precocial birds.

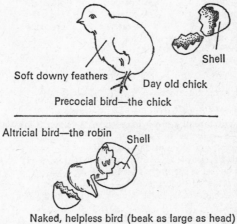

Shell

Soft downy feathers

Day old chick

Precocial bird—the chick

Altricial bird—the robin   Shell

Naked, helpless bird (beak as large as head)

Figure 115

Each species of bird lays a characteristic number of eggs, distinct in size and colour from other species.

Birds are of great economic importance to man. Some are useful because they eat insects harmful to man's person and to his crops. Others are of value because they serve as food for man. Some eat large quantities of weed seeds; others are scavengers.

Because of their usefulness and beauty, man has been making efforts to preserve native birds. There are laws in most countries protecting many species of birds and their offspring. There are numerous private organizations also dedicated to their protection.

In the autumn some birds migrate—that is, fly to a more comfortable climate where there is a greater food supply, returning the following spring. Some are year-round residents who are able to adapt themselves to changes in seasons and weather.

Classic examples of birds that migrate great distances and overcome many hazards on their journey are the Arctic tern and the swallow. The Arctic tern, a water bird, makes its nest and bears its family in the Arctic region, after which it migrates to the Antarctic region to spend the winter and back to the Arctic to continue the life cycle—a 22,000 mile return trip.

The swallow builds its nest and lays its eggs in Europe in the spring, and winters in South Africa. It makes this 6,000 mile trip each way, annually.

Scientists have not been able to solve the riddle of why animals like the monarch butterfly, the salmon, the Sargasso eel and some birds migrate. Is it instinct? What exactly is instinct in animals lower in the scale than man? No one has ever succeeded in finding a satisfactory answer to these questions.

VOCABULARY

feathers	syrinx	birds of prey
plumage	vocal cords	altricial
beak	seed-eaters	migrate
crop	insect-eaters	precocial
gizzard	perching	

Exercise No. 32

Complete the following statements:

1 Bright red gills in a fish indicate the presence of fresh ——.
2 The body temperature of a fish is like that of the water it lives in. It is therefore considered a —— blooded animal.
3 —— are the organs of locomotion of the fish.
4 The lateral line, a series of nerve cells, enables the fish to detect —— in the water.
5 The webbed hind feet of a frog are adaptations for ——.
6 Adult frogs breathe by means of (a) —— and (b) ——.
7 Thin tissues holding the digestive organs in place in the abdominal cavity are called ——.
8 The chamber of the heart which is adapted to pump blood to the lungs and to other parts of the body is called the ——.
9 The young water-living, fish-like baby frog is called a ——.
10 The newly-hatched baby frog gets its food from the ——.
11 Frogs go into an inactive period in the mud during the winter months. This condition is known as ——.
12 The scales, on the under surface of a snake, used for locomotion are known as ——.
13 The fusion of the backbone and ribs forms the —— of a tortoise.
14 —— are lizards which change colour readily to match the colour of their immediate environment.
15 The hollow-biting teeth of poisonous snakes are called ——.
16 —— were prehistoric reptiles.
17 Reptiles breathe by means of ——.
18 Alligators and crocodiles have a heart with —— chambers.

Exercise No. 33

Match a number in Column *A* with a letter in Column *B*.

	A		*B*
1	feathers	a	voice-box of bird
2	syrinx	b	travelling of birds during change of season
3	gizzard	c	organs of flight
4	migration	d	cover body of all birds
5	precocial	e	part of digestive system where food is stored
6	vocal cords	f	naked, helpless young
7	breast bone	g	home of birds
8	wings	h	bones of bird—for buoyancy
9	crop	i	part of digestive system—grinds food
10	hollow bones	j	young that are able to move independently
11	altricial	k	centre bone—attachment of wing muscles
12	nest	l	cords that produce sound in syrinx

MAMMALS

Mammals are the most highly developed and structurally specialized vertebrate animals on earth. It is the group to which man belongs.

Duck-billed platypus

Spiny anteater

Figure 116 Egg-laying mammals

The term mammal is a Latin word for breast. The group encompasses all animals whose young are fed or suckled by milk from the **mammary glands** of the mother.

Other distinguishing features of this group are:

1 Mammals have hair or fur growing from the skin.

2 Mammals are warm-blooded.

3 They breathe by means of lungs after birth.

4 The young are born alive from tiny eggs fertilized within the body of the mother, and resemble the parents. The unborn embryo receives nourishment from the body of the mother.

5 The body of a mammal is divided into three regions: namely, head, chest and abdomen.

6 The chest region is separated from the abdomen by a muscular partition called the diaphragm.

7 Few offspring are born at one time.

8 There is a relatively long period of parental care.

9 Sweat glands are present.

Mammals are classified into sub-groups according to their modes of living, their feeding and breeding habits. The least mammal-like animals resemble lower forms of vertebrates because, instead of bearing their young alive, they lay eggs in similar fashion to the birds and reptiles. This appears to be some proof that mammals were descended in some dim past from an ancestor also common to birds and reptiles. The duck-billed platypus is an example. It lays eggs instead of bearing its young alive.

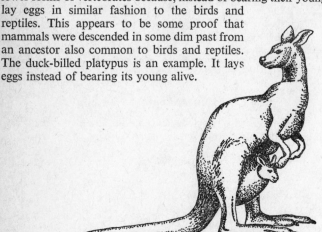

Figure 117   Mammal with pouch—kangaroo

The sub-groups of mammals are, in general, the following:

Egg-laying Mammals—Simple, primitive mammals. Eggs are laid outside of the mother's body, as with birds and reptiles. Examples are the duck-billed platypus and spiny ant-eater. See Fig. 116.

Mammals with Pouches—After their birth the young are placed in an external pocket (pouch) of the female. Here they are fed from the mammary glands until they are able to obtain their own food. They also are protected by the mother and kept warm. Examples: the opossum and kangaroo.

Placental Mammals—Their young develop in a special structure, the uterus inside the female's body. They obtain food and oxygen through the placenta and are born alive. They can be divided into several orders.

Armadillo—toothless mammal
Figure 118

Toothless Mammals—The armadillo (found in South America) is an example. It gets its name from the scale-like armoured plates that cover its body.

The young are usually produced in twos or fours (twins and quadruplets). The sloth of South America is another such mammal. See Fig. 118.

Mammals that Eat Insects—Among the better known of this group are the hedgehogs, shrews and moles. Hedgehogs have long protective quills and eat small insects. Moles and shrews eat grubs (the larvae of beetles) which they dig out of the ground.

Sea-living Mammals—Dolphins, porpoises and whales exemplify this group. Although they live in water, they breathe by means of lungs and so must

Aquatic mammal   Bottle-nosed dolphin

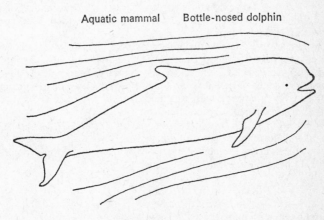

Figure 119

surface in order to obtain air. The whale is the largest living animal ever to have existed.

Carnivorous (flesh-eating) Mammals—Some live in water, for example, seals, walruses and sea lions; and some live on land, for example, bears, raccoons, dogs, cats, wolves, foxes, tigers, lions, weasels, skunks, mink and related animals. These mammals have long, sharp eye-teeth (canines) for holding and tearing flesh. They are all fleet of foot and well able to protect themselves and their young. The land forms have extremely keen sense of hearing, smell and sight.

Gnawing Mammals, Rodents—Mammals in this group are distributed all over the world, in every type of habitat. Included in the group are mice, rats, squirrels, voles, chipmunks and beavers (Fig. 120). The front, cutting teeth (**incisors**) are very sharp and

Figure 120 Water vole

strong. They never wear out because, as they are used and worn down, they continue to grow. They maintain their sharpness because the front enamel surface of the teeth is extremely hard, whereas the back surface is softer and wears down more easily.

The teeth of the beaver are so strong, that the animal is able to gnaw through thick trunks of trees to secure logs for damming up a waterway and for building colonies of houses made of poles and mud.

Rats are found in most parts of the world where man lives. The brown rat is very destructive to cereal and other grains in warehouses. Some rats are responsible for serious epidemic diseases such as bubonic plague which is transmitted by the rat flea.

Mammals with Hoofs—To this group belong horses, cows, pigs, sheep, deer, hippopotamuses and rhinoceroses. Bone and fossil remains prove that the modern horse is a descendant of a very small fleet-of-foot horse (about the size of a fox terrier dog) that existed in prehistoric times. The outstanding characteristic of these animals is their horny, hoof-enclosed toes. They are all herbivorous (vegetable eaters).

Cows, deer and sheep chew the cud or ruminate. Partially chewed food is swallowed and partially digested. It is then regurgitated (brought into the mouth again), chewed and swallowed a second time to be completely digested.

Mammals that Fly—The bat is the only known member of this group. Its mouse-like body is covered with very fine hairs. A thin, rubbery membrane stretches between the fingers of the fore-limbs, hind-limbs and tail, forming wings with which the animal flies during the night-time. Although bats have poor eyesight, they are extremely sensitive to the nearness of solid objects and avoid flying into them. There is a similarity between radar and the supersonic impulses emitted by the bat. These act as an echo-locating device to determine the position of a possible obstacle in its path.

The bat

Figure 121 Flying mammal

In tropical countries, there are a few species of bats called vampires which suck blood from human beings as well as from other large mammals.

Mammals with Trunks—To this group belongs the largest land animal in existence, the elephant. The trunk of the elephant consists of the drawn out nose and upper lip.

This lumbering creature shows great intelligence, one of the reasons for its use as a spectacle in circuses. Elephants travel in herds in their native Asian and African habitats.

Primates—Mammals with flexible fingers, the family of man. Mammals belonging to this group have an especially well-developed brain. Best developed is the brain of man.

Primates have five toes and fingers on the limbs, the big toe and thumb of each being opposable (able to grasp). The eyes are set in the head so that they look forward. Most primates can stand erect. In this group are the lemurs, monkeys, chimpanzees, gorillas, baboons, and man.

Man is the most highly developed of all mammals because he possesses the best-developed brain, the ability to reason, and the power of speech. *Homo sapiens*, the scientific name man has applied to his species, means wise man. Control of his environment and the establishment of cultures and societies make man the supreme animal on earth today.

Economically, mammals are important to man.

Useful

Domesticated animals for food and food products. (Cows, horses, sheep, pigs, goats, deer, moose, etc.)

For hides, leathers and furs. (Cows (hide), pigs (skin), seals, beavers, mink, squirrels, etc.)

For beasts of burden. (Horse, mule, camel, elephant, etc.)

As companion (cats, dogs) and protectors.

To destroy harmful insects (bats, moles and others).

Provide oil and bone (whale).

Harmful

Rats and mice carry diseases and destroy grains.

Wild rabbits, and deer, destroy vegetable crops.

Squirrels destroy seeds of valuable trees, eggs and young birds.

SUMMARY

Vertebrates are animals which have an internal backbone and usually two pairs of appendages. A nervous system consisting of a brain, spinal cord and branching nerves is characteristic. They have chambered, muscular hearts which pump red blood through blood vessels throughout the body.

Fish are the simplest form of vertebrates which live in water, breathe by means of gills and are cold-blooded.

Frogs, toads and other cold-blooded amphibians spend part of their lives in water and part on land. The central nervous system is similar in structure and function to the central nervous system of man. Amphibians hibernate in the mud during the winter.

Reptiles are cold-blooded vertebrates with thick, scaly skins. They breathe by means of lungs. A four-chambered heart appears for the first time in alligators and crocodiles.

Birds are warm-blooded vertebrates whose bodies are covered with feathers and whose bones are hollow adaptations for flying. The song of a bird is produced in a voice box (syrinx) much like the voice box of man. Some birds migrate annually.

Mammals are the most highly developed and specialized vertebrates. They suckle their young on milk produced in mammary glands. The young are born alive (with two exceptions). The bodies of mammals are covered with hair or fur. Man is the superior mammal with the best developed brain.

VOCABULARY

mammal	carnivorous	ruminate
mammary gland	herbivorous	regurgitation
suckle	canine	opposable
diaphragm	incisor	Primate
pouch	cud	Homo sapiens

Exercise No. 34

Complete the following statements:

1 Vertebrates whose young are suckled by the female from mammary glands are called ——.

2 The chest cavity is separated from the abdominal cavity in mammals by a muscle called the ——.
3 The duck-billed platypus is considered a distant relative of birds and reptiles because it ——.
4 An example of a mammal with a pouch for its young is the ——.
5 The whale is an example of an —— mammal.
6 The common brown rat is economically harmful because it eats —— and is responsible for ——.
7 The front gnawing teeth of the beaver are called ——.
8 The sharp eye teeth of the cat that are used to tear flesh are called ——.
9 The —— carries the germs that cause bubonic plague.
10 Cows, sheep and deer chew the ——.

Exercise No. 35

Write paragraphs explaining:

1 How a bat navigates.
2 The meaning, with examples, of the terms carnivorous and herbivorous.
3 How you would prove that whales and dolphins are not fish.
4 What animals belong to the Primates and what features they have in common.

CHAPTER X

THE HUMAN BEING:
HIS LIFE FUNCTIONS AND ADAPTATIONS

So far, we have concentrated on an understanding of the plant world and of the animals lower in the scale of animal life than man. We have stressed the interrelationship between plants and animals, their dependence upon one another and, finally, their relationship and importance to man.

The human body like all other living organisms, must carry on the life processes characteristic of protoplasm in order to live successfully. Like other animals, man is structurally adapted to carry on these functions.

Since man has the best-developed brain—can reason, speak and write—he has many advantages over most other animals. With observation, study and experimentation, he has been able to learn the physical structure of his body and the manner in which his body functions. Scientists have analysed the chemical changes that result in co-ordination of body functions to make a healthy human body and mind.

Let us consider each of the body's functions and its structural adaptations.

INGESTION OR FOOD GETTING

Every animal has a distinctive means or adaptation for ingestion. Simple animals have simple methods of food-getting. More complex animals have more highly specialized structures for this function.

Man is well equipped with highly developed sense organs to discriminate among foods, to take food to his mouth and to prepare it for simplification by the digestive organs.

The eyes and nose serve as organs of discrimination. Man uses his hands to bring food to his mouth. Within the mouth, the tongue and teeth work together to prepare the food for the process of digestion by juices.

In the tongue there are tiny taste buds, nerve endings, which distinguish sweet, sour, bitter and salty tastes.

The mouth is lined with a membrane (a thin layer of cells) which is kept moist by a fluid called saliva which is produced by glands distributed around the mouth. The secretion, saliva, serves two purposes: it keeps food moist for ease of swallowing and it contains a digestive enzyme.

Let us consider the important role the teeth play in the preparation of food for digestion.

The human animal is provided with two sets of teeth, the temporary set or milk teeth, which are replaced by a permanent set. In the mature adult, there are thirty-two teeth in a permanent set, sixteen in each jaw.

The upper jaw is stationary, an immovable part of the skull, while the lower jaw is connected by a hinge-like joint under each ear. This is the movable

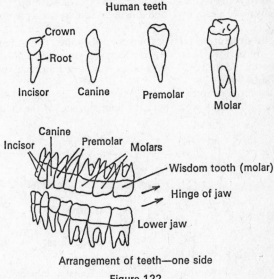

Human teeth

Arrangement of teeth—one side

Figure 122

part of the skull. Feel your jaws during the chewing motion and discover this for yourself.

The teeth are arranged quite efficiently according to their function. There are four different tooth types, each type adapted for a different job. The four types are:

Incisors—four in the centre of each jaw. They are flat from front to back, sharp and chisel-like, adapted for biting, and cutting food.

Canines—two in each jaw. These are sharp and pointed, adapted for holding and tearing food.

Premolars—four in each jaw. They are known as **bicuspids** because there are two hill-like projections or cusps on their surfaces. These are adapted for grinding and crushing food.

Molars—six in each jaw, if all form. They have a larger surface than premolars. They are also adapted for grinding and crushing food. The four large molars that may grow at the hinge end of each jaw, are commonly known as wisdom teeth because they appear last, when the human body reaches maturity. See Fig. 122.

There are twenty temporary or milk teeth which start growing through the gums (sometimes painfully) from the time the child is about six to nine months old. The front incisors are usually first to develop, followed by the canines.

These are then replaced by the second set which have molars in addition. The first molars appear when the child is about six years old and are therefore referred to as the six year molars. The second premolars appear at about the twelfth year and are called the twelve year molars; wisdom teeth cut through the gums at about the eighteenth to twenty-fifth year of life—in adulthood.

There frequently is too little room for the wisdom teeth to cut normally through the gums. They then stop growing, become lodged in the jawbone and are said to be impacted. Often, because of their position, they are little used and difficult to clean, and food lodges in their crevices, possibly resulting in decay.

The general structure of all types of teeth is the same. There are three parts: the crown—the part which is exposed above the gum; the neck—which is just below the gum; and the root—which is the means of anchoring the tooth in a socket in the jawbone.

The tooth is well adapted internally to serve its function. The very centre contains the pulp cavity which receives nourishment for the entire tooth. It

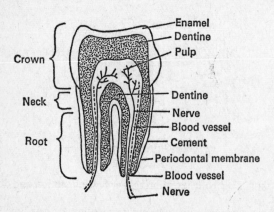

Figure 123   Structure of a tooth—molar

contains blood vessels and nerves. Surrounding the pulp is a bone-like material known as **dentine**. The dentine in the crown is covered by a hard surface called enamel.

The loss of the first set of teeth, the temporary teeth, is natural in the course of growing up. The loss of the permanent second set can take place through neglect or faulty care.

The much publicized precaution 'see your dentist at least twice a year' is a sound one. He will remove the tartar (a phosphate concretion that coats the teeth) so that bacteria of decay in the mouth, working on fermenting sugar and acids that adhere to the teeth, will not cause **dental caries** (tooth decay).

Acids in the mouth that accumulate on the surface of the teeth, wear away the enamel. Bacteria of decay then lodge in the dentine and thrive on sugars wearing down the dentine. A cavity in the enamel and dentine of a tooth may not be unusually painful except when pressure is exerted on the pulp cavity below or when extreme heat or cold touches the dentine. As soon as the decay reaches the pulp, however the soft tissue containing nerves and blood vessels are exposed and a severe toothache results.

Teeth and gums can be kept clean and healthy by daily, thorough brushing, with a toothpaste that is free of harsh abrasives. A balanced diet, complete with milk, fresh fruits and vegetables, and other foods containing vitamins and minerals important to the body will help keep teeth in good health. A clean healthy tooth is less vulnerable to decay than a tooth which is cleaned infrequently and which is suffering from malnutrition.

DIGESTION

Food is composed of many compounds which cannot be used by the body in their edible form. The process of digestion breaks them down into the different elements that the body needs to build new tissues, to repair old and worn tissues, and to provide fuel for the energy to live.

During digestion they are changed into a soluble state so that they can pass through cell membranes, by the process of diffusion, to become part of protoplasm.

STRUCTURE OF DIGESTIVE SYSTEM

The human digestive system or alimentary canal consists of a continuous tube of about 30 feet long, most of which is folded neatly and held firmly by **mesenteries** within the abdominal cavity.

Food enters the mouth and, after being throroughly chewed, is swallowed down into the gullet or oesophagus in the throat. Another tube, the trachea in front of the oesophagus, opens into the mouth. The trachea is the passage way for air from the mouth and nose into the lungs. There is a flap of tissue called the epiglottis that covers the trachea, preventing food from entering the respiratory tract during swallowing. See Fig. 124.

After the food is swallowed, it passes down into the oesophagus. Muscular contractions called **peristalsis** force the food through the oesophagus into the sac-like stomach. A full stomach can hold about three pints of food or liquid.

Between the oesophagus and top of the stomach is a ring of muscle, called the **cardiac sphincter** (so called because it is next to the heart) that prevents backflow of food. Sometimes, when the stomach is overloaded or disturbed, vomiting follows the opening of this muscle.

After some food elements are digested in the stomach by enzymes, they pass into the small intestine. There is another ring muscle at this junction, called the **pyloric sphincter,** that prevents food from leaving the stomach to enter the intestine before digestive changes take place.

The small intestine is a tube about 20 feet long and about an inch in diameter in the adult body. It is much coiled and folded so that it can fit in the relatively small abdominal cavity. Mesentery tissues hold the intestines in place. Digestion of the remaining undigested food is completed in the small intestine. It is in this organ that the blood absorbs digested (soluble) food and carries it to all parts of the body.

Any indigestible food substances and solid wastes enter the large intestine. Solid waste products leave the large intestine, aided by peristaltic action, through an enlargement at the base called the rectum.

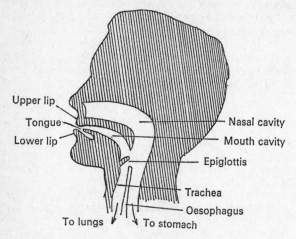

Figure 124   Throat structure

Between the small and large intestine is a small blind pocket called the appendix. When the appendix becomes unduly sore, inflamed and swollen, the condition known as appendicitis results. Sometimes surgery is necessary to remove this possible source of general body infection. The appendix is known as a vestigial organ because it has no function in the erect mammal, man. Its existence in man seems to be evidence of four-footed ancestry. See Fig. 125.

There are auxiliary organs called digestive glands related to the digestive system. These structures produce the digestive juices containing enzymes which make food soluble. Digestive enzymes act only on specific types of food, and are particular about the medium in which they work (see Chart).

Digestion of starch compounds starts in the mouth. As the food is chewed, and rolled around in the mouth by the tongue, it is mixed with saliva. This fluid contains the digestive enzyme **ptyalin** which is produced by salivary glands in the mouth. Ptyalin acts chemically on cooked starch in food and changes it to a soluble sugar.

In the stomach wall, there are many small digestive glands called gastric glands, which produce enzymes that digest proteins in food.

Final digestion takes place in the small intestine. Here in addition to the intestinal juices, enzymes from the pancreas and bile from the liver digest the remaining starches, sugars, proteins and fats.

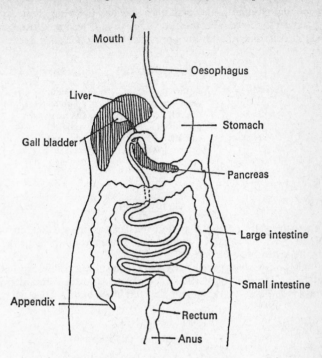

Figure 125 Human digestive system

DIGESTIVE ENZYMES

ENZYME	LOCATION	ACTION
Ptyalin	In saliva (alkaline)	Changes cooked starch to sugar
Pepsin	In stomach (acid—hydrochloric acid)	Starts digestion of proteins
Trypsin	In pancreatic juices (alkaline)	Continues digestion of proteins
Amylase	In pancreatic juices (alkaline)	Continues digestion of starches
Lipase	In pancreatic juices (alkaline)	Digests fats
Erepsin	In juices of small intestine (alkaline)	Completes protein digestion
Maltase, sucrase	In juices of small intestine (alkaline)	Completes starch and sugar digestion

End products of digestion:
    Proteins become soluble amino acids.
    Starches become soluble sugars.
    Fats become soluble fatty acids and glycerine.

The gall bladder serves as a storage place for bile which is the digestive juice produced by the liver. Bile is a fluid which plays a role in digestion by emulsifying fats.

Except for the mouth and oesophagus (which is in the chest cavity) the entire alimentary canal is in the abdominal cavity, separated from the chest by the muscular diaphragm through which the oesophagus passes.

VOCABULARY

saliva	tartar	appendix
incisor	dental caries	appendicitis
canine	mesenteries	gastric gland
premolar	peristalsis	vestigial
impacted	cardiac sphincter	taste buds
pulp	pyloric sphincter	enamel
dentine	rectum	enzyme

ABSORPTION

In discussing the process of digestion, the fact was stressed that food is made soluble so that it can be carried by the blood stream from which it enters body cells by the process of diffusion.

The small intestine is specially adapted for the process of absorption. Tiny, finger-like projections called **villi** (singular: villus) extend inward from the intestinal wall. These are richly supplied with blood vessels. Digested proteins

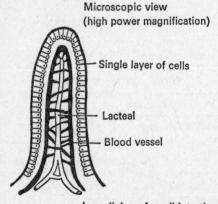

Microscopic view
(high power magnification)

— Single layer of cells

— Lacteal

— Blood vessel

Inner lining of small intestine
A villus—organ of absorption in the small intestine
Figure 126

and sugars pass through the thin membrane of each villus, enter the tiny blood vessels by the process of diffusion and are carried by the blood to all other body cells. Fats are absorbed into lacteals (small lymph vessels) in the villi that eventually empty into large blood vessels.

The rhythmic contraction of the intestine (peristalsis) plays a large part in the distribution of digested food to the villi for absorption.

As the blood passes into the liver, some of the soluble sugar is removed, changed by the liver cells into glycogen (called animal starch). It is stored there for future use as fuel for the body. One of the major functions of the liver, then, is to keep a uniform amount of sugar in the blood.

When digested food in the blood reaches the body cells, each cell selects the kind of food it needs and changes it into protoplasm, or combines it with oxygen to produce energy.

In animals of one cell only, food is digested within the cell protoplasm and dispersed to all parts of the cell by the natural flowing movement of the protoplasm. Within the cell protoplasm, the digested food is then assimilated or changed into more protoplasm.

Undigested food and water pass into the large intestine. Water is absorbed into the walls of the large intestine and the solid wastes (faeces) leave the body through the rectum.

Elimination of solid wastes is important to the well-being of the body. Bacteria in the large intestine cause decay of waste materials and the formation of poisons which may enter the bloodstream and affect the entire body.

VOCABULARY

absorption	lacteal	faeces
villus	glycogen	lymph
villi	assimilation	

CIRCULATION

In simple one-celled animals, the process of circulation of digested food and oxygen and the removal of wastes is a simple one—just a matter of protoplasmic motion within the cell membrane. In animals of many cells, specialization of tissues, then organs and finally systems, becomes increasingly greater.

For example, in fish, red blood is circulated through simple blood vessels that bring deoxygenated blood (blood from which some oxygen has been removed) to the gills for replenishment. Oxygenated blood (blood with oxygen restored) is carried directly from the gills to all parts of the body. Gas waste, carbon dioxide, is brought by the blood from all active body cells back to the gills where it is released into the water. The heart is a simple, two-chambered organ, with a muscular ventricle (lower chamber) separated from the auricle (upper chamber) by a valve that ensures against backflow of blood.

In the frog, another cold-blooded animal, the heart is more advanced in structure. There are two separated auricles and a single muscular ventricle. Deoxygenated blood from the active body cells passes through the lungs where it takes in fresh oxygen. From here it returns to the heart to be pumped by the ventricle through blood vessels to all parts of the body.

In warm-blooded animals, the heart has four separate chambers, two auricles and two ventricles. Blood vessels known as arteries carry blood to the body cells and veins carry blood back to the heart. Capillaries, microscopic blood vessels, with walls of one-celled thickness, provide the connexion between arteries and veins. It is between blood in the capillaries and the cells of tissues that the exchange of soluble food and gases (by the process of diffusion) takes place.

In man, the functions of the circulatory system are the same as they are in all other warm-blooded animals, namely—to carry digested food from the digestive system to all parts of the body; to carry blood containing fresh oxygen from the lungs to all body cells; to carry gas and liquid wastes from all cells in the body to the organs from which excretion takes place; to regulate all body processes by distributing hormones (chemical messengers) produced by ductless glands; to carry antibodies that help fight disease, and to distribute heat to keep body temperature even.

THE HUMAN CIRCULATORY SYSTEM

The human circulatory system consists of a four-chambered heart, arteries, capillaries, veins and red fluid, the blood. In the living body, blood flows in a continuous circuit, from the heart through blood vessels, to various organs and back to the heart.

The human heart, contrary to popular belief, is not on the left side of the chest. It is lodged in the centre of the chest, just underneath the breast bone. It lies between the two lungs and above the diaphragm, which is the muscle separating the chest from the abdominal cavity.

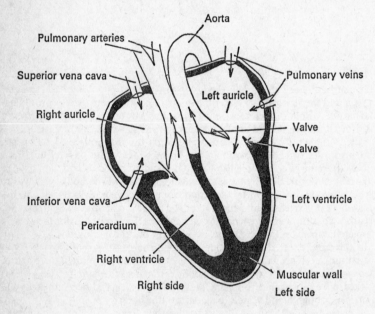

Figure 127   Human heart (diagrammatic)

The heart is roughly triangular in shape, about double the size of a man's fist, with its narrow end pointing towards the left side of the body. It is a thick, muscular organ, divided internally into four chambers. The upper two chambers, the **auricles** or **atria** (singular: atrium) receive blood from all over the body. The lower two chambers, **ventricles,** contract rhythmically to pump blood to all parts of the body.

Observe a chicken's heart or a pig's heart (both closely resemble the human heart). Make a cut vertically through the centre and compare the internal structure with the diagram of the human heart.

Note, in the diagram, that the left side of the heart is completely separated from the right side. Observe the valves that separate the left auricle from the left ventricle, and the right auricle from the right ventricle. These valves prevent backflow of blood into the auricles when the ventricles contract to pump blood out of the heart to the rest of the body.

Look at Fig. 127. Let us briefly enumerate the functions of each labelled part of the human heart:

1 **Pulmonary veins**—carry oxygenated blood from the lungs to the left auricle.

2 **Left auricle**—receives blood with fresh oxygen from the lungs.

3 **Valve**—opens to allow blood to be pumped from the left auricle into the left ventricle, then closes to prevent backflow of blood when left ventricle contracts.

4 **Left ventricle**—receives blood from left auricle and pumps (by rhythmic contractions) this blood to all parts of the body except the lungs.

5 **Aorta**—largest artery in the body; carries blood from left ventricle to all parts of the body except the lungs.

6 **Superior and inferior venae cavae**—large veins which carry blood from all other parts of the body back to the right auricle.

7 **Right auricle**—receives deoxygenated blood from all parts of the body.

8 **Right ventricle**—receives blood from right auricle to be pumped to the lungs.

9 **Pulmonary arteries**—carry deoxygenated blood pumped from the right ventricle back to the lungs for fresh oxygen supply.

10 **Pericardium**—a sheath of tissue that protects the muscular heart.

In a normal person, the ventricles contract to pump out blood about seventy times each minute. This periodic contraction is called the heart beat. Each time the heart beats, blood is pumped into the arteries in a rhythmic wave of motion. This is known as the pulse. Count the number of heartbeats by feeling the pulse. The number of waves you feel when you place your finger-tips on the wrist artery indicates the number of heartbeats per minute. Other arteries that are close to the skin surface, such as the temple and neck arteries, may also be used for this purpose.

Active physical exercise and emotional stress increase the pulse rate which indicates faster heart action. During illness, when the blood attempts to overcome body infections and disease, the heart beats faster—the pulse rate is higher.

The layman should not attempt to diagnose or treat any heart condition when there appears to be a disturbance or variation in the normal function of this vital organ. He should consult a doctor when such disturbances occur. One of the instruments used in examination of the activity of the heart is an **electrocardiograph** machine. This records, electrically, the beat of the heart over a period of time, on a graph. The picture resulting is called an **electrocardiogram.** A doctor can often read this picture and discover a deviation from the norm.

Science has made great progress in methods of diagnosing, treating, and curing heart conditions. Delicate and successful surgery is being performed on heart ailments as a matter of course.

BLOOD VESSELS

The blood vessels are well adapted for their special jobs in the body. There are three types of blood vessels, namely, arteries, capillaries and veins. An artery is a blood vessel which carries blood away from the heart to all parts of the body. The aorta is the largest artery in the body. It leads directly from the left ventricle of the heart with a large supply of oxygenated blood.

Arterial blood generally appears bright red due to its supply of oxygen.

The term 'blood pressure' refers to the force of the blood within artery walls. The doctor uses an instrument called a sphygmomanometer to measure this force. A rough standard for normal blood pressure has been established depending upon the sex and age of the individual. Any deviation above the norm is called high blood pressure or hypertension. Continuous physical and mental strain, calling for overactivity on the part of the heart, may result in hypertension.

As an individual grows older all the muscles of the body become less elastic. The muscular walls of the arteries, as well, lose their elasticity and gradually become hardened. As they become less flexible, the passageways in the arteries become smaller, the pressure of the blood against these walls increases and the heart has to work harder to pump blood through them.

In order to reach all cells of the body, the vessels carrying the blood must necessarily branch from larger into smaller tubes. Thus large arteries branch into smaller arteries and finally into very tiny branches called capillaries.

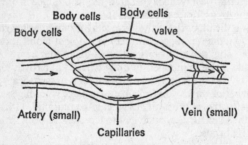

Figure 128 Artery, capillary and vein (diagrammatic)

These are vessels with walls of one-celled thickness, allowing digested food and oxygen to pass directly into the cells which they surround by the process of diffusion.

Gas and liquid wastes from the cells enter the bloodstream in these capillaries and are carried by veins into which they branch. Tiny veins join up to form larger veins until they become main veins, the superior and inferior venae cavae, which enter the heart.

Veins are blood vessels which carry blood back to the heart from all organs of the body. These are relatively thin-walled and inelastic. Within them are small valves that prevent backflow of blood, especially where the blood has to flow against the pull of gravity (that is, from the lower trunk, legs and arms). Blood in the veins is generally purplish because it contains less oxygen. It is generally on its way back to the heart to be sent to the lungs for oxygenation.

Let us trace the blood through the circulatory system.

Blood, with fresh oxygen, returns to the left auricle of the heart through the pulmonary veins. It passes through valves into the left ventricle. From here it is pumped with great force into the largest artery, the aorta, which branches into smaller arteries and finally into capillaries. Oxygen and digested food enter the cells of the body; waste gases (carbon dioxide) and liquids leave the cells and diffuse into the thin-walled capillaries. Blood, carrying these substances, enters small veins which branch into larger veins. Blood from the

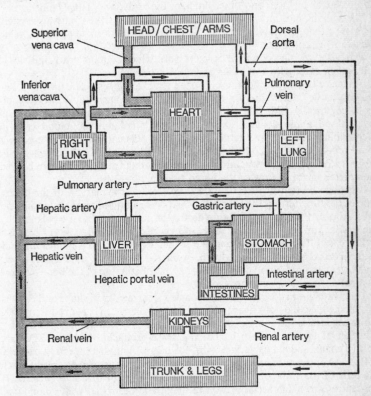

Figure 129   Circulation in human body (diagrammatic)

lower part of the body returns to the right auricle of the heart through the large, vein, the inferior vena cava. Blood from the upper part of the body returns through the superior vena cava into the right auricle; the blood passes through valves into the right ventricle. From here it is pumped directly through the pulmonary artery into the lungs where the waste gas carbon dioxide is given off together with water vapour and fresh oxygen is taken in. Oxygenated blood then returns to the left ventricle of the heart via pulmonary veins and the cycle is repeated rhythmically.

Liquid wastes are extracted from the blood as it passes through the kidneys in its circuit round the body. Note that all the deoxygenated blood from the stomach and intestines passes to the liver in the hepatic portal vein before passing to the interior vena cava in the hepatic vein. In the liver the blood sugar level is controlled.

THE BLOOD

Water is the major substance of all living bodies. Man's body mass consists of about 60 per cent water. In fact, the water contains the same salts which are dissolved in ocean water and in approximately the same proportions. Perspiration, urine and blood, and other fluids of the body, are highly saline.

The actual job of carrying food, oxygen and wastes in the circulatory system is done by the semi-liquid tissue, blood. There are about six quarts of blood in the average adult body.

The blood consists of a fluid called **plasma,** which contains many individual cells called **corpuscles** and other bodies called **platelets.**

There are two types of corpuscles, each type having a specific function. The red corpuscles contain an iron compound known as **haemoglobin** which combines chemically with oxygen in the lungs to form **oxyhaemoglobin** which gives blood a red colour. There are about 5 million red blood cells in each cublic millimetre of blood. These blood cells carry and release oxygen to all other tissues of the body. Red blood cells are disc-like and concave in shape with a constant structure and have lost their nuclei. They are carried along in the natural flow of the liquid plasma.

It is believed that new blood cells are formed in the marrow of the bones. One of the functions of the liver is the final destruction of worn-out red blood cells. About 10 million red cells are destroyed per second, but are balanced by the production of an equal quantity of new red blood cells.

The condition known as anaemia may occur when there is an insufficiency of the iron compound, haemoglobin, in the red corpuscles; and also from an insufficiency of red blood corpuscles or a malfunctioning of the bone marrow as a result of disease or other factors.

The white blood corpuscles or leucocytes are irregular in shape and colourless. Some have the power to move about in the plasma. There are about 7,000 white corpuscles per cubic millimetre of blood. They defend the body against invasion of foreign protein including disease-producing bacteria. They are able to engulf and eat bacteria as Amoeba engulfs and digests a food particle.

Because of their ability to move, white blood corpuscles can emerge between the cells of the walls of the blood vessels to surround invading bacteria. A concentrated whitish accumulation of living and destroyed white blood corpuscles and dead bacteria plus dead body cells at the point of an infection, a cut or wound of any sort, is called **pus.** If the white cells are strong enough to overcome the bacteria in the given area, the pus dries and healing takes place. If the bacteria prove the stronger, infection spreads by means of the bloodstream, and may become serious.

The platelets are very tiny bodies with no nuclei. They serve some function in coagulation or clotting of blood. See Fig. 130.

The fluid part of the blood is the straw-coloured plasma which is about 90 per cent water. Besides being the vehicle for conveying blood cells, it has other specific functions. Plasma contains digested food substances, dissolved minerals, enzymes, hormones and antibodies.

It also contains a protein substance called **fibrinogen,** which hardens into a close meshwork of fibres called **fibrin,** which prevents flow of blood from even

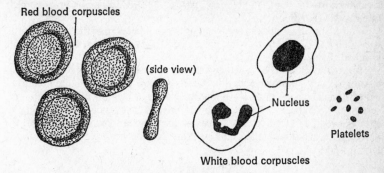

Figure 130   Human blood cells (magnified)

the smallest cut in the skin. When a cut occurs the platelets that rush to the area, begin to dissolve and produce an enzyme that encourages the fibrinogen to harden into fibrin. The yellowish liquid of the blood that remains after clotting takes place is called serum.

Recently, it was discovered that the presence of vitamin K (found in green, leafy vegetables such as spinach, kale and cabbage and also in tomatoes and chestnuts) is important in blood-clotting. Vitamin K is often injected during surgical operations to prevent great loss of blood.

The rare disease of the blood, **haemophilia,** is a condition in which blood does not clot even after the slightest cut has been inflicted, and from which there is danger of bleeding to death. It is an hereditary condition which manifests itself in the human male.

Just as individuals differ in external physical characteristics, inheriting these differences from preceding generations, so do they differ in blood types. There are four different types of blood A, B, AB and O depending upon the presence or absence of a blood protein antigen on the red-corpuscles. Before a transfusion (transferring of blood from one individual to another) can be made, the blood types of the donor and that of the recipient must be determined. Unless the types are the same the recipient may die, by causing the donor blood to clot.

Blood banks have been established in which the four different types of blood plasma have been collected and stored for future use, especially in emergencies in hospitals before and during surgery. During the Second World War, many lives were saved by the administration of blood plasma. One method of preserving blood plasma is by a drying process. Dried plasma is packed in air-tight containers. The addition of sterile water to the dried plasma makes the latter ready for on-the-spot transfusions, especially valuable on fields of battle and in other emergencies.

Another important factor in blood has recently been brought to light. Because experimentation on rhesus monkeys has determined this factor, it has been named the **Rhesus (Rh) factor.** About 15 per cent of the world's white population is lacking the Rh factor (known as Rh negative); 5 per cent of the negroid, and 10 per cent of the mongoloid populations also lack it. An Rh negative woman may have difficulty in pregnancy.

It has not yet been determined what causes the lack of this factor, nor how it can be introduced into the blood as part of the chemical make-up of heretofore negative Rh blood.

Some of the blood plasma seeps out of the capillaries to bathe the body cells with fluid and supply them with oxygen and food substances. This body fluid is called tissue fluid.

This is collected up by open-ended lymph vessels and returned to the circulatory system in the neck region. On its journey back, the tissue fluid, now called lymph, passes through numerous glands, or lymph nodes, containing special cells similar to the white blood corpuscles. The function of these glands is to destroy harmful bacteria. In cases where much infection is present, the glands may become swollen and painful. Swollen neck glands are infected lymph nodes.

VOCABULARY

corpuscle	haemophilia	sphygmomanometer
platelet	anaemia	phagocyte
oxygenated	transfusion	haemoglobin
deoxygenated	pulmonary	oxyhaemoglobin
auricle	pericardium	fibrinogen
ventricle	pulse	fibrin
artery	plasma	pus
vein	serum	capillary
electrocardiogram	Rh factor	hormone

Exercise No. 36

Match a number in Column *A* with a letter in Column *B*.

A	*B*
1 saliva	a part of tooth containing blood vessels and nerves
2 milk teeth	b changing food to protoplasm
3 taste buds	c vestigial organ in man
4 impacted	d on tongue
5 pulp	e rhythmic contractions of muscles of digestion
6 sphincter muscles	f muscle separating chest and abdomen
7 dental caries	g temporary teeth
8 alimentary canal	h prevent backflow of food in alimentary canal
9 gall bladder	i digestive tube
10 appendix	j tooth lodged in jaw
11 small intestine	k organ of absorption
12 diaphragm	l cavities in teeth
13 peristalsis	m digestive juice in mouth
14 villus	n projection in small intestine for absorption
15 assimilation	o storage for bile

Exercise No. 37

Select the correct word or phrase for each of the following:

1 Blood minus all cells and fibrin: (a) corpuscle; (b) capillary; (c) serum; (d) platelet.
2 Blood cell that carries oxygen to the body cells: (a) red corpuscle; (b) white corpuscle; (c) platelet; (d) Amoeba.

3 Hereditary disease condition in which the blood fails to coagulate: (a) anaemia; (b) colour blindness; (c) haemophilia; (d) plasma.

4 Vitamin in blood important for the part it plays in coagulation: (a) Vitamin A; (b) Vitamin D; (c) Vitamin E; (d) Vitamin K.

5 Disease resulting from lack of or malfunctioning of haemoglobin in the blood: (a) anaemia; (b) fainting; (c) haemophilia; (d) diabetes.

6 Cells in blood that destroy invading disease-producing bacteria: (a) platelets; (b) skin cells; (c) red corpuscles; (d) white corpuscles.

7 The wave of heart beat is called: (a) tick; (b) beat; (c) flow; (d) pulse.

8 The largest artery in the body is the: (a) vena cava; (b) aorta; (c) capillary; (d) ventricle.

9 The instrument used to measure blood pressure is a: (a) electrocardiogram; (b) watch; (c) sphygmomanometer; (d) arm band.

10 The smallest blood vessel in the body is a: (a) capillary; (b) vein; (c) artery; (d) red corpuscle.

11 A blood vessel which carries blood back to the heart is: (a) artery; (b) vein; (c) capillary; (d) platelet.

12 The largest percentage of the body composition is: (a) bone; (b) skin; (c) blood; (d) water.

13 The liquid which bathes the body cells is known as: (a) blood; (b) water; (c) tissue fluid; (d) saliva.

14 Blood is pumped from the heart to the entire body by the: (a) ventricles; (b) lungs; (c) auricles; (d) nerves.

RESPIRATION

All living things require oxygen with which to burn food (oxidation) to produce energy needed to carry on life functions.

$$\text{Sugar} + \text{Oxygen} \longrightarrow \text{Energy} + \text{Carbon Dioxide} + \text{Water}$$

Breathing is the process by which oxygen is taken in and the waste gas carbon dioxide is given off.

All animals are adapted structurally for this process. Recall that a simple animal, like Amoeba, absorbs oxygen directly through its cell membrane, from air dissolved in the water of its environment. An earthworm absorbs oxygen through its moist skin. Air containing oxygen enters the grasshopper through holes, spiracles, on its body and penetrates the body in branching tubes called tracheae. A fish possesses gills in which the blood extracts oxygen from the water that passes over these organs. All land-living vertebrate animals, including man, are adapted with lungs into which they breathe air containing the necessary oxygen.

The process of respiration and circulation are closely related in man. It is the red corpuscles in the blood which are responsible for transporting oxygen from air in the lungs to the individual cells of the body.

The term breathing refers to the mechanical act of taking air into the lungs and releasing air from them. The breathing organs of man that make up the respiratory system are the nose and mouth, trachea, two **bronchi** or bronchial tubes (main branches of the trachea, one leading to each lung), **bronchioles** (branches of bronchi) and finally air sacs (pouch-like ends of smallest bronchioles).

We normally breathe air in through the nose (sometimes through the mouth). It passes down over the vocal cords in the **larnyx** (voice box) and into the trachae. This structure has external rings of cartilage which keep the passageway upen and protect the soft tissue. There is a tiny flap of tissue called the epiglottis which closes the opening to the trachea when food is being swallowed.

Air from the trachea flows through each bronchial tube, into the bronchioles of the lungs and finally into the millions of air sacs at the end of each smallest bronchiole.

The air sacs are surrounded by blood capillaries. It is here that the exchange of gases takes place. Oxygen from the air passes into the bloodstream by

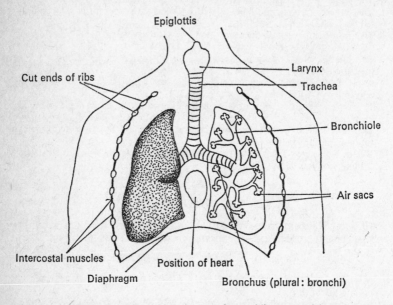

Figure 131   Breathing organs of man (diagrammatic)

diffusion and carbon dioxide passes out of the bloodstream into the air sacs, to be breathed out. Blood freshly furnished with oxygen is bright red whereas blood with little oxygen and much carbon dioxide is less red, sometimes appearing purplish in the veins.

The actual mechanism of breathing can be demonstrated in the laboratory and at home using a model as in Fig. 132.

Inspiration (intake of air) takes place when the diaphragm contracts and moves downward, expanding the chest cavity from top to bottom. The muscles between the ribs pull the ribs upward and outward, expanding the chest cavity from front to back. This series of automatic actions creates a lowered air pressure in the lungs and air actually rushes in and fills the lungs. See A—Fig. 132.

As the diapgragm and rib muscles relax, and the size of the chest cavity is reduced, air is forced out of the lungs in the act of expiration. See B—Fig. 132.

The average normal rate of breathing is about eighteen times per minute. This increases with increased physical activity. It also decreases with age, being very rapid in babies but slow in old people.

Normally, breathing is not a voluntary act. We do not consciously think about breathing in and out. The presence of the waste gas carbon dioxide in the blood stimulates the nerve centre in the brain stem that controls the muscles of our breathing apparatus and we breathe.

Suffocation occurs when the tracheal opening is closed by a gas, by water or by some other obstacle, thus preventing normal breathing. Artificial respiration may be successful in removing the obstacle and in stimulating the

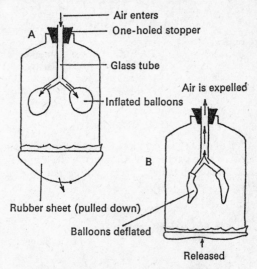

Figure 132   Breathing mechanism

muscles to restart the breathing process. A machine, the pulmotor, is used to administer oxygen mixed with a small percentage of carbon dioxide in the attempt to stimulate the nerves to start natural breathing again.

Tuberculosis is a lung disease in which specific bacteria may destroy lung tissue and which eventually, if unchecked and untreated, causes death. The disease can be halted completely if diagnosed and treated in early stages. Streptomycin in carefully prescribed doses, is administered in combination with rest, sunshine and proper food treatment.

Poliomyelitis, is closer to being controlled now by Salk vaccine. It sometimes paralyses the nerve centres controlling breathing. The iron lung, a machine which mechanically administers artificial respiration over a period of time to the victim, is used to help these cases.

In these days of high flying, man encounters changing conditions of air pressure and content that are not a normal part of his daily living and to which his body is not accustomed.

Our bodies function best at sea-level, that is, we are structurally adapted for such an environment. Above sea-level the air we breathe decreases in pressure and there is a gradual decrease in oxygen content. An inadequate supply of oxygen in an area of low pressure, 12,000–15,000 feet above sea-level, is one of the causes of air sickness.

Above 15,000 feet, a pilot in a plane who does not make use of his oxygen mask, suffers dizziness, unsteady vision, loss of hearing and lack of muscular co-ordination. This may result in complete blackout.

The value of periodic chest X-ray in a clinic, by a doctor, or in a health centre especially designed for this function, has been stressed and demonstrated. It is often easier and less costly to prevent disasters to the good health of our bodies and minds than to cure them.

VOCABULARY

respiration	air sac	larynx
breathing	epiglottis	suffocation
trachea	vocal cords	pulmotor
bronchi	inspiration	tuberculosis
bronchiole	expiration	poliomyelitis

EXCRETION

The elimination of waste gases, liquids and solids from the body is necessary for the general well-being of the body. Carbon dioxide is a result of the oxidation of food compounds containing carbon. Nitrogenous wastes are the result

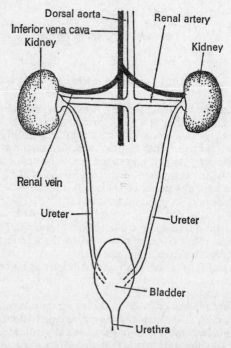

Figure 133 Organs of excretion

of the breakdown of excess proteins which cannot be stored in the body. Excess water is also excreted.

Our bodies are structurally adapted for the elimination of all these wastes in the process of excretion. We have already discussed a function of the lungs as an organ of excretion, that is, the excretion of carbon dioxide in expiration. In addition excess water, in the form of water vapour, is given off from the lungs in exhaled air.

Excess protein is changed, by the liver, into a soluble substance called **urea.** This is carried in the blood and eliminated dissolved in water from two systems of the body—the kidneys as urine and, to a lesser extent, the skin as sweat.

The human kidneys, bean-shaped organs (about 4 inches by $2\frac{1}{2}$ inches), are located one on each side of the spinal column in the small of the back. As the

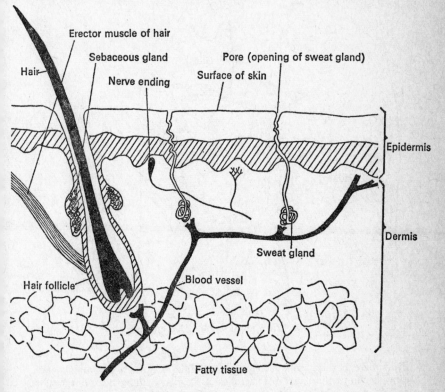

Figure 134 Section through skin

blood passes through the kidneys, from the body cells where it has picked up liquid wastes, these wastes pass by diffusion into the kidney tubules. The wastes containing a high percentage of water collect in small tubes which empty into two larger tubes, **ureters,** which empty into the bladder. From here, the waste, urine, is eliminated from the body. See Fig. 133

The skin is another organ of elimination of nitrogenous liquid wastes and soluble mineral salts in small quantities. The presence of water in the body is important for this process to take place.

During the process of elimination of liquid wastes from the surface of the skin (otherwise known as perspiring or sweating) the skin serves another function, namely, that of regulating body temperature. It is adapted for this purpose by the presence of sweat glands scattered throughout the skin.

A sweat gland consists of a coiled tube with a long duct and opening on the surface of the skin. Liquid wastes plus a small amount of mineral salts enter the sweat glands by diffusion from the blood in the surrounding capillaries.

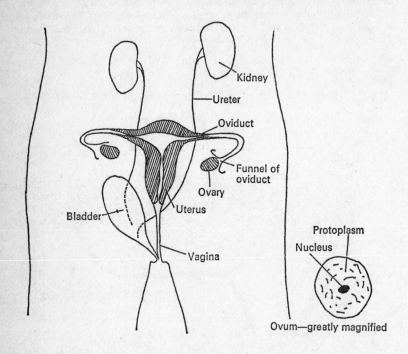

Figure 135 Female reproductive organs

From there they are brought to the surface of the skin where the water evaporates, leaving a thin layer of mineral salts. Regular bathing cleanses the salts and dried sweat off the skin and keeps the pores clear for necessary constant elimination. See Fig. 134.

Evaporation of perspiration reduces heat of the skin and of the blood in the capillaries of the skin, thus gradually reducing the entire body heat. Our skin acts as a self-regulating cooling system.

During excessive perspiration, when a great deal of necessary salt which is dissolved in the body waste fluid is lost, there is danger of heat exhaustion and other consequences. To avoid this, concentrated salt tablets are administered.

REPRODUCTION

The female reproductive organs are the ovaries which produce egg cells or **ova** (singular: **ovum**). Close to each **ovary** is the funnel-shaped opening of the **oviduct,** the tube down which the ova pass when they are released from the ovary. The oviducts open into the **uterus,** in which the developing embryo is

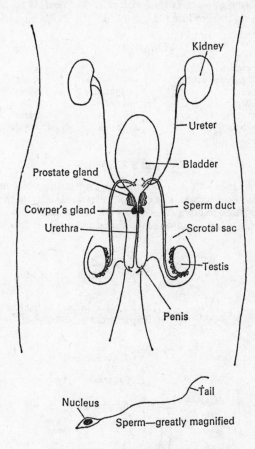

Figure 136 Male reproductive organs

housed and which communicates with the outside through a muscular tube, the **vagina.** See Fig. 135.

Between the ages of eleven and sixteen, the ovaries become active and begin to produce mature ova, one ovum being released from alternate ovaries every four weeks. This process is called **ovulation.** Immediately following ovulation, the walls of the uterus become thickened with extra blood vessels in order to provide nourishment for a possible embryo. Fertilization occurs in the oviduct. If this does not take place, the egg, together with the now unnecessary uterine lining, passes out of the body in the menstrual flow.

The male reproductive organs, the two **testes** (singular: **testis**), lie outside the abdominal cavity in the scrotal sacs. **Sperms** are manufactured in the testes, travel along the sperm duct and are released through the **urethra**. The **prostate gland** and **Cowper's gland** secrete a fluid medium in which the sperm can swim by lashing movements of their tails. The penis is an erectile organ whose function is to introduce the sperms into the female body. See Fig. 136.

VOCABULARY

excretion	bladder	urine
nitrogenous wastes	sweat glands	ureter
urea	perspiration	kidney
ovary	uterus	testis
ovum	vagina	sperm
oviduct	ovulation	prostate gland

DUCTLESS GLANDS

In man's adaptations for life functions, there are glands which manufacture essential chemical substances. For example, gastric glands and the liver pour digestive juices through tubes called ducts into the stomach and intestine respectively to bring about digestion of food substances. Sweat glands in the skin

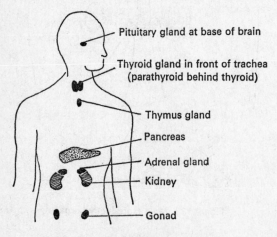

Figure 137　The ductless glands

and salivary glands in the mouth are other glands with ducts. The juices produced by these glands with ducts are called secretions.

During the 1920's scientists discovered that there are other glands in the body which have no ducts, and are therefore called ductless or **endocrine glands.** They produce or secrete chemicals called **hormones** (chemical messengers) directly into the blood stream. Hormones travel from the gland in which they are manufactured through the blood stream to the organ or organs they affect. See Fig. 137.

Normal functioning of all the endocrine glands results in normal functioning of the cells of the body and general well-being.

The endocrine glands control our body activities. Some of their functions are generally familiar—e.g. the disorder in which the neck is much enlarged and pouchy-looking and the eyes seem bulging. This swollen condition is known as goitre and is probably caused by an over-active **thyroid** gland in the neck region around the voice box. The thyroid secretes a hormone called **thyroxin** which controls the rate at which food is oxidized in the body (metabolism). The basal metabolism test determines this rate. Thyroxin contains iodine as part of its chemical make-up.

Abnormalities occur in the body where there is an insufficient production of thyroxin as well as where there is an overabundance of this hormone.

In children, lack of thyroxin results in abnormal physical and retarded mental growth. The condition is known as cretinism and the child is called a cretin. Cretinism can sometimes be overcome by treating with injections of thyroxin compounds (containing iodine) or by oral medication. In regions of the country where there is a lack of iodine in the soil and water, iodized salt is used.

A lack of thyroxin in adults results in bloating of the body and loss of energy. The mental processes become sluggish and the general physical appearance is one of premature old age and deterioration. Doses of thyroxin, under supervision of a doctor, can overcome this condition, which is known as myxoedema.

An over-active thyroid may produce a goitre. It also results in extreme tension, nervousness and loss of weight. Until recently the only way to treat such a condition was by surgery. At present the injection of radioactive iodine to decrease the over-secretion of the thyroid has been successful.

The **pituitary** gland, called the master gland, is located at the base of the brain. It merits its name because it seems to control other endocrine glands. Specifically, its functions are to control growth of the bony skeleton, to regulate metabolism of food, to regulate the muscles of some internal organs, and to regulate the functioning of the kidneys.

Overactivity of the pituitary gland in childhood results in giantism—the famous giants of the circus. Underactivity of the master gland results in the opposite deformity, namely, dwarfism.

At the back of the thyroid gland and resting against the sides of the windpipe are two pairs of **parathyroid** glands. These glands regulate the use of calcium and phosphorus in bones and teeth. They also provide calcium to the skeletal muscles. Insufficient calcium causes great pain and lack of muscular control.

The **thymus gland** is located at the base of the trachea. Comparatively little is known of its specific action, but it is thought that it plays a role in the build-up of antibodies.

Earlier in the chapter we noted the function of the **pancreas** as a digestive gland with a duct. It has another function—that of an endocrine gland. Within the body of the pancreas are groups of specialized cells (from which there are no ducts) called the **islets of Langerhans,** named after the scientist who discovered them and their significance. These cells secrete the hormone **insulin** directly into the blood which carries it to the liver. Here it serves the purpose of regulating the uptake of sugar from the blood by the liver to be stored as animal starch or glycogen.

When there is an insufficiency of insulin, the disease diabetes results. When a urine analysis (examination of the composition of the urine) shows excessive amounts of sugar, it is usually indicative of lack of insulin resulting in diabetes.

In the early 1920's, two Canadian scientists, DR. FREDERICK G. BANTING and DR. CHARLES HERBERT BEST, were successful in isolating insulin from animal pancreas. Injection of controlled and prescribed doses of insulin in the human body suffering from diabetes is effective in controlling but not in curing the disease.

The paired **adrenal** glands are located on top of each kidney. Extreme emotional disturbances—such as fright, fear, anger and joy, stimulate the **medulla** (centre of the gland) to produce the hormone **adrenalin.** This secretion activates the liver to pour forth more sugar into the blood for rapid oxidation in the muscles and in the brain cells—this results in more rapid, sometimes immediate, thinking and muscular responses. Thus it works in antagonism to insulin.

Adrenalin also aids in blood clotting by constricting blood vessels, decreasing shock and stimulating heart action. It helps relieve asthmatic conditions due to constriction of the trachea and bronchial tubes.

Adrenalin may be synthesised from animal secretions and is sometimes injected into the body during operations where there is apt to be excessive bleeding, and directly into the heart muscles in cases of heart failure.

The adrenal **cortex** (outer layer) secretes several hormones affecting salt retention, blood sugar concentration and the ability to withstand stress.

The reproductive organs are double-duty glands, that is, they function with ducts and as endocrine glands. Hormones become active especially during adolescence and then in adulthood, regulating external characteristics and the sexual functions particularly menstruation and pregnancy.

In the small intestine, there are cells which secrete a hormone called **secretin,** which stimulates the pancreas and liver to produce digestive juices.

Secretions produced by endocrine glands affect all the systems of our body and are the chemical regulators of all body functions.

VOCABULARY

endocrine	secretin	thymus
hormone	cretin	islets of
secretion	cretinism	Langerhans
thyroid	pituitary	insulin
iodized	giantism	adrenal
myxoedema	parathyroid	adrenalin

SKELETAL AND MUSCULAR SYSTEMS

The internal skeleton (endoskeleton) of man consists of more than two hundred bones, some of which are movable and others, immovable. There are two main functions of the skeletal system: (1) to provide places of attachment of body muscles for movement; (2) to protect and support the internal, soft body organs.

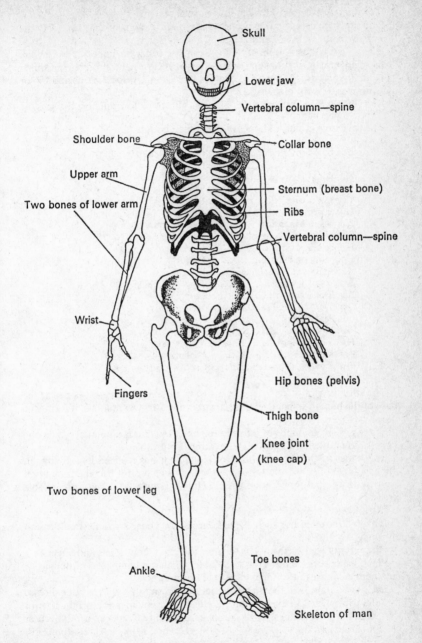

Skull

Lower jaw

Vertebral column—spine

Shoulder bone

Collar bone

Upper arm

Sternum (breast bone)

Two bones of lower arm

Ribs

Vertebral column—spine

Wrist

Hip bones (pelvis)

Fingers

Thigh bone

Knee joint
(knee cap)

Two bones of lower leg

Toe bones

Ankle

Skeleton of man

Figure 138

The human skeleton is divided into general regions:

The **skull**—encases and protects the brain and organs of the face. Only the lower jaw is movable and is attached by a hinge joint.

The **spinal column**—consists of thirty-three separate bones or **vertebrae.** This segmented structure supports the head, encloses and protects the spinal cord (main nerve from the brain), serves as attachment for the ribs and hip or **pelvic** bones. It is the main axis of the body.

The **limbs**—fore-limbs or arms and hind-limbs or lower limbs, the legs.

The following is a list of bones of the human body:

Bones of top of head	Cranial bones (cranium)
Collar bone	Clavicle
Shoulder blade	Scapula
Breast bone	Sternum
12 pairs of ribs	Ribs
Upper arm	Humerus
2 bones in lower arm	Radius and ulna
Bones of spinal column	Vertebrae
Hip bones	Pelvis
Upper leg or thigh	Femur
Knee cap	Patella
2 bones of lower leg	Tibia and fibula
Bones of wrist	Carpals
Bones of the hand	Metacarpals
Bones of fingers	Phalanges
Bones of ankle	Tarsals
Bones of the foot	Metatarsals
Bones of toes	Phalanges
Fused bones at base of spine	Coccyx

The **coccyx,** a tail-like structure, a fusion of several vertebral bones at the base of the human spine, is a vestigial structure. In lower animals, it forms the tail.

There are several kinds of joints in the body. A joint is a point at which one bone joins another and may be immovable or movable.

The bones of the skull are immovable after it has reached its full size. In infancy and early childhood the separated bones have not become fully fused because of the nature of bone tissue. Thus a baby's skull has 'soft' pliable areas.

Movable joints are of three types:

Ball and **Socket** joints, such as the bones of the upper arm and shoulder and the upper leg and hip.

Hinge joints, such as the bones forming the jaw, elbow, knee, and fingers.

Plane joints such as the wrist and ankle which are composed of numerous small bones whose flat surfaces glide over one another.

Lack of vitamin D in the diet of a child may result in a serious bone disease and deformity called rickets. Natural sunshine stimulates the production of this vitamin in our bodies. The vitamin assists the body in the metabolism of calcium and phosphorus needed for bone structure. Milk, liver, eggs and fish liver oils (cod and halibut) are rich sources of vitamin D.

Bands of tissues called **ligaments** connect bones of movable joints. A sprain results when a sudden too-sharp movement occurs that tears a ligament. A strain occurs when a ligament is stretched beyond its natural endurance.

The skeleton of our body has not always been hard bone nor is it completely bony even in adulthood. As an unborn child develops in the body of the mother, the endoskeleton is at first composed of soft, pliable, pre-bone tissue known as **cartilage.**

Since both cartilage and bone are tissues, they must be composed of cells.

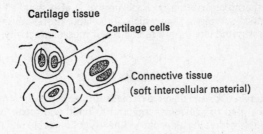

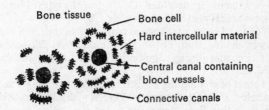

Figure 139   Cartilage and bone tissues

Cartilage cells are scattered throughout a soft connecting substance called connective tissue. As we grow older, the soft tissue becomes hard due to the deposits of calcium phosphate minerals, and the cells are replaced by bone cells.

Throughout life, in some regions of the skeleton, cartilage remains unchanged. Since this tissue is comparatively soft and resilient, it has a cushioning effect that helps to withstand shock and provides easier movements of joints. Pads of cartilage fill the spaces between the vertebrae of the spinal column providing ease of movement and protection against shock to the nerve cord.

There are pads of cartilage in the nose and ears that give shape to those organs and afford protection because of their pliability. Feel your nose and an ear. You can bend either structure quite freely without danger of breaking.

The smooth, translucent, flexible part of the breast bone of a chicken or part of the knuckle bone of a lamb which is commonly referred to as gristle is cartilage.

The muscles in the body provide the basic means of all movement. They cover the skeletal frame, give contour to the body and are found in the walls of several internal organs such as the heart and stomach. They are attached to bones and other structures by strips of connective tissue called **tendons.**

There are two types of muscles, those which we consciously activate, voluntary muscles, and those over which we have no conscious control, involuntary muscles. Muscles of the legs, arms and neck are examples of voluntary muscles. Muscles of the heart and digestive tract are involuntary.

All muscles are deep red in colour due to the rich supply of blood that flows through the many branching blood vessels. Digested food and oxygen are supplied to the muscle cells where these substances are combined in oxidation to produce the necessary energy. Each muscle is also supplied with nerves from the central nervous system which, in collaboration with the hormones from the parathyroid glands, aid in control of muscular activity.

SUMMARY

Food is prepared for and digested or made soluble in the digestive system before it can be used to provide energy and to build and repair body tissues. Digestive glands within the alimentary canal (digestive tube) and the pancreas and liver aid in the digestion of food.

The villi are structures in the lining of the small intestine which are adaptations for absorption of digested food. Cells select the type of food they need. Digested food is assimilated in the body cells.

Digested food and oxygen are carried to all cells in the body and wastes are carried away by the blood in the process of circulation. Blood is in constant motion as it circulates through the body. There are four different types of human blood.

For the process of respiration, oxygen is inhaled and the waste gas carbon dioxide is exhaled. Living things require oxygen with which to oxidize food to provide energy to live. Breathing refers to the mechanism of taking air into the lungs and expelling it. The red blood cells (corpuscles) transport oxygen from the lungs to all body cells.

The lungs are the organs of excretion of carbon dioxide and excess water vapour; the kidney and skin are organs of excretion of liquid wastes and mineral salts, and the large intestine is the organ of elimination of solid wastes. The temperature of the body is regulated by the skin.

Ductless or endocrine glands produce hormones which control all body functions.

The bony endoskeleton of man is composed of more than two-hundred movable and immovable bones which provide places of attachment for muscles, means of locomotion, protection and support for internal organs. The muscles provide the basic means of all body movement.

VOCABULARY

skeleton	vertebrae	cartilage
endoskeleton	spinal cord	tendon
skull	pelvis	ligament
spinal column	joints	rickets
vertebral column	coccyx	

Exercise No. 38

Complete each of the following statements:

1 The organs of respiration in man are the ——.
2 The actual exchange of gases takes place in the —— of the lungs.
3 When a supply of oxygen is cut off from an individual —— results.
4 The (a) —— closes the entrance to the (b) —— when food is swallowed. This prevents (c) ——.
5 A lung disease which can now be almost completely controlled is ——.
6 The organ which stores and eliminates nitrogenous wastes is the ——.
7 The glands in the skin which produce perspiration are called ——.
8 The organs which extract liquid wastes from the blood are the ——.
9 The organ for elimination of solid wastes is the ——.
10 The regulator of the body temperature is the ——.

Exercise No. 39

Which *one* term in each of the following includes the other three.

1 skull, spine, endoskeleton, pelvis
2 ball and socket, joint, hinge, plane joint
3 tissue, bone, muscles, cartilage
4 involuntary, voluntary, heart, muscles
5 bone, skull, ribs, vertebra
6 ductless gland, thyroid, thymus, pituitary, ovary
7 diabetes, islets of Langerhans, sugar control, pancreas
8 myxoedema, dwarfism, glandular malfunctioning, cretinism
9 adrenalin, secretin, insulin, hormone
10 secretions, chemical regulators, hormones, enzymes

CHAPTER XI

FOOD

In the chapters on human body functions, frequent references were made to the use of food to provide body energy. One must consume food to live, and certain food substances to live successfully. The term to live refers to the carrying on of all life functions.

Food serves several purposes in our bodies: it provides energy for the life processes; provides material for building and repairing cell protoplasm; regulates body processes.

CLASSIFICATION AND VALUE OF FOODS

All food substances can be divided into two general groups:

Organic foods—those which are produced by living organisms. Carbohydrates (sugars and starches), fats and proteins are organic food substances. Carbohydrates and fats are energy-producing, containing the elements carbon, hydrogen and oxygen. Proteins are cell-building, containing nitrogen in addition to the three elements found in carbohydrates.

Inorganic foods—those which come from rocks, soil and the seas. Mineral compounds of calcium, phosphorus, iron, sulphur, iodine and copper are needed to assist in cell-building and repairing (especially bone, teeth and muscle tissue) and in the general regulation of body functions.

Water is a compound essential to all body processes. It is not considered a food substance but is present in large quantities in many of the foods we eat. About two-thirds of man's body weight is the water in the tissues of his body. This compound of hydrogen and oxygen (H_2O) dissolves food, oxygen and wastes; makes up a large part of the blood; it is the basis for glandular secretions (both of ducted and ductless glands); and helps regulate body temperature.

Vitamins are chemical substances found in some foods that are also necessary for the well-being of the entire body. The lack of any one or many vitamins in the body results in specific diseases, and in some cases malformations of the skeleton and general disability.

The food substances, carbohydrates, fats and proteins are referred to as nutrients. Mineral compounds, water and vitamins are called accessory foods.

Some foods found in most normal diets are rich in proteins; some excel in carbohydrates, others in fats or minerals or water, still others in vitamins. Most foods contain a combination of two or more nutrients and accessory foods.

Here is a chart listing familiar foods, classified according to the outstanding nutrient or food accessory content (except vitamins).

CARBOHYDRATES	FATS	PROTEINS	MINERALS
Cereals	Butter	Lean meat	*Calcium*
Bread	Lard	Cheese	*Milk
Potatoes	Bacon	Eggs	Cheese
Spaghetti and	Fatty meats	Fish	Green vegetables
related products	Oils	Beans	*Iron*
Rice	Nuts	Peas	Lean meats
Sugar	*Milk	Gelatine	Liver
Chocolate	Margarine	Liver	Eggs
Cake		Wheat products	Raisins and other
*Milk		Peanuts	dried fruits
		*Milk	Beans
			Phosphorus
			Green, leafy
			vegetables
			*Milk
			Sulphur
			Egg yolk
			Green, leafy
			vegetables

* Notice that milk contains all nutrients plus the minerals. It is also rich in cholesterol which produces vitamin D when irradiated (exposed to the sun or an ultra-violet ray lamp).

Make a list of all the foods you have eaten during a day. Check with the chart and determine how well-balanced your day's diet has been. Generally, a diet for the day should include all the nutrients plus the necessary minerals, vitamins, water—about 6 glasses or its equivalent—and a certain amount of roughage. Roughage consists largely of the indigestible cellulose of plants which adds bulk to the food, and enables the gut muscles to grip it and keep it moving by peristalsis, particularly in the large intestine.

BALANCED DIET

A balanced diet might include one or more servings daily from each of the following basic groups:

1 Milk—at least 1 quart for a child; a pint for an adult.

2 Vegetables—at least two, a green leafy vegetable at least five times each week.

3 Potatoes—at least once daily.

4 Fruit—cooked or uncooked at least once daily.

5 Cereal products—whole cereal for breakfast; bread and other cereal products.

6 Meat, fish, poultry, eggs or cheese—at least once daily.

7 Butter, margarine or other fat—on bread or in cooking.

8 Sugar or some other sweet.

The specific amounts of a serving of each of these recommended basic foods should depend on the age of the individual, his occupation (if an adult), and the amount of physical activity in which he participates.

A **Calorie** is a heat-measuring unit. Chemists have devised a method of measuring the number of units of heat or Calories given off by food substances when they are oxidized. They have determined the number of Calories used per hour for each pound of body weight, depending upon the activity of the body. The number of Calories of food a person requires is determined by multiplying the hours spent in each activity through an average day by the weight of the person and by the Calories used per hour per pound.

Consult the following tables, list your activities in a typical day and determine the approximate number of Calories your body requires.

ACTIVITY	CALORIES USED PER HOUR PER POUND OF BODY WEIGHT
Sleeping	0·5
Sitting	0·7
Working with hands while sitting	0·8
Standing still	0·9
Walking (moderate speed)	1·5
Mild exercise	1·8
Extreme physical exertion	2·5

Use the following example as a guide to planning your own calorific needs.

Richard weighs 85 lbs. In a typical 24-hour day, he sleeps 10 hours, sits and reads about 2 hours, works at his desk in school about 5 hours, stands about 1 hour, walked at moderate speed 3 hours, and engages in vigorous sports for about 3 hours. Here is how to compute approximately the number of Calories he needs to provide sufficient energy for such a day.

ACTIVITY	NO. OF HOURS ×	RICHARD'S WEIGHT ×	NO. OF CALORIES PER HR. PER LB. =	CALORIES NEEDED
Sleeping	10	85	0·5	425·0
Sitting	2	85	0·7	119·0
Working at desk	5	85	0·8	340·0
Standing	1	85	0·9	76·5
Walking at moderate speed	3	85	1·5	382·5
Playing vigorously	3	85	2·5	637·5

Total number of Calories needed for that day.   TOTAL: 1,980·5

If you are in doubt as to whether you are consuming enough energy-producing food to provide you with the proper number of Calories for your age, sex, weight and occupation, consult a reliable, scientific book on nutrition (the science of foods and their relationship to the growth and repair of tissues and provision of energy in the body).

TESTS FOR FOOD NUTRIENTS

Chemists have devised simple means of identifying nutrients in common foods. You can make these tests at home, using easy-to-secure apparatus and chemicals.

Test for the presence of starch in a food:

Take a small piece of potato or flour, place it in a test tube and add to it a drop of a weak iodine solution. Notice a blue-black colour appearing. This indicates that starch is present.

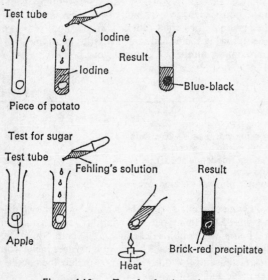

Figure 140　　　Test for food nutrients

If, when the iodine solution is added to a food, it does not turn this colour, you can deduce that starch is not present in that food.

Test for the presence of sugar in a food:

Place a small piece of apple or grape in a test tube. Add a blue-green chemical called Fehling's solution. (Can be purchased at a chemist.) Tilt the test tube away from your face and hold it over a gas or Bunsen burner until you see bubbles appear in the fluid. Do not allow it to boil over.

The colour will change from blue-green to a deep brick red with the appearance of a solid, or precipitate, indicating the presence of sugar in that food.

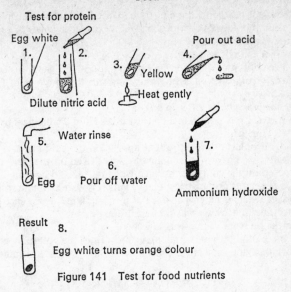

Figure 141   Test for food nutrients

If there is no change in colour, you can deduce that sugar is not present.
Test for the presence of protein in a food:
Place a piece of hard-boiled egg white in a test tube. Add a few drops (enough to cover the food) of dilute nitric acid (extreme caution should be exercised in using acids). Heat slightly. Then rinse off the acid with water and add ammonium hydroxide.

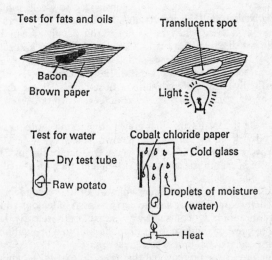

Figure 142   Test for food nutrients

After the egg is heated with the nitric acid, a yellow colour appears. On the addition of ammonium hydroxide, the yellow colour changes to orange, indicating the presence of protein.

Test for fats and oils in a food:

Rub a piece of butter or bacon on brown paper. Note the translucent spot that appears. (Hold up to a light.) This indicates the presence of fat or oil. See Fig. 142.

Test for the presence of water in a food:

Place a piece of raw potato in a dry test tube. Hold a cold glass over it and heat the test tube gently.

Notice the droplets of moisture that appear on the cold glass.

This is water in the form of vapour that was driven off the piece of potato and condensed on the cold glass surface. See Fig. 142. To be really scientific, you should also test this moisture to make sure it is water. Obtain some **cobalt chloride** paper which is blue when dry but turns pink in the presence of water. Use this to show that water was present in the potato.

Test for the presence of minerals in a food:

Place a piece of potato in a small pyrex dish. Burn the potato. A grey-white ash appears that does not burn. This indicates the presence of minerals.

VITAMINS AND THEIR VALUE

Testing for the presence of vitamins in food is not a simple matter. It is usually done in a laboratory. These tests are performed on animals like white mice, guinea pigs, and monkeys.

The animals are divided into two groups for experiment and control. A food to be tested for its vitamin content is fed to one group, over a period of time, and not to the other. Results indicate the effects of a deficiency of the vitamin on the bodies of the animals.

The discovery of these chemical food substances now called vitamins has an interesting background. History relates that many of the sailors who were part of Magellan's crew when he explored the Pacific Ocean became ill with an unknown disease. These sailors lived on hard tack and salted meats because these foods remained unspoiled longest throughout a voyage. After weeks at sea, the sailors became listless, their muscles weaker and weaker and finally they suffered serious nose-bleeds. Some died. Others who had stronger constitutions survived and went ashore when the ships reached land.

Sailors who ate the fresh fruits that grew native to the shore on which they landed, recovered from the illness later known as scurvy.

It was discovered that English sailors who were fond of the juice of lemons or limes did not succumb to scurvy. Or if they did, they recovered when fed lemon or lime juice regularly.

Although British Navy officials were unaware of the reasons for this, they passed a law that required every ship to carry a cargo of lemons and limes for the crew's consumption. Of course, it was difficult in those early days before refrigeration to prevent spoilage of fresh foods. But this precaution did help to prevent the occurrence of scurvy to a great extent.

At the same time, it was discovered that the Chinese and Japanese seamen whose diets consisted mainly of polished rice and fish, succumbed to a disease which they named beriberi (Japanese for 'I cannot! I cannot!'). The disease affects the muscles, weakening and finally paralysing them.

Japanese doctors discovered that beriberi could be relieved and even prevented by the addition of vegetables, meat and condensed milk and whole, unpolished rice to the diet.

To this day, in parts of the Far East, the people whose nourishment consists of polished rice and fish, suffer from beriberi.

Finally, after years of study and experimentation, scientists in various countries concluded that there are certain chemical substances in foods which are necessary to regulate all body functions and to prevent disease not caused by bacteria. These substances were named vitamins. The diseases that result from a lack of or total absence of vitamins are called vitamin deficiency diseases.

At present, the value of foods containing vitamin A, D complex (a group of vitamins with similar characteristics which are found in the same foods), C, B complex, E and K are known.

Science has been able to synthesize in pill or liquid form all of these vitamins. In many cases, supplementary vitamins can be recommended by a doctor to overcome mild deficiencies due to faulty or unbalanced diet or other causes.

There follows a chart of the vitamins, foods in which they occur and deficiency illnesses.

VITAMINS

VITAMIN	GOOD SOURCE	EFFECT OF DEFICIENCY	REMARKS
A	Fresh green vegetables, milk, butter, fish-liver oils, liver	Reduced resistance to disease, night blindness	Not destroyed by heating
D	Fish-liver oils, milk, egg-yolk, liver	Malformation of bones, e.g. rickets	Can be made in skin when exposed to sunlight
B_1 (thiamin)	Yeast, Marmite, wheat germ	Fatigue, muscular wasting, nervous disorders, beriberi	Destroyed by heat
B_2	Yeast, milk, meat, green vegetables	Skin diseases, nervous disorders	Destroyed by heat
C (ascorbic acid)	Oranges, lemons, black-currants, tomatoes, green vegetables	Poor healing of wounds, anaemia, lowered resistance to infection, scurvy	Destroyed by heat
E	Wheat germ, butter	Sterility proved in rats but not in humans	
K	Vegetables, especially cabbage and spinach	Failure of blood to clot	

Most vitamins are easily lost or destroyed by heat, or by exposure to oxygen (become oxidized), and by being dissolved out of food into water. To prevent the loss of vitamins, it is recommended that as little water as possible be used in cooking vegetables and fruits. Use this cooking water (in which vegetables and fruits have been cooked and into which some vitamins have been dissolved) again for making soups, sauces and gravies. Prepare salads and peeled or cut fruits just before serving to prevent exposure to oxygen and oxidation of some vitamins.

Foods rich in vitamins B and C should be cooked only a short time to prevent their destruction by heat.

It was seen that milk is included under almost all food sources of nutrients, minerals and vitamins. It is almost a complete food—easily digested, with no waste matter.

The sources of milk vary. In most English-speaking countries cow's milk is drunk. In some parts of South America, milk from the llama is used. Buffalo's milk is commonly used in India; whereas in Europe, goat's milk is used. In Russia, some people use mare's milk, while in desert regions, the milk of the camel is used.

GUARDING OUR FOOD

Throughout the ages people have attempted to profit by the adulteration of food. For example, water has been added to milk to increase its quantity. Sometimes harmful chemicals have been used.

From the middle of the eighteenth century, acts have been passed to protect various commodities such as tea, coffee and cocoa.

The Food and Drugs Act of 1938 prohibits the adulteration of food and the addition of harmful substances. It gives the Government power to inspect and analyse all food, and insists on hygienic conditions of food manufacture throughout the country.

In this way, the public welfare, so far as food and drug consumption is concerned is largely protected by law against adulteration and other malpractices.

SUMMARY

Food we eat contains substances which provide energy, material for building and repairing protoplasm and regulation of body processes.

Food substances are organic or inorganic.

Carbohydrates and fats provide energy for the body when they are oxidized.

Proteins provide materials for growth and repair of protoplasm.

Minerals, vitamins and water are food accessories needed to assist in building protoplasm and regulating all body functions.

Water makes up two-thirds of the body weight. It is an essential part of food.

Milk is a universal and almost complete food.

The Food and Drugs Act seeks to protect the public against adulterated foods and drugs.

VOCABULARY

nutrient	Fehling's solution	scurvy
vitamin	nitric acid	beriberi
nutrition	ammonium hydroxide	rickets
Calorie	translucent	irradiation

Exercise No. 40

Match a number in Column *A* with a letter in Column *B*.

	A		*B*
1	Calorie	a	chemicals in food that regulate body processes and prevent dietary diseases
2	nutrients	b	expose to ultra-violet rays of sun
3	carbohydrates	c	originally from living matter
4	vitamins	d	composes two-thirds of body weight
5	protein	e	food substance that builds and repairs tissues
6	milk	f	unit of heat measurement
7	irradiate	g	sugars and starches
8	adulterate	h	almost complete food
9	organic	i	to make a food inferior
10	water	j	food substances that provide energy and materials for growth of protoplasm

Exercise No. 41

Select the correct word or phrase for each of the following:

1 Juices from citrus fruits are used to cure: (a) pellagra; (b) rickets; (c) beriberi; (d) scurvy.
2 The vitamin needed to aid in blood clotting is: (a) vitamin A; (b) vitamin B; (c) vitamin K; (d) vitamin D.
3 The sunshine vitamin prevents the deficiency disease of: (a) scurvy; (b) beriberi; (c) rickets.
4 A good source of vitamins A and D is: (a) whole cereal; (b) cod liver oil; (c) yeast; (d) water-melon.
5 The minerals needed to keep bones and teeth in good condition are: (a) iodine and iron; (b) calcium and phosphorus; (c) sulphur and copper; (d) zinc and lead.

CHAPTER XII

THE NERVOUS SYSTEM: THE SENSE ORGANS

The governing system in our bodies, which works in close co-ordination with the hormones secreted by ductless glands, is the nervous system. It controls our physical actions, our thinking processes and our emotional behaviour.

TROPISMS

Simple plants and animals respond to changes in stimuli in the environment. The sensitivity of protoplasm causes it to respond to the presence of food, water, light, lack of light, heat and the presence of enemies.

Plants respond to stimuli although they have no nervous systems. These responses are known as **tropisms** which are growth responses to directional stimuli. If the tropism is towards the stimulus, it is known as a positive tropism. If the tropism is away from the stimulus it is called negative tropism. For example, roots of plants grow in the direction of water and downward towards the pull of gravity. These responses are known, respectively, as positive

hydrotropism and positive **geotropism.** Leaves and stems of plants grow towards the sunlight in positive **heliotropism.** Roots grow away from the sunlight, in the direction of darkness, hence the response is negative heliotropism.

Tropism in plants

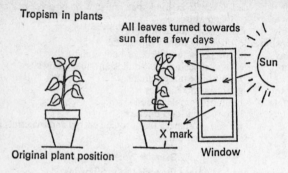

All leaves turned towards sun after a few days

Sun

X mark

Original plant position

Window

Figure 143a Positive heliotropism

Responses of plants to light are called **phototropisms,** to contact or touch **haptotropisms,** to chemicals **chemotropisms.**

To observe heliotropism in plants, place a potted plant on a shelf near a window. Leave it for a day or two. (Mark the side of the pot that is facing the

Leaves and stem grow up

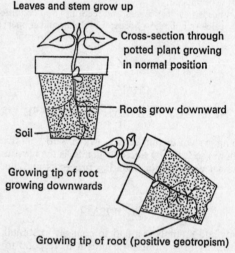

Cross-section through potted plant growing in normal position

Roots grow downward

Soil

Growing tip of root growing downwards

Growing tip of root (positive geotropism)

Figure 143b Tropism in plants

sunlight.) Notice how the leaves seem all to be facing in the direction of the window. Turn the pot round so that the side opposite the mark is facing in the direction of the window. Allow this to stand for a day or two. Observe that the leaves on their leaf stems and the main stem itself has turned to grow towards the sunlight, showing positive heliotropism.

To observe geotropism, place a young potted plant, that has been growing in normal position on its side for several days. Notice how the stem and leaves have turned to grow upward (negative geotropism) and the roots have turned to grow downward towards the centre of gravity (positive geotropism). See Fig. 143b.

Plants like the Venus fly trap and pitcher plant are sensitive to the touch of

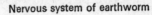

Nervous system of earthworm

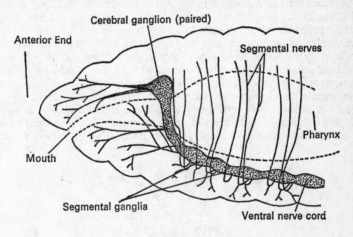

Nervous system of grasshopper

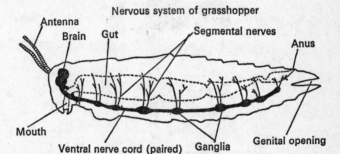

Figure 144

an insect. They close upon contact. This is not a growth response but is caused by changes in the water pressure of the cells and is called a **nastic** movement. The reaction of plants like mimosa where the leaves close up is a nastic response to vibrations. A number of flowers, mainly of the daisy family, close when light fades, and re-open next day. This again is a nastic movement.

We have already observed the importance of the chemical regulators, hormones, in body responses and functions.

Plants, too, have a hormone called **auxin**, the importance of which was discovered by F. W. WENT in 1928. This growth-promoting chemical appears to activate cells of plants to their characteristic responses to stimuli, by its uneven distribution resulting in uneven growth in response to certain stimuli. Just as animal physiologists have been able to isolate animal hormones, and to prepare some synthetically, so plant physiologists have done the same with auxin. Their commercial uses include weed killers, to prevent premature fruit drop and to produce seedless fruits.

NERVOUS SYSTEM OF SIMPLE ANIMALS

Protozoa, such as Amoeba and Paramecium, respond negatively to light and other harmful conditions, and positively to the presence of food. The sensitive properties of protoplasm make this possible.

In simple multicellular animals, we begin to see evidence of a nervous system, in primitive form. Responses to stimuli are effected and controlled by specialized cells called nerve cells or **neurons,** without any central control organ.

Among animals higher in the scale of life, the earthworm has the beginnings of an organized and specialized but simple nervous system. See Fig. 144.

There is a large nerve cord that extends along the ventral surface of the body just below the digestive tube. In each segment of the earthworm's body the nerve widens into a collection of nerve cells called a **ganglion.** Smaller

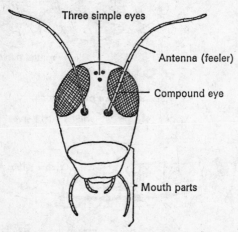

Head of grasshopper showing sense organs

Figure 145

nerves branch from each ganglion to all parts of the body. At the anterior end is a large ganglion as this is the part of the animal which most needs to be sensitive to the presence of food and light. Many nerve endings of touch located in the skin of the animal, especially around the mouth region, are sensitive to the touch of any objects in its pathway. Although earthworms have no eyes, there are other nerve endings in the skin that are sensitive to light, from which the animal withdraws when possible.

The nerve system of the grasshopper is similar to that of the earthworm except that in the former there are specialized sense organs—the feelers or antennae, two compound eyes on the top of the head, and three tiny, simple eyes.

The thin antennae are organs that are sensitive to smell and feeling. The three single eyes (**ocelli**) are sensitive to the change from light to dark. The pair of compound eyes are composed of thousands of small facets (six-sided lens-like structures). They are sensitive to light, motion and colour. Each facet shows only one part of an image—an entire picture being viewed by the grasshopper as a mosaic. See Fig. 145.

The nervous system of the fish, a simple vertebrate, shows marked advance in structure. It consists of a well-developed brain, a spinal cord and nerves branching from the brain and spinal cord to all parts of the body.

Sense organs in this animal are better developed than those of the grass-hopper. The paired eyes, with no lids, are slightly movable and can see for short distances. There are sensitive organs of smell within the nostrils. A series of nerve cells in the skin called the 'lateral line' just under the scales and extending the length of the body, is a special organ for sensitivity to depth of water and changes in water-pressure. The semicircular canals, the inner, and only part of the ear present in a fish maintain the balance of the fish.

THE HUMAN NERVOUS SYSTEM

The human nervous system is extremely highly developed and adapted for complex behaviour. It is one of the first systems of the body to develop in the embryo. It is the control system for all our thinking and doing.

The central nervous system in man consists of an extremely well-developed brain and spinal cord; the many nerves branching from and returning to the brain and spinal cord comprise the peripheral nervous system. See Fig. 146.

Let us consider each part of the central nervous system and the adaptations for its highly specialized and complex functions.

THE BRAIN

The brain is the control centre. It receives stimuli and sends out commands for responses to these stimuli. This vital organ has three main divisions, each having its own particular function in controlling our physical and mental activities. See Fig. 147.

Cerebrum—This is the largest and best developed section of the brain in man. Its functions are to control our actions and our thoughts. It is divided into areas whose responses to stimuli result in reasoning, speaking, hearing, seeing, memory, and direction of muscular activity.

Cerebellum—This is a small section of the brain just at the base and under the large cerebrum. Its functions are to regulate the activity of muscles after the cerebrum has thought about them and also to control body balance.

Medulla Oblongata—This is an enlarged area at the top of the spinal cord and just under the centre of the cerebrum. Its functions are to control the activities of our internal organs, for example: peristaltic action of the diges-tive tube, beat of the heart and breathing, and to regulate all involuntary muscles, those over which we have no conscious control.

The spinal cord, the main nerve trunk, of the body has many paired nerve branches leading from it to all parts of the body. It is the go-between of the body parts and the brain. It is not always necessary for a stimulus to reach the brain before a reaction or response takes place. A reflex reaction occurs almost immediately after the message or impulse gets to the spinal cord and back to a muscle (for example, touching a hot stove and removing the finger).

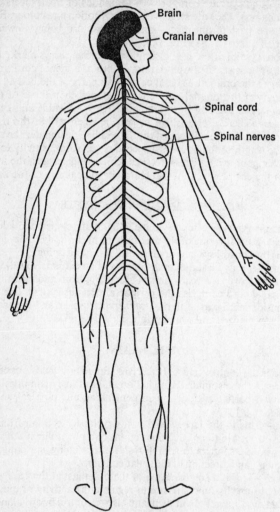

Figure 146   Nervous system in man

NEURON—SMALLEST UNIT OF NERVOUS SYSTEM

The smallest unit of the nervous system is a neuron or nerve cell. These cells are very specialized. A nerve cell is made up of three parts, each of which has a special function:

Section through brain

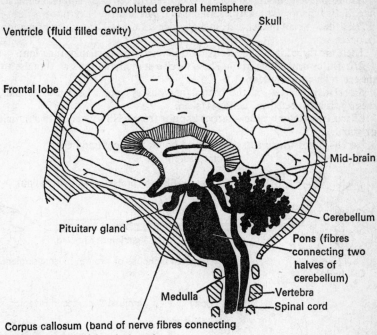

Ventricle (fluid filled cavity)

Convoluted cerebral hemisphere

Skull

Frontal lobe

Mid-brain

Cerebellum

Pons (fibres connecting two halves of cerebellum)

Pituitary gland

Medulla

Vertebra

Spinal cord

Corpus callosum (band of nerve fibres connecting the two cerebral hemispheres)

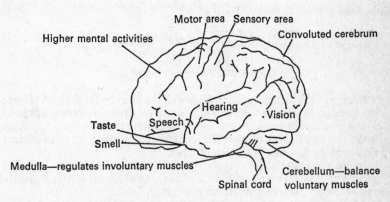

Higher mental activities

Motor area   Sensory area

Convoluted cerebrum

Hearing

Vision

Taste

Speech

Smell

Medulla—regulates involuntary muscles

Spinal cord

Cerebellum—balance voluntary muscles

Figure 147 Areas of the human brain

Cell body—irregular in shape, with branches leading from it. Its function is to regulate the activities of the entire cell.

Axon—one long insulated fibre leading from the cell body and branching at its end. Its function is to relay a stimulus to the next nearest neuron.

Dendrites—small branches from many sides of the cell body. Their function is to receive stimuli.

There are three kinds of neurons, each adapted for a particular function:

Afferent or sensory neuron—These receive stimuli and send an impulse to the central nervous system.

Associative neuron—in the central nervous system, where the stimulus message is interpreted and action is taken.

Efferent or Motor neuron—carries impulse from CNS for action to a muscle or gland.

Nerve—fibres which run parallel and bound in a common coat.

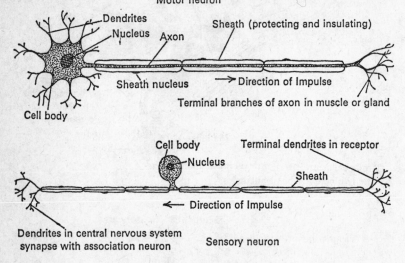

Figure 148   Neurons or nerve cells

Neurons do not actually connect one with the other by touching. A **synapse** is formed, over which an impulse jumps very much like electricity will jump over a small space between open ends of wires that almost touch. A synapse is the very small space between the terminal ends of the axon of an afferent nerve and the dendrites of an efferent nerve.

In order to have control over the body and to adapt it to the environment, nerve pathways have been established within man's nervous system. Some responses made to stimuli are voluntary; others are involuntary.

All voluntary responses occur after a message is brought by a sensory nerve to associative nerves in the area of the brain concerned with the response. The type of response depends on the order from the brain which is carried by the motor nerve to the muscle that will cause motion or the gland that will send forth secretions to control muscles or to activate responses.

For example, when the telephone bell rings, the sound enters the ears. The impulse is carried along sensory nerves in the inner ears and then to the brain. In the brain, the sound is interpreted and several associations are made with different motor nerves; (1) carrying a message to the muscles of the legs and we walk to the telephone; (2) carrying a message to the hand and we raise the receiver to the ear; and (3) carrying a message to the organs of speech and we say 'Hello'.

REFLEXES

A natural reflex act is a rapid response for our protection against sudden danger in the environment. The reflex act is instantaneous without necessitating thought or judgement.

Let us refer to the situation in which one touches a hot stove with the finger. The stimulus of extreme heat affects the nerve endings of touch in the skin. The impulse is carried along afferent or sensory nerves to the spinal cord where it connects with cell bodies and is transferred to motor nerves which

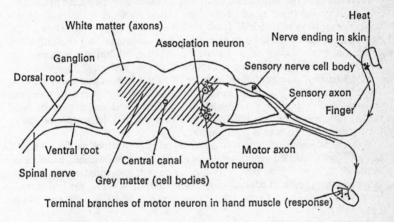

Figure 149 Transverse section of spinal cord to show a reflex arc

carry the impulse back to the muscles of the hand and finger and arm. Result: you pull your finger away without thinking about it. This constitutes a **reflex act** or **arc**.

Sometimes reflexes are learned or acquired over a period of time. Such a response, in which the presence of a new stimulus results in the same response as the original stimulus of a natural reflex, is known as a conditioned reflex.

Early in 1900, a Russian scientist, IVAN PAVLOV, directed experiments on dogs to discover the steps in learning or acquiring a conditioned reflex. One of his experiments was based on the fact that as soon as a dog smells or sees food, his mouth waters or fills with saliva, a natural reflex act.

Pavlov placed a dog in an empty room where he fed it at a set time each day. Each time, just before a dish of food was placed before the animal at feeding time, a bell was rung. The dog's mouth watered at the sight and smell of the food. This procedure was repeated every day over a period of time.

At the end of this time, a bell was rung at each feeding time, but no food was placed before the dog. The dog's mouth continued to water at the sound of the bell without the presence or scent of the food.

After repeating this and other similar experiments many times and with many different dogs, Pavlov came to a conclusion. He concluded that a 'new or substitute stimulus (ringing of the bell) had become associated with the original stimulus (the food) and resulted in the same response (mouth-watering) as the original stimulus (just food)'. He named the response a **conditioned reflex.**

Other scientists have followed up Pavlov's experiments with similar investigations on other animals and on man as well. They refer to a conditioned reflex as a conditioned reaction because a new stimulus is able to result in a given reaction.

After Pavlov reached his conclusions concerning conditioned reflexes or reactions, he set his next goal at discovering whether or not the reactions were permanent.

With the same dog who was conditioned to salivate at the sound of the bell, Pavlov extended the trial of ringing the bell at meal-time, but without accompanying it with a dish of food. Gradually, the amount of saliva in the dog's mouth decreased until its mouth did not water (salivate) at all, thus deconditioning a response or, as Pavlov described it, inhibiting a response. An inhibition, then, is the stopping or suppressing of a response.

Many natural reflexes that seem to be inherited in man and other animals are called instincts. The sucking of an infant at its mother's breast, sneezing, yawning and crying are a few examples in man. Nest-building of birds at mating time is another example of an instinctive action. Migration of eels to the Sargasso Sea to spawn is still another.

A learned response differs from a natural reflex with which we are born. We acquire many learned responses throughout our lives without even being aware of it. We develop new responses to stimuli and situations in our environment as a result of conditioning. As we meet new situations and stimuli, we develop definite reactions or behaviour patterns which become part of our personality.

As we grow older, we acquire other conditioned responses, form new associations and are constantly experiencing new conditioning—we are learning. As we learn, we are able to respond to better advantage, to the stimuli in our environment. We are able to change or alter our responses, when necessary, to the same stimuli or to different environments.

INTELLIGENCE

Intelligence in man is thought of as the ability to learn and to adjust to his environment. It by far supersedes the same attribute in other mammals. The cerebrum of man—which controls reasoning, memory and speech—is the largest part of the brain and much larger in proportion than the cerebrum of any other animal. Man is able to use a spoken and written language to express his ideas and is capable of reflective thinking (thinking in abstract terms) and the solution of intricate problems. And man is able to inhibit and control his instinctive drives.

We have been speaking of intelligence in general terms. It is understood that individuals differ in intelligence just as they differ in the colour of their eyes and the shape of their fingernails.

Much attention has been focused, in recent years, on the means of testing an individual to determine his intelligence. Psychologists have devised tests which determine the average performance of any age group.

The I.Q. (intelligence quotient) of an individual can be determined by comparing his individual performance on a given test with the average performance of his age group. The score he makes on this type of test indicates his mental age. The I.Q. is determined by dividing the mental age (M.A.) by the actual or chronological age (C.A.) and multiplying the result by 100.

$$\frac{\text{M.A.}}{\text{C.A.}} \times 100 = \text{I.Q.}$$

For example, if a test indicates that Billy, who is eight years old (C.A.), has a mental age (M.A.) equivalent to the average for an eleven year old, his I.Q. is figured as follows:

$$\frac{\text{M.A.} = 11}{\text{C.A.} = 8} \times 100 = 137 \cdot 5 \text{ I.Q.}$$

It has been established that the normal I.Q. is about 90–110.

These tests are not by any means infallible but they do perhaps give a general clue to the intelligence of an individual as compared with the average intelligence for his group.

Thus, I.Q. serves, among other factors, as a grouping in school classes within an age group; and as a placement factor, combined with aptitude tests that indicate the kind of work one is best suited to do.

VOCABULARY

tropism	efferent	synapse
hydrotropism	reflex	impulse
geotropism	conditioned reflex	axon
heliotropism	learned response	dendrite
phototropism	neuron	intelligence
haptotropism	ocelli	inhibition
auxin	compound eye	intelligence quotient
sensory	cerebrum	mental age
afferent	cerebellum	chronological age
motor	medulla oblongata	

Exercise No. 42

Complete each of the following statements:

1 A root of a plant grows downward. This is known as ——.
2 —— is the hormone that controls plant growth.
3 The response of leaves to the sunlight is called ——.
4 The unit of structure of the nervous system of man is the ——.
5 The major parts of our nervous system are ——.
6 A simple, automatic response of higher animals is known as a ——.
7 A neuron which carries an impulse to the brain is called an ——.
8 The function of the cerebellum is ——.
9 The organs of smell and feeling in the grasshopper are ——.

10 The neuron which carries a message for action to a muscle or gland is known as an ——.
11 —— is the Russian scientist who experimented with conditioned reflexes in dogs.
12 An example of an animal which has no nerves is ——.
13 Blushing is an example of a —— act.
14 Driving a car is an example of a ——.

THE SENSE ORGANS

The organs in man which are especially adapted to receive and respond to stimuli from the environment are called sense organs. The human sense organs are the eyes, the ears, the nose, the tongue and the skin. The list of basic sensations (sight, sound, smell, taste and touch) has been variously extended, detailed, and qualified, and there does not seem to be universal agreement among scientists.

THE EYES

The eyes are structurally adapted to receive light rays and to respond to them.

The eyeball which fits into a protective socket in the skull and is also protected by eyelids and eyelashes, has several parts:

The **sclerotic coat**—protective tissue around the outside of the entire eye; the white of eyeball.

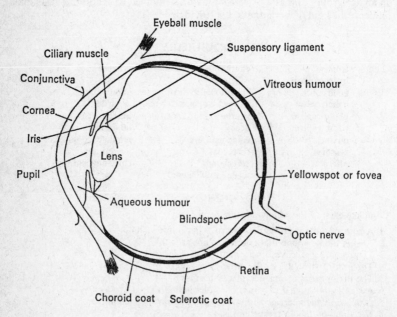

Figure 150   The human eye

The **choroid coat**—just under the sclerotic coat; contains blood vessels for providing nourishment to the organ; it is pigmented to prevent reflection of light rays.

Iris—coloured part of the choroid coat.

Ciliary body—thickened, muscular edge of the choroid layer and around the lens; suspensory ligament holds the lens in position.

Pupil—round opening in the choroid coat, surrounded by the muscular iris; regulated in size by responses to degrees of light.

Cornea—front of eyeball; part of the sclerotic coat that is transparent to allow light rays to enter.

Conjunctiva—thin membrane lining the eyelids and covering the cornea.

Lens—double convex and flexible portion of the eye, just beyond the iris; part of the eye through which light rays pass and are bent to be focused on the retina.

Retina—thin layer of tissue on the inner surface of the eye; contains nerve cells called rods and cones which respond to light rays that are focused on it by the lens.

Fovea—area of clearest vision on the retina.

Optic nerve—nerve of sight; enters the eyeball at the back to supply the retina with rods and cones; carries sensory impulses to the brain.

Blind spot—point at which the optic nerve enters the retina; no rods or cones on this area so that light impulses cannot be received at this point.

Aqueous humour—liquid in the space between the iris, part of the lens and cornea; keeps the lens moist; protects the eyeball from physical shock.

Vitreous humour—transparent, gelatin-like substance filling the large inner cavity of the eyeball; helps keep the shape of the eyeball; protects the retina and its nerve endings.

The principles of the camera were fashioned after the structural adaptations of the eye.

The sensation of seeing involves many steps. Light rays enter the transparent cornea, pass through the aqueous humour through the pupil and to the lens. The lens is shaped so that light rays are bent as they pass through and meet, are focused, at a point on the retina after having passed through the vitreous humour.

The nerve cells, rods and cones on the retina receive light stimuli and send impulses along the optic nerve to the area of sight in the cerebrum of the brain. Here the impulses are interpreted into images or pictures that we see.

Several sets of muscles control the eye and many of its parts. There are muscles which turn the entire eyeball part of the way in its socket. There are those which control the iris, that nearly close the pupil if light is intense and relax the pupil (opening it) if the light is dim. The ciliary muscles control the shape of the lens so that it can accommodate to focus light rays from near and distant objects. Muscles of the eyelids close and open them to protect the eyeball.

Glasses are used to correct abnormalities or deficiencies of the eye lens or shape of the eyeball. The most common eye defects are astigmatism, near-sightedness and far-sightedness.

Astigmatism is due to improper shape of either the cornea or the lens of the eye so that the eye is unable to focus a number of points at the same time. Crossing black lines of equal intensity will appear sharply black in one direction and grey or indistinct in another. Pictures or images appear partially indistinct. Lenses with curvatures to equalize eye lens or cornea curvatures are used.

Near-sightedness is due to an elongated eyeball and a lens that is too

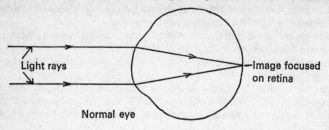

Normal eye

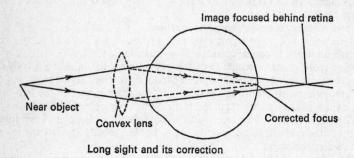

Long sight and its correction

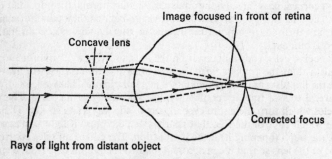

Short sight and its correction

Figure 151   Common eye defects and their corrections

rounded. The image resulting is indistinct because it is focused in front of the retina instead of on the retina. Corrective lenses must necessarily be concave to bring the focus of light rays to the retina.

Far-sightedness is due to a foreshortened eyeball and a flat eye lens. People who are far-sighted see distant objects without difficulty but close objects are not clear because they are focused behind the retina instead of on it. Lenses must be convex to correct this abnormality.

Most of us are born with normally shaped and normal functioning eyes. It is to our advantage to protect, not abuse these sense organs. Proper lighting, good posture, sufficient rest, good diet and medical care when necessary will help keep the eyes functioning correctly.

The designations of those who deal professionally with diseased or defective eyes are often confused. The **ophthalmologist** is the doctor who diagnoses and treats diseases and defects of the eyes. The **oculist,** who is not a doctor, prescribes for glasses without the use of drugs; and the **optician** makes and sells glasses.

THE EARS

The organs of hearing in man are his ears, which are complex structures of three divisions.

1 The **Outer Ear**—consisting of the shell or **pinna** that directs air waves into the ear canal to the eardrum or **tympanum.**

2 The **Middle Ear**—contains three movable little bones. One of the bones, the hammer (**malleus**), is connected to the eardrum. The hammer is connected

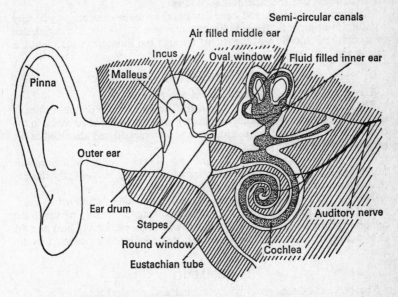

Figure 152 The human ear (diagrammatic)

to the anvil (**incus**) which is connected to the stirrup (**stapes**). The **Eustachian tube** leads from the middle ear to the back of the mouth. This adaptation ensures equal air pressure on each side of the eardrum. The acts of swallowing and yawning help to equalize the pressure. Keeping the mouth slightly open while in an ascending lift helps to keep the pressure equalized and to prevent the clogged feeling in the ears.

The **Inner Ear** (deepest in the skull)—contains two very delicate structures, the **cochlea** and the **semicircular canals**. The cochlea, a snail-shell-like organ, is filled with a fluid and contains nerve endings. These nerve endings receive vibrations from the fluid and transfer impulses to the area of hearing in the cerebrum of the brain via the **auditory nerve** (nerve of hearing).

The semicircular canals, three arched tubes at right-angles to each other, are also filled with fluid and lined with nerve endings that transmit impulses to the cerebellum of the brain where the centre of balance is located. Severe, unaccustomed rocking or whirling motion will disturb the fluid in the canals and will result in the sensation of dizziness.

The sensation of hearing involves all of the structures of the ear except the semicircular canals. Vibrations of air (sound waves) enter the ear canal and are directed to the sensitive eardrum, which vibrates. This causes the hammer, the anvil and the stirrup to vibrate. Vibrations of the stirrup are transferred to the membrane of the inner ear and to the fluid in the cochlea. Here, nerve endings receive and transmit sound impulses to the centre of hearing in the brain where they are interpreted as the sounds we hear.

The soft wax that forms in the ear canal protects the delicate middle and inner ears. The wax and the tiny hairs in the ear canal protect the rest of the ear from water, dirt and other foreign bodies.

Infection of the middle and inner ears or injury to the eardrum may be very painful. If not properly treated, deafness may result. Infectious material, due to a cold, may travel from the throat through the Eustachian tube into the middle ear.

ORGANS OF TASTE, SMELL AND TOUCH

The sensations of taste and smell are closely related.

The tongue is the organ of taste in man. The little bumps on the surface of the tongue contain nerve endings that carry impulses to the taste centre in the cerebrum of the brain. Here the impulses are interpreted and identified as the sensation of sweet, sour, bitter or salt.

The organ of smell in man is the nose. Small nerve endings in the mucous membrane lining of the nose receive stimuli. Olfactory nerves carry the impulses to the brain for interpretation and we smell.

The skin is a widespread organ of touch. Nerve endings scattered in every part of the skin receive stimuli, send impulses along the sensory nerves to the cerebrum of the brain and we feel pressure or pain, sensations of heat or cold. Our muscles react to these sensations (motor responses) as directed by the brain.

SUMMARY

The nervous system governs our mental and physical activities and our emotional behaviour. Man's is the most highly specialized in the animal kingdom.

Tropism is the name given to the growth response of plants to stimuli in the environment. Auxin is a recently discovered plant hormone that controls growth of plants.

Intelligence in man is the ability to learn and adjust to the environment.

The sense organs of man are his eyes, nose, ears, tongue and skin, each structurally adapted to respond to specific stimuli in the environment.

VOCABULARY

sclerotic coat	optic nerve	eardrum
choroid coat	blind spot	anvil
iris	aqueous humour	stirrup
pupil	vitreous humour	hammer
cornea	astigmatism	cochlea
lens	near-sightedness	auditory nerve
retina	far-sightedness	olfactory nerve
rods and cones	oculist	semicircular canal
	optician	

Exercise No. 43

Complete the following chart.

PART OF EYE	FUNCTION
1 Sclerotic coat	
2 Choroid coat	
3 Cornea	
4 Optic nerve	
5 Iris	
6 Pupil	
7 Lens	
8 Retina	
9 Aqueous humour	
10 Vitreous humour	

Exercise No. 44

Match a number in Column *A* with a letter in Column *B*.

A	*B*
1 blind spot	a tube connecting ear with back of mouth
2 astigmatism	b organ of taste
3 optician	c part of retina that cannot receive light impulses
4 Eustachian tube	d organ of touch
5 cochlea	e nerve of smell
6 balance	f one who makes corrective glasses
7 auditory nerve	g function of semicircular canals
8 skin	h eye abnormality
9 olfactory nerve	i organ of hearing in inner ear
10 tongue	j nerve of hearing

CHAPTER XIII

DISEASE: ITS CAUSES AND CONTROL

Tremendous advances have been made since the beginning of medical history. Every day we learn of new efforts to reduce physical and mental suffering caused by diseases. Many diseases that were at one time the scourges of mankind, have ceased to exist entirely—recorded only in history. Others will disappear as we progress in medical science.

From the beginning of man's existence on earth there have been illnesses of every nature. Long ago, these illnesses were attributed to evil spirits which had entered the body and had to be driven off by inflicting physical suffering. A magician or medicine man was called upon, and even worshipped, to frighten the evil spirits by prayers and incantations, by flaying or other cruel inflictions and by the administration of malodorous concoctions or brews of herbs, honeybee stings, entrails of animals, alligator claws and other wildly imaginative medications.

Sometimes the patients or, rather, victims, recovered in spite of these treatments, because of the body's natural tendencies to fight disease-producing organisms. Sometimes the herbs that were used actually had a curative effect. In all probability years of experience in treating a common complaint or ailment did teach the early physicians some medical knowledge. Later, with the advance of medical knowledge, some of the healers became physicians.

Even our immediate ancestors held what we now know to be old wives' tales and superstitious beliefs regarding the prevention and cure of disease. It was quite common for people to wear strong-smelling talismans (camphor bags, garlic and onion strings) somewhere on their persons to ward off evil spirits which were believed to cause epidemic diseases. They believed, too, and for the same reason, that only horrible-tasting medicines could be effective in treating and curing ailments. Although much of this 'witchcraft' was ineffective, a good deal of practical knowledge came from it. The value of parts of plants in treating some sicknesses has been indisputably demonstrated by scientists.

BRIEF HISTORY OF MEN AGAINST DISEASE

VAN LEEUWENHOEK's microscope made possible the beginnings of the study of disease-causing organisms. But although he saw and made written descriptions of bacteria, and other micro-organisms, he did not associate them with disease.

In the middle of the eighteenth century, an Italian scientist, LAZORO SPALLANZANI, performed experiments which proved that decay, believed to be caused by tiny living things, did not occur when food had been properly sterilized and sealed against contamination.

It was not until the end of the eighteenth century that the English physician, EDWARD JENNER, first used a vaccination against smallpox. Although he knew little about bacteria or viruses, he believed that cowpox in cattle was another form of the dreaded smallpox in human beings. He believed and proved that rubbing a little serum taken from a cowpox pustule (blister) into a scratch in the arm of a person would either immunize that person (prevent his succumbing to the disease), or cause a future attack of the disease to be milder.

About sixty years later, LOUIS PASTEUR, a French scientist, now known to the world for the establishment of the Germ Theory of Disease and the process of pasteurization, performed experiments on fermentation of beet pulp and grape juices used to produce wine.

He demonstrated that unsuccessful wine and beer production was due to the destruction of the yeast plants, responsible for the fermentation, by small rod-like organisms he called microbes.

About the same time, the silk industry in France was threatened with ruin due to disease of silkworms. Pasteur proved that the disease of these silkworms (larvae of silkworm moths) was caused by another type of microbe.

After experimentation he also concluded that the diseases anthrax, which affected and often killed sheep and cattle, and chicken cholera, were caused by still other microbes or micro-organisms.

Pasteur's research and experiments with these diseases led him to the discovery that inoculations into healthy animals of a solution of weakened disease-producing microbes would immunize them against the specific diseases. He obtained the weakened cultures from the blood of animals suffering from the disease. Disease-causing agents were referred to as germs about this time.

Another contribution Pasteur made to the control of disease was the discovery of the cause of and cure for rabies.

Pasteur's conclusion that all diseases are caused by specific microbes or germs and that they may pass from one living thing to another and thus spread diseases, was a most important contribution to the welfare of mankind.

The Germ Theory of Disease is responsible for the discovery of the causes for, and control of, almost all known diseases, the introduction of aseptic surgery and the development of the science of public health.

SIR JOSEPH LISTER, an eminent British surgeon, contributed some conclusive evidence to substantiate Pasteur's germ theory. He proved that infections that developed after surgery were due to microbes or germs that were present on the surgeon's hands, on his instruments, on the linen, and in the air he and his assistants exhaled.

He is credited with being the pioneer in aseptic surgery. Lister proved that infections can be avoided by sterilization of all surgical equipment with dilute carbolic acid, thorough cleaning of surgeon's and assistant's hands, and the wearing of gauze masks over nose and mouth during an operation.

About the same time that Pasteur made his discoveries, the scientist ROBERT KOCH, working independently in Germany, discovered that specific bacteria cause anthrax in cattle and the lung disease tuberculosis.

He made a substance called tuberculin from an extract of the tubercle bacillus which he thought could be administered to cure tuberculosis. Unfortunately it did not cure the disease, but it did provide a test for the presence of tuberculosis in both cattle and human beings.

Koch's most important contributions, other than the discovery of anthrax and tuberculosis bacteria, was the method he established in studying disease-causing bacteria. The steps in his method are still used today. There are four consecutive steps:

1 Find and isolate the organisms believed to cause disease, from the tissues of the victim.

2 Grow the organisms by themselves outside of the tissues, in a culture or pure food medium.

3 Produce the same disease, by injection of the organisms from the pure culture, in a healthy animal.

4 Isolate and grow in pure culture, the organisms causing the disease in the second victim.

In this way it can be proved beyond doubt that a specific micro-organism causes a specific disease.

Bacteriology, one of the most important biological sciences, has demonstrated that some bacteria produce diseases in man and in other animals and others are extremely useful to man and necessary for his physical and economic well-being.

Bacteria are found almost everywhere—on, in and above the earth; in air, in soil, and in water. They thrive in all animals and plants. They have been found temporarily inactive, encased in spore cases, in icebergs and in natural hot water springs.

STUDYING BACTERIA IN THE LABORATORY

Bacteria may be collected and grown in the laboratory for observation and experimentation. For bacteria to grow and multiply successfully, certain favourable conditions must be present. Bacteria, like other living organisms, must have food. In addition, they require a limited amount of oxygen, moisture, some heat, and the absence of direct sunlight (they prefer darkness).

To raise a pure bacterial culture in the laboratory, food in the form of liquid broth or gelatin made from agar agar, a sea weed, and beef extract or sugar solution is used. This combination is boiled until it is free of any microorganisms.

The containers in which the food medium is prepared as well as those in which the bacteria will be planted must also be freed of living organisms by

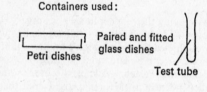

Containers used:

Petri dishes

Paired and fitted glass dishes

Test tube

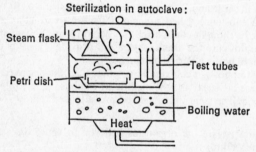

Sterilization in autoclave:

Steam flask

Petri dish

Test tubes

Boiling water

Heat

Figure 153a Preparation of bacteria cultures

sterilization. An autoclave (type of steam sterilizer) is used to sterilize flasks, Petri dishes, test tubes, etc.

After the food is prepared and containers sterilized, the food is poured into a Petri dish or test tube. A Petri dish (JULIUS PETRI, 1852–1922, German bacteriologist) is a flat round glass dish with a large exposed surface. The cover fits loosely but adequately over the dish and can easily be removed. If the food is a gelatin it must be allowed to set.

To prepare a culture, bacteria from a chosen source must be introduced to the food contained in the Petri dish or test tube. If the culture is to be of bacteria from human saliva, a sample is collected in a sterile test tube. A needle is sterilized by holding it in a flame, allowed to cool, then dipped into the saliva. This is touched to the agar agar gelatin or into the liquid broth

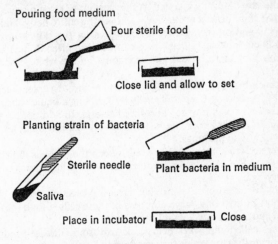

Figure 153b   Preparation of bacteria cultures

and the containers are immediately covered to prevent contamination from the air. The bacteria have been planted or the medium has been inoculated.

In the laboratory, the culture is then placed in an incubator where the warm darkness is favourable to the growth of bacteria. Here they multiply rapidly and frequently by fission until colonies are formed in a day or two.

The nature of the bacteria is determined by the colour and the outline of the colony they produce (among other factors) and by examination of a stained sample under the microscope.

PATHOGENIC BACTERIA

Pathogenic or disease-producing bacteria cause disease in two manners:

Body tissues may be destroyed. (Example: tuberculosis bacteria destroy lung tissue.)

They may produce **toxins** (poisons) which disturb normal body function and result in symptoms of the disease. (Example: scarlet fever bacteria produce toxins that result in a very sore throat, high fever, red spots, etc.)

Some pathogenic bacteria cause communicable diseases—diseases which can be spread from one individual to another through the air, in water, in food and by physical contact with the body or towels, handkerchiefs or articles of clothing of the affected individual. The bacteria of such diseases (diphtheria, pneumonia, influenza, whooping cough, mumps and other children's diseases) get into the human body by way of the nose, mouth and other body openings.

When a person sneezes or coughs, he sprays out droplets of moisture carrying thousands of bacteria. When the moisture evaporates, the bacteria cling to dust particles in the air and become dispersed.

NATURAL BODY PROTECTION AGAINST BACTERIAL INVASION

Our bodies are naturally adapted to some extent to resist disease-producing bacteria. The skin forms a protective wall over the entire body. Hairs growing from the skin and oil secreted from glands within the skin keep its surface protected. Bacteria which enter a break in the skin often do not get any further because they are attacked and overcome by the white blood cells, the phagocytes.

Mucous membranes lining the digestive and respiratory tracts keep the inner surfaces of these organs moist and sticky by secreting a liquid substance called **mucus.** This serves as a trap for invading bacteria. In addition, little hairs in the nose strain out dirt carrying bacteria before the incoming air enters the trachea on its way to the lungs.

Tears secreted from glands in the eyelids keep the eyeballs moist and, with the aid of the eyelids and lashes, protect the eyes against invasion of foreign bodies carrying bacteria.

The white blood corpuscles provide natural protection. When bacteria invade any part of the body, large numbers of these cells rush to the focal point of invasion and attempt to devour the bacteria.

Substances called **antibodies** help to destroy some disease-producing bacteria or to neutralize the toxins they produce.

Some bacteria which are swallowed with food or water are destroyed when they reach the stomach by acids in the digestive juices and by bile in the small intestine.

VOCABULARY

cowpox	chicken cholera	culture
smallpox	rabies	autoclave
anthrax	microbe	Petri dish
Germ Theory	tuberculin	communicable disease
toxin	aseptic	

Exercise No. 45

Match a number in Column *A* with a letter in Column *B*.

A	*B*
1 van Leeuwenhoek	a aseptic surgery
2 Spallanzani	b germ theory of disease
3 Edward Jenner	c decay is caused by living organisms
4 Louis Pasteur	d early microscope
5 Robert Koch	e cause of tuberculosis
6 Joseph Lister	f first vaccination against smallpox
7 Petri	g paired dish for bacteria cultures

NATURAL AND ACQUIRED IMMUNITY

It is common knowledge that some people are immune to certain diseases produced by bacteria—that is, they are able to resist these diseases. Others are susceptible to diseases—that is, they lack the ability to resist.

Immunity may be natural or acquired. If natural immunity is present, it indicates that the person was born with the ability to resist a certain disease. For example, we are all born with a natural immunity to the bacteria which cause distemper in dogs.

Another type of immunity is known as acquired immunity. This is a resistance one develops during one's lifetime. Such an immunity may be acquired in two different manners:

Active acquired immunity—This type develops after an individual has recovered from a disease. During the illness, specific antibodies (chemicals) are built up in the blood which aid the white blood corpuscles in destroying bacteria or viruses and toxins of a specific disease. Example: recovery from smallpox, yellow fever, scarlet fever, chicken pox, mumps usually makes the body immune to subsequent attacks because of the development of antibodies specific to the disease.

Passive acquired immunity—This type may not last a lifetime because it involves introduction of foreign substances which the body tends to get rid of in the natural process of elimination. It may be acquired in several ways:

Injection of a serum containing antibodies (an antitoxin) taken from an animal which has recovered from the disease. The once universally fatal disease diphtheria is now controllable by use of diphtheria toxin-antitoxin. For this an injection of small quantities of weakened and harmless diphtheria toxins (poisons released by diphtheria-causing bacteria) in combination with antitoxin (taken from a serum of a horse that has recovered from induced diphtheria) develops acquired immunity. An injection of tetanus antitoxin prevents the disease but does not cure it.

Another method to induce acquired immunity is by vaccination. A vaccine is a substance which confers immunity when it is injected into a person. Vaccines may be made from the serum of a person or animal that had the disease. It contains dead or weakened bacteria or viruses (i.e. smallpox, typhoid, epidemic meningitis, whooping cough). Vaccines may be prepared by chemically treating disease-causing bacteria in culture to destroy their strength.

Either type of vaccine will stimulate the blood to form antibodies to prevent the specific disease-producing bacteria from thriving and causing damage.

There are several tests which may be administered to an individual to discover whether or not he is susceptible to a particular disease. (They are named after the scientist credited with their discovery.)

Schick Test—Test to determine susceptibility to diphtheria. A small amount of dilute diphtheria toxin is injected just under the skin. A small red area will appear around the point of injection if a person is susceptible.

Dick Test—Test to determine susceptibility to scarlet fever. The same as for the Schick Test, using scarlet fever toxin. (Robert Koch used tuberculin with the same method when testing for susceptibility to tuberculosis.) The **Wassermann Test** for syphilis is a similar test.

Widal Test—This is used to discover the presence of typhoid fever in an individual. Blood is taken from the suspect and the serum removed. Living typhoid bacteria (from a culture) are then added to the serum which has been diluted with salt water. Antibodies in the serum will cause the typhoid bacteria to form clumps.

At present, children and adults can be immunized against many diseases. Paediatricians recommend immunization of children against diphtheria, whooping cough, measles and tetanus at the age of four months. A series of three injections, spaced about a week apart, of combined diphtheria and whooping cough toxin-antitoxins, may be administered. This may be effective for adults who are preparing for extensive travel in countries where sanitary conditions are possibly inadequate.

Vaccination against smallpox is compulsory for entry into a large number of countries.

A routine activity of all branches of the Armed Forces is immunization against typhoid, typhus, yellow fever, smallpox, influenza, cholera and epidemic meningitis.

The havoc created by some disease-producing bacteria can be avoided in our everyday existence by cleanliness at all times, by the use of antiseptics and disinfectants such as iodine and peroxide, by sterilization of possibly infectious articles or foods and isolation of ill persons to prevent the spread of infectious diseases.

THE VIRUS

There are some communicable diseases that are caused by what are known as filterable viruses as they are so small that they will filter through even the finest porcelain filter.

Viruses were first demonstrated in 1892. With the aid of the **electron microscope,** they are seen to be mainly spherical or ovoid in shape, consisting of the typical nuclear protein. They can multiply only at the expense of living host cells; are very specific about their host, and even the type of cell within which they will reproduce, and are responsible for a wide range of infectious diseases. They can be isolated in the form of crystals.

It is believed that viruses cause smallpox, chicken pox, mumps, measles, influenza, poliomyelitis, rabies and even the common cold.

The tobacco mosaic, a tobacco leaf disease is thought to be caused by a specific virus. DR. W. M. STANLEY, working at the Rockefeller Institute in Princeton, New Jersey, used a powerful electron microscope to view the virus crystals he was able to abstract from the juice of a tobacco leaf afflicted by the mosaic disease.

Isolation of virus crystals from infected living tissues have made vaccinations against measles, and similar infections, possible.

The common cold, the most universal illness, is least understood thus far. Some hold the view that it is caused by a type of filterable virus which enters the body either through the nose or mouth and throat. It weakens or destroys tissues of the nose and throat, leaving them susceptible to attacks by some disease-producing bacteria, and producing symptoms that are most uncomfortable and difficult to get rid of.

It is believed by some scientists that a virus is a possible cause of cancer.

VOCABULARY

immunity	vaccine	communicable
susceptibility	disinfectant	electron microscope
antitoxin	antiseptic	virus

Exercise No. 46

Complete each of the following statements:

1 A person is said to be —— if he cannot contract a specific disease.
2 An —— is a substance built up in the blood after a siege of a specific disease, to help the phagocytes combat a subsequent attack.
3 Vaccination provides —— immunity against a specific disease.
4 To prevent diphtheria, a doctor injects —— in three doses into children about four months of age.
5 The harmful poisons given off by some pathogenic bacteria are known as ——.
6 The Schick test is the test for susceptibility to —— whereas the Dick test is for susceptibility to ——.
7 The presence of typhoid fever in an individual can be determined by the —— test.
8 A chemical substance such as iodine or peroxide that can be used on the body to slow up the growth of bacteria is an ——.

PARASITIC DISEASES

Some diseases are caused by specific parasitic protozoa.

The most common is malaria, literally meaning bad air. At one time it was considered that swampland night air was the cause of malaria. The most typical symptoms of the disease are high fever alternating with chills. These eventually debilitate the victim.

Early in 1880, CHARLES LAVERAN, a French scientist, discovered that swamp fever, as it was then called, was caused by a parasitic protozan that is amoeboid in appearance. In 1895 SIR RONALD ROSS, a member of the British Medical Service, serving in India, discovered that the protozan causing malaria needs two hosts to survive. He proved that the alternate host to man was the female Anopheles mosquito. The protozoan is now called **Plasmodium.**

After intensive study, Ross discovered the life history of the malarial parasite in the female Anopheles mosquito, the means of transmission to man, and the continuance of its life history in the bloodstream of man. See Fig. 154.

When a female Anopheles mosquito bites a person suffering from the disease, it sucks into its digestive tract the blood corpuscles infected by the protozoa.

After about 12 days in the stomach of the mosquito, the sexual phase of the parasite develops. The egg and sperm cells unite to form a fertilized egg from which a group of dormant or temporarily inactive spores develop.

The spores enter the salivary gland of the mosquito where they remain until the insect feeds on another human being.

When the mosquito attacks a human being, saliva, containing an anticoagulant substance, is first injected into the skin. The parasitic spores thus enter the bloodstream.

The parasites invade the red blood corpuscles of the victim and multiply rapidly. About every 24 hours the spores burst out of the red blood cells and each enters a new red blood corpuscle where it divides and repeats that part of the cycle. Many red blood cells are destroyed in this manner.

Another female mosquito which bites this victim of malaria repeats the cycle.

The Anopheles mosquito is native to many parts of the world. Before the use of quinine (from the bark of the cinchona tree) and then later synthetic products, millions of people suffered from the disease and from frequent recurrences. During the Second World War there was a large incidence of malaria among the Armed Forces in the South Pacific theatre of operations. In some cases the malarial protozoan lived dormant in its victim, probably in

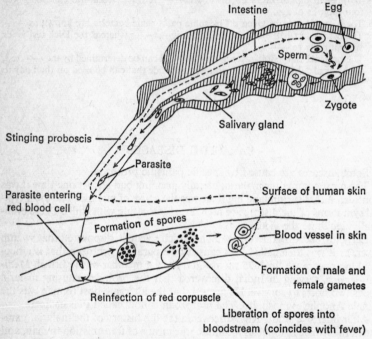

Figure 154   Life history of malarial parasite—Plasmodium

the liver, so long as the victim took drugs. A recurrence of the symptoms of malaria occurred after the soldiers discontinued the treatment.

In parts of Africa and India a large percentage of the civilian population suffers from malaria as a normal course of living. Indeed, a recent estimate of world figures showed that there were not less than 3 million malarial deaths, and at least 3,000 million cases of malarial fever each year throughout the world.

The control of the Anopheles mosquito is the most effective means of preventing the disease it transmits. All mosquitos lay their eggs and go through their early development in ponds, swamps, shallow lakes or sluggish streams.

Destroying the breeding places by draining swampy waters when feasible, or covering their water surfaces with oil to shut off the supply of air, is effective in destroying the immature stages of the parasitic animal.

Sometimes poisons, such as D.D.T. are used to destroy the adult form of the mosquito. Fine screening in windows and doors and fine mesh-netting covering beds should be used in areas where the Anopheles abound.

Adequate and proper treatment of people suffering from malaria can also help prevent the spread of the disease.

The harmful female Anopheles can be distinguished from the harmless but annoying common Culex mosquito. When the Culex stings, her body remains parallel with the surface of the skin. When the Anopheles stings, her body slants upward.

The positions of the larval stages of both insects are somewhat different. The Culex lays eggs in a raft-like arrangement in large numbers on the water's surface. The Anopheles larva lies parallel to the surface of the water with breathing tubes from both ends of the body above the surface.

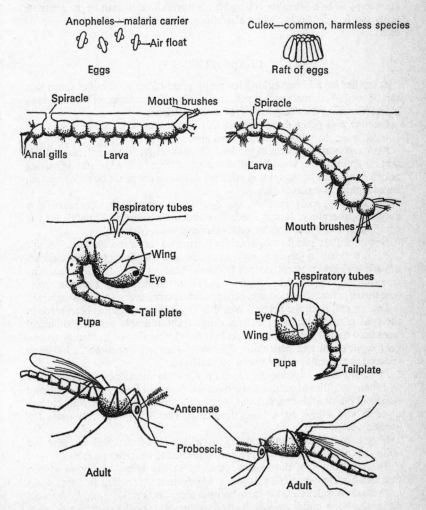

Figure 155 Metamorphic stages of mosquitoes

DR. WALTER REED, together with volunteer human guinea pigs worked in Havana and the Panama Canal Zone (about 1900) to discover the cause, prevention and cure of yellow fever. One of his colleagues died, a victim of the disease.

Through his untiring experiments and observations, he discovered that yellow fever is carried by another type of mosquito, the female Aëdes, which transmits it to human beings through her sting. He was successful in destroying the breeding places of these insects and instructing people in methods of protecting themselves against the mosquitoes.

It was not until many years later that the actual cause of yellow fever was discovered to be a filterable virus which is transmitted to man by the alternate host, the female Aëdes, when she stings. Protective vaccines have proved effective.

CHEMOTHERAPY

Scientists have been working for many years trying to discover drugs that can be used to combat specific parasitic diseases. This science of **chemotherapy** is fast becoming a leading branch of medical science.

Quinine and other drugs are used in treating malaria. Quinine was discovered more than three hundred years ago.

PAUL EHRLICH, the father of modern chemotherapy, discovered, about 1910, that an arsenic compound he called salvarsan (that he used in staining living cells for microscope study) was effective in killing the parasitic protozoa that cause syphilis, a venereal disease.

In Germany, early in 1900, the dye sulphanilamide was prepared in a chemical laboratory. It was used, very much the same as Ehrlich's arsenic compound, as a dye in staining cells for convenience of study.

Not until 1935 was it recognized (in Germany) that a specific water-soluble sulphur compound (**neonprontosil**) could be used effectively to treat and cure diseases caused by streptococcus bacteria. This cut down fatalities resulting from pneumonia, child-bed fever, a type of meningitis, 'strep' (streptococcus) sore throat, a form of dysentery, peritonitis and septicaemia (blood poisoning).

During and since the Second World War much progress has been made in the field of chemotherapy. Sulpha drugs (**sulphathiazole** and **sulphadiazine**) were used on the battlefield to treat burns and wounds and in surgery to prevent septicaemia and peritonitis. The death-rate from pneumonia has been reduced considerably by the use of sulpha drugs.

Penicillin and streptomycin have already been mentioned in Chapter VI and many additional antibiotics have been prepared from moulds and from tissues of plants and some animals. At present aureomycin, bacitracin, chloromycetin and others have been developed, each being effective against a specific disease.

Undoubtedly, more antibiotics will be discovered that will increase our ability to control diseases that previously seemed to be unconquerable.

There is danger of unforeseen reactions in the human body to sulpha drugs and antibiotics. There is also the unfortunate fact that frequent doses of these chemicals cause them to become less effective. This may be because either the body builds up a resistance to the drugs or the disease-producing organism itself builds a greater tolerance for or immunity to the drugs.

DISEASES—A SOCIAL PROBLEM

Some diseases are a social problem. Statistics tend to prove that the lower the economic standards and the poorer the people, the higher the rate of illness and death. Where there is inadequate housing, unsanitary living conditions, improper and insufficient nourishing foods and notably poor working conditions, health suffers.

Among people who live under these undesirable circumstances the incidence of tuberculosis, cholera, dysentery and dietary deficiency-diseases is greatest.

The individual family can do its part to help prevent epidemics of infectious diseases in a given community. A doctor should be consulted to diagnose and treat cases of chicken pox, diphtheria, measles, German measles, influenza, mumps, pneumonia, poliomyelitis, whooping cough and scarlet fever or any other infectious disease. He will advise isolation of the sick person for the safety of other members of the family and instruct admittance into hospital, if the case is severe.

Schools should be notified of the occurrence in a child of any of these diseases so that, if necessary, preventative serums and vaccines may be administered to members of a class who have been exposed to the infectious child during the incubation period of the disease. The incubation period is the time between which disease-producing organisms enter the body and the time symptoms appear. This is the period when the disease can be most infectious and communicable. The incubation period varies with the disease.

Since water and milk may contain many types of disease-producing organisms, both are protected in many countries by laws regulating purification and standards for content.

Typhoid fever and cholera bacteria flourish in unpurified water. Diphtheria, dysentery and other diseases of the digestive system have been traced directly to polluted water supply.

Before water reaches us in the towns and cities, it goes through a series of purification processes to rid it of any possible pathogenic organisms. It is filtered through beds of rough and fine sand to strain out filterable foreign substances. Following that, it is sprayed into the open air so that bacteria may be killed by sunlight and the oxygen. Finally, before it enters pipes for distribution, small quantities of chlorine (not enough to spoil the taste) or activated charcoal are added as a further precaution against the possible presence of disease-producing organisms.

Periodically, samples of reservoir water are studied to determine purity or possible presence of foreign substances. If there is any doubt tests are made, investigations are set in action and immediate steps are taken to clear the water of any contamination.

Milk supply is most carefully guarded against the presence of bacteria which cause typhoid fever, tuberculosis, diphtheria, undulant fever and other diseases. All dairy farms are carefully inspected at frequent intervals—all cows, cowhands, dairy equipment and cow-sheds. If standards of cleanliness are not approved by inspectors, the milk and other dairy products may not be marketed.

Careful handling and proper refrigeration of milk during transportation from farms to cities must be observed.

The process of pasteurization of milk is an important means of safeguarding health. Disease-producing bacteria (of undulant fever, tuberculosis and typhoid fever) are destroyed during the process. To pasteurize milk, it is heated to 145° F., not boiled, for 15 minutes and then cooled rapidly. Immediately afterwards it is bottled under absolutely sterile conditions.

Science has gone far in controlling many diseases caused by bacteria, viruses and by parasitic animals. There are still, however, organic diseases that remain to be conquered. But great strides have been made that promise success in their treatment and prevention. Organic diseases of the heart and kidneys, rheumatic fever, arthritis, and cancer take high priority in scientists' endeavours to control disease.

SUMMARY

The introduction of the microscope made possible the science of bacteriology. In the middle of the eighteenth century, it was proved that decay was caused by 'living things'.

The Germ Theory of Disease was established by Louis Pasteur. Bacteria are found everywhere in all environments under almost every condition. Disease-producing bacteria are known as pathogenic. Certain organs and tissues in our bodies (skin, mucous membranes, tears, phagocytes and antibodies in the blood) offer natural protection against invasion of pathogenic organisms.

Immunity to disease (either natural or acquired) means the inability to contract a disease; susceptibility means the inability to resist disease. Vaccines develop immunity by stimulating the blood to form antibodies. The use of antiseptics, disinfectants and sterilization are precautions in everyday life against the undesirable effects of pathogenic bacteria.

Some communicable diseases are caused by viruses. A virus is a disease-producing substance which grows and multiplies within living tissues but which cannot be isolated outside of living tissue except as a mineral-like crystal.

Malaria is caused by parasitic protozoa, yellow-fever by a virus. They are transmitted to man by the Anopheles and Aëdes mosquitoes, respectively. Quinine and synthesized drugs are used as specifics in the treatment of malaria.

Chemotherapy is the science of treating disease chemically with drugs and antibiotics.

VOCABULARY

malaria	Aëdes mosquito	antibiotic
Plasmodium	quinine	penicillin
Anopheles mosquito	sulpha drugs	incubation
Culex mosquito	filterable virus	pasteurization
	chemotherapy	

Exercise No. 47

Select the correct word or phrase for each of the following:

1 Pasteurization of milk destroys: (a) butter fat content; (b) all vitamins; (c) pathogenic bacteria.

2 The alternate host to man in the life history of the malarial parasite is: (a) an earthworm; (b) a housefly; (c) Anopheles mosquito; (d) Aëdes mosquito.
3 The malaria-causing protozoan attacks: (a) red blood corpuscles; (b) the skin; (c) the heart.
4 Penicillin is an example of: (a) a disinfectant; (b) a sulpha drug; (c) an antibiotic.
5 The scientist who is responsible for the discovery of penicillin is: (a) Fleming; (b) Ehrlich; (c) Pasteur.
6 The chemical substance used in the treatment of malaria is: (a) iodine; (b) salversan; (c) quinine.
7 The chemical substance which has proved successful in the treatment of pneumonia is: (a) a sulpha drug; (b) quinine; (c) antibodies.
8 Streptomycin has been used successfully in the treatment of: (a) yellow fever; (b) tuberculosis; (c) blood poisoning.
9 Injections of toxin-antitoxin or toxoid serum is given to prevent: (a) diphtheria; (b) smallpox; (c) chicken pox.
10 The common harmless mosquito is known as a: (a) Anopheles; (b) Aëdes; (c) Culex.

CHAPTER XIV

REPRODUCTION

Mankind has always been curious about his beginnings. The ancient Hebrews recorded their beliefs concerning creation in the Book of Genesis. The early Greeks and Romans believed that living things arose spontaneously from the non-living things in their surrounding environment.

SPONTANEOUS GENERATION

Later, the Greek philosopher Aristotle held that although animals like frogs, toads and snakes arose spontaneously, they came from mud that was activated by the sun's heat and light. Others of his time believed that living things grew spontaneously from dead, decaying animals, from filthy rags, from dew on the grass, sluggish water and rains from the heavens. This **Theory of Spontaneous Generation,** that living things can arise directly and suddenly from non-living things or dead things, was held by most scientists until late in the seventeenth century.

About this time, scientists began to observe certain phenomena which they had not trained themselves to notice before. It was previously believed that fly maggots grew spontaneously from dead, decaying animal flesh, and that flies grew spontaneously from these maggots. Around 1650 a British surgeon, SIR WILLIAM HARVEY, expressed his opinion that all living animals came from eggs. Then in 1680, the Italian scientist REDI observed a fly laying eggs in a decaying piece of meat. This set him thinking and experimenting.

He took three jars all equal in size and cleaned them thoroughly. In each he placed a piece of decaying meat. One jar he covered securely with a piece of parchment; the second with fine-meshed gauze, and the third he left entirely uncovered. He set these aside for several days in the sunshine.

He observed that there were no flies around Jar A (parchment covered), and no maggots in the meat; that the smell of the decaying meat attracted a cluster

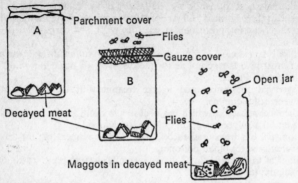

Redi's Experiment—To disprove the theory
of spontaneous generation   Figure 156

of flies outside Jar B (gauze covered) but no maggots appeared in the meat;
and that flies swarmed in and around the open Jar C and that maggots appeared in this meat.

This was the first real attempt to disprove the Theory of Spontaneous
Generation. Many similar experiments followed. Pasteur's experiments (about
1860) convinced scientists that all living things come from other living things,
and, further, that living things come from living things of the same kind.

All living things grow old, and, in time, die. It is now an accepted fact that,
in order for a species of plant or animal to continue and survive, it must reproduce itself. The production of new individuals from previous individuals
of the same species is known as reproduction.

There are two methods of reproduction: (1) **asexual reproduction,** in which

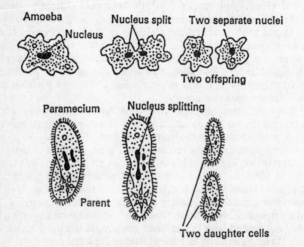

Asexual reproduction—binary fission—simple animals
Figure 157

the new individual develops from a single parent (example: binary fission in Amoeba and budding of yeast); and (2) **sexual reproduction,** in which two specialized reproductive cells or gametes are needed to produce an offspring (example: seeds produced by flowering plants, mammals).

In either type of reproduction, the function of the nucleus of the cell is most vital. (This was discovered by ROBERT BROWN.) The nucleus carries the characteristics of the species (inherited characteristics) and activates the process by which a cell divides to reproduce itself.

ASEXUAL REPRODUCTION

Simple plants and animals reproduce in the simplest manner, by asexual reproduction. There are three types of asexual reproduction: binary fission, budding, and spore formation (sporulation).

In the process of binary fission, when the cell has reached its maximum size the nucleus divides in half, and activates the rest of the cell protoplasm to do

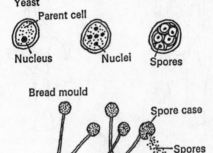

Asexual reproduction—sporulation (spore forming)

Figure 158

the same. This results in the formation of two cells about equal in size and content. See Fig. 157.

The simplest forms of the animal world, e.g. Amoeba and Paramecium, reproduce by binary fission; and of the simple plants, bacteria and Pleurococcus do so also.

Another type of asexual reproduction is budding. In this process, a small projection of protoplasm containing part of the nuclear material grows from the parent cell. As this projection, the bud, increases in size, a wall is formed between it and the parent cell. The bud finally separates from the parent, and becomes an independent individual. Sometimes a small part of the body of a multicellular individual grows out as a bud and becomes a new individual.

Examples of this type of asexual reproduction are found in yeast and Hydra (a member of the jellyfish family). See Fig. 159.

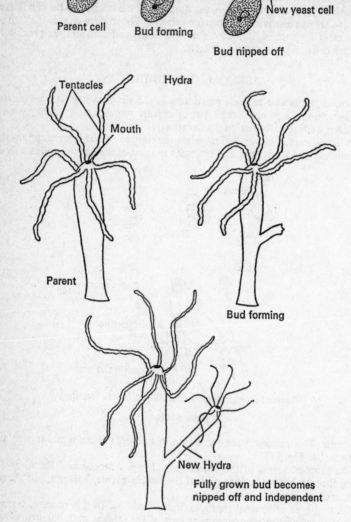

Yeast

Parent cell   Bud forming

New yeast cell

Bud nipped off

Hydra

Tentacles

Mouth

Parent

Bud forming

New Hydra

Fully grown bud becomes
nipped off and independent

Figure 159 Asexual reproduction—budding

In some animals like sponges and corals the buds often remain attached to the parent organism, reach full growth and produce buds of their own. A colonial formation results.

Still another type of asexual reproduction is asexual spore formation or sporulation. Yeasts, as well as bread moulds, reproduce in this manner.

Common bread mould develops spore cases, **sporangia,** in which tiny spores develop. Each of these spores contains nuclear and protoplasmic material which will enable it to develop into a new mould plant when environmental conditions are favourable. See Fig. 158.

Spores are encased in a thick protective coat which may keep the protoplasmic content alive for many years, under very unfavourable conditions. Almost all fungi reproduce by spores—one reason why mildews, plant rusts and smuts are so hard to destroy and cause so much economic damage.

Many pathogenic bacteria produce spores which enable them to survive extremes of temperature and lack of food and moisture, making them almost impossible to combat by the usual methods of sterilization, drying, and canning. Bacteria which cause **botulism,** food poisoning, and also those which produce **tetanus,** lockjaw, are examples of spore-producing bacteria.

VEGETATIVE PROPAGATION

Another type of asexual reproduction in which only one parent is involved is known as vegetative propagation. This refers to the production of a new organism or portion of an organism from a part of a living thing that is usually not the organ of reproduction. For example, the flower of flowering plants usually contains the organs of reproduction. However, new plants may be produced from leaves, stems and roots of flowering plants either in nature or by man.

Bulbs—miniature plants enclosed in large, food-storage leaves, which grow underground from a short, thick stem. Examples are: tulip, lily, narcissus, hyacinth, onion.

Purchase two narcissus bulbs or two onions. Cut one vertically down the middle and observe the structures. Plant a few bulbs in glass jars and note how the roots grow from the bottom of the bulb. Watch the leaves grow up—some turning green, while others wither when their stored food has been used by the growing plant. See the flower stem grow from the main stem.

Rhizomes—horizontal stems, partly underground, from which whole new plants will grow at intervals. Examples are: many grasses, iris and Solomon's seal.

Runners or Stolons—stems which grow parallel to but above the ground, and from which grow roots and an entire new plant where the plant makes contact with the soil. Examples are: strawberries, blackberries.

Tubers—enlarged underground stems containing stored food, with eyes or buds from each of which an entire new plant will grow. Examples are: potato, Jerusalem artichoke.

Cut a piece of potato on which there is an eye and plant it in a glass jar. Watch the roots, stems and leaves of a new potato plant growing. This vegetative method of producing potatoes is much faster than reproduction from the seeds of the plant.

Root-Stocks—parts of underground roots, from which an entire new plant will grow. Ferns are examples of plants which have this structure.

Regeneration in animals is another type of vegetative propagation. Most animals are able to replace damaged cells and tissues by repairing the cells and adding new tissues. For example, torn or damaged skin, mucous membranes, cartilage, bone and blood tissue may be replaced. But regrowth

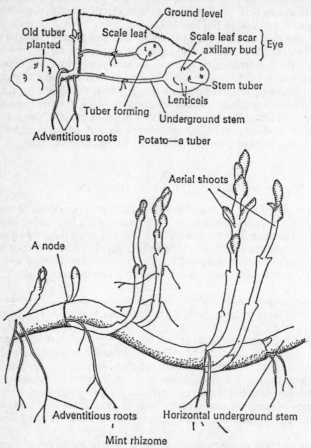

Figure 160a   Vegetative propagation

or regeneration of entire organs or sections of an animal is not usual; only in the simpler animal forms is such regrowth possible. For example, the starfish can regenerate an arm if it has been severed from the rest of the body. Another classic example is the flatworm Planaria. It can be cut into many pieces, many of which will regenerate themselves into new animals.

Lobsters and crabs regenerate a claw or antenna which has been lost or severed from the body. Some lizards are able to regenerate tails.

Man has made good use of his knowledge of vegetative propagation. The natural sponge industry is a fine example of artificial propagation by regeneration. Sponges are cut up into pieces and returned to their native waters, where each piece will regenerate into a new sponge animal. This process is a speedier method than waiting for the natural budding process.

Farmers, agriculturists and horticulturists are able to ensure speedier continuance of the desirable characteristics of a chosen fruit, flower or vegetable-bearing plant by propagation, using cuttings or slips from the chosen plant. To do this, a piece of stem or branch is cut from the plant, dipped in hormone

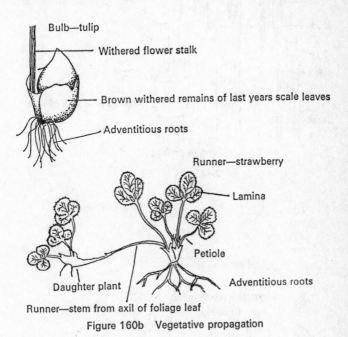

Bulb—tulip

Withered flower stalk

Brown withered remains of last years scale leaves

Adventitious roots

Runner—strawberry

Lamina

Petiole

Adventitious roots

Daughter plant

Runner—stem from axil of foliage leaf

Figure 160b   Vegetative propagation

powder and placed in water or well-moistened sand until roots appear. Then it is planted in fertile soil containing minerals necessary for successful growth into a new plant. Each new plant has the same desired characteristics as the parent plant from which the cutting or slip was taken.

Another method of artificial propagation is by grafting. This is accomplished by cutting a branch from a tree (known as the scion) chosen for its desirable characteristics, and attaching it in a special slit or groove to a related tree known as the stock. The point of juncture of the two parts is carefully covered with treated wax or waxed cloth to prevent harmful infection by bacteria, fungus spores, and the loss of water and tree sap. After a while, the two tree parts grow together, and the scion continues to produce its original leaves, flowers and fruits; but it gets its water and minerals for food manufacturing from the hardy chosen stock. See Fig. 161.

Vegetative propagation—Grafting
(cleft grafting)

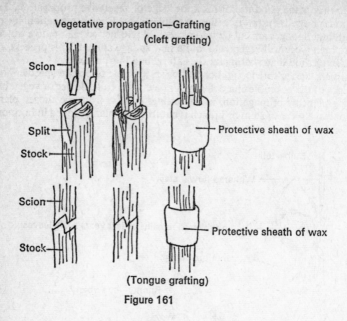

Scion

Split

Stock

Protective sheath of wax

Scion

Stock

Protective sheath of wax

(Tongue grafting)

Figure 161

Vegetative propagation
Budding

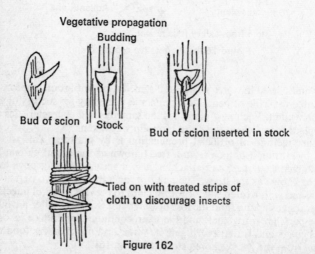

Bud of scion   Stock

Bud of scion inserted in stock

Tied on with treated strips of
cloth to discourage insects

Figure 162

The advantages of this method of artificial propagation are: to produce varieties of seedless fruits; to combine the most desirable characteristics of scion and stock, and to obtain a variety of fruits on a single tree. Apple, peach, apricot and pear trees are often grafted.

Artificial budding is another method of artificial vegetative propagation used to improve fruit or flower production. This is done by cutting a bud complete with its bud stem from a chosen tree (scion) and attaching it under the bark of another related tree (stock). The juncture is carefully sealed, and, after a while, the bud grows into a new branch, or becomes the trunk of a new tree. This method is used for cherry, plum, and some types of peach trees and grapevines. See Fig. 162.

Grafting of animal tissues has been successful. For example, grafting of skin is done to replace injured or seriously burned skin on a human body. Healthy bone sections may be grafted to replace broken or diseased portions. Normal, healthy eye corneas may be grafted to replace injured or diseased corneas without affecting the eyesight of the individual. There are cornea banks in some large hospitals, to which people have willed their eyes for future use in cornea-grafting operations.

VOCABULARY

spontaneous	stolon	root-stock
generation	tuber	grafting
reproduction	cutting	budding
asexual	slip	regeneration
sexual	botulism	vegetative
sporulation	offspring	propagation
sporangia	parent	rhizome
runner	scion	bulb
	stock	

PRIMITIVE SEXUAL REPRODUCTION

In the case of Paramecium, an exchange of nuclear material, to strengthen the species, often occurs before fission. This process is known as conjugation.

Two Paramecia exchange nuclear material, then each of the animals involved in the exchange splits eventually producing four new Paramecia. See Fig. 163.

Spirogyra grows in ponds in a string-like series or filaments of many independent cells. The filament may reproduce asexually by splitting into shorter pieces between the cells. This is fragmentation. They may also produce filaments as a result of conjugation. See Fig. 164.

During conjugation, a conjugation tube develops to join two cells of Spirogyra in adjoining filaments. The contents of these cells change to form **gametes,** one of which passes through the conjugation tube to fuse with that of the opposite cell and form a **zygote.** The zygote, in turn, forms a **zygospore,** which falls off the filament, and develops into a new filament, when conditions are favourable. One of the original parent cells is called the active or male gamete, and the other is called the female or passive gamete.

Spirogyra exhibits a simple and basic type of sexual reproduction—that is, the fusion of two similar cells (parent cells—gametes) to form a third cell (zygospore) which will grow into the new individual or offspring.

Conjugation in Paramecium

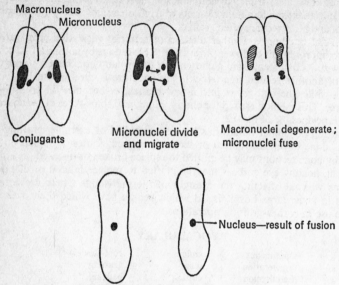

Macronucleus
Micronucleus

Conjugants

Micronuclei divide
and migrate

Macronuclei degenerate;
micronuclei fuse

Nucleus—result of fusion

Conjugants separate and divide again by binary fission

This is a simplified version of a more complex process
Figure 163

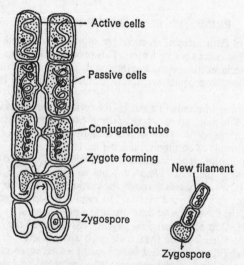

Active cells

Passive cells

Conjugation tube

Zygote forming

New filament

Zygospore

Zygospore

Figure 164   Conjugation—Spirogyra

SEXUAL REPRODUCTION—THE FLOWERING PLANT

Flowering plants reproduce sexually: that is, two sexes are involved in the process of reproduction. In this most highly developed representative of the plant word, the flower is the reproductive organ. A typical flower is composed of the following parts, starting from the outside: refer to Fig. 82

Sepals (Calyx)—green, leaf-like structures at the base of the flower. Their main function is to form a protective sheath around the bud.

Petals (Corolla)—colourful parts of the flower that attract insects and protect the vital parts of the flower.

Stamens—male reproductive organs. Each consists of: (a) **filament**—stalk which supports; (b) **anther**—in which pollen grains are produced and held until they are ripe; (c) **pollen grains**—each containing two male gametes.

Pistil—the female reproductive organ, usually in the centre of the flower. It

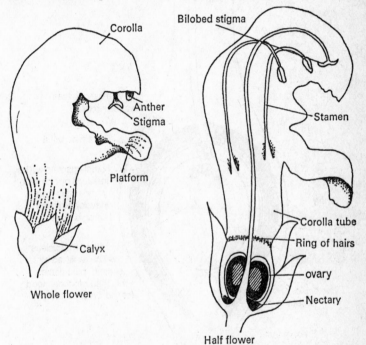

Figure 165   Insect pollination—dead nettle flower

consists of: (a) **stigma**—top of pistil, on which pollen lands; (b) **style**—narrow structure down which the pollen grows for passageway of the male gamete; (c) **ovary**—base of pistil. It contains the egg cells (female gametes).

Receptacle—swollen tip of flower stalk, to which all parts of the flower are attached.

In order for a new plant to develop, a male gamete must combine with a female gamete (egg cell). Each pollen grain contains a male gamete. The ovary of the pistil contains one or more egg cells.

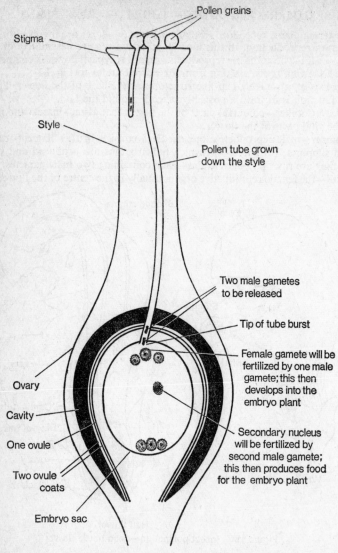

Pollen grains

Stigma

Style

Pollen tube grown
down the style

Two male gametes
to be released

Tip of tube burst

Female gamete will be
fertilized by one male
gamete; this then
develops into the
embryo plant

Ovary

Cavity

One ovule

Two ovule
coats

Secondary nucleus
will be fertilized by
second male gamete;
this then produces food
for the embryo plant

Embryo sac

Figure 166   Pollination and fertilisation of an ovary with only *one* ovule

Before a male gamete can combine with an egg cell, pollination (transfer of pollen from the anther of the filament to the stigma of a pistil) must take place. This may come about in one of three manners:

1. **Self-pollination**—in which the pollen of a flower lands on the stigma of the same flower.

2. **Cross-pollination**—in which the pollen of one flower is transferred to the stigma of another flower of the same species—by the wind, water, insects, birds, or other animals.

Insect pollination. The beautiful colours and scents of flowers are not for our benefit, but to attract insects which know that they will find nectar there. In the process of collecting this, grains of pollen become attached to their

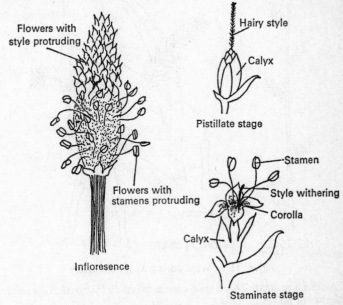

Figure 167   Wind pollination—greater plantain

hairy bodies, to be deposited later on another flower of the same species. Some flowers show remarkable adaptations to specific insects. The dead nettle flower is a good example. See Fig. 165.

Notice the platform especially designed for the bee; the **nectary** deeply placed so that the bee must enter the flower to reach it; the position of the stamens ensuring that they will brush against the bee's back and deposit their pollen there; the ring of tiny hairs to prevent smaller insects robbing the nectary.

Wind pollination. Flowers which rely on wind to scatter their pollen have no colour, scent or nectar, but produce huge quantities of light pollen since much will inevitably be wasted. Grasses and trees such as willow, hazel and elm have flowers of this type. Pussy willow and catkins are the male pollen-carriers of the willow and hazel trees respectively.

The greater plantain, a common lawn weed, has flowers modified to aid the transfer of pollen by wind. The flowers of this plant are borne in a spike-like infloresence and open in succession from below upwards. Each flower is first in a female stage with feathery stigmas to trap pollen grains floating in the air. Later, when the stigmas have withered, the stamens ripen. The anthers are well exposed and loosely attached to long filaments so that the slightest air movement shakes them and carries away large quantities of tiny pollen grains.

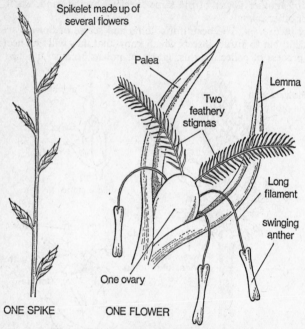

Figure 168   Wind pollinated grass flowers

3. **Artificial pollination**—wherein man aids nature by transferring pollen to the stigmas of flowers.

After pollination, the pollen grain produces a pollen tube and two male nuclei. The pollen tube grows down the style and into the ovary of the pistil. Here one male nucleus unites with one egg nucleus in an embryo sac to form a fertilized egg or **zygote**. The other nucleus fuses with a secondary nucleus in the ovary to form the endosperm. The union of a male nucleus with an egg nucleus is known as fertilization.

After fertilization, the zygote starts to divide into many cells, and finally becomes the seed containing the embryo or baby plant. It also contains food for the new plant to use until it is able to manufacture its own food—after it has developed into an independent plant with roots, stems and leaves.

SEXUAL REPRODUCTION—VERTEBRATE ANIMALS

Reproduction in vertebrate animals such as the fish, frogs, birds, reptiles and mammals (including man) is basically the same. Two parents are required to produce male gametes or sperm cells and female gametes or egg cells. The parents are adapted with their respective reproductive organs for the production of unlike gametes.

Fertilization of the eggs of most fish, and frogs takes place just after the eggs leave the body of the female. Hence development of the embryo is usually outside the body of the female.

Fertilization of the eggs of mammals takes place within the body of the female. Therefore, the embryo develops within the body of the female or mother.

The embryo plant or animal develops after the egg cell is fertilized. In many-celled forms of life, the fertilized egg cell begins to divide into many cells, which remain, however, attached. A differentiation of cells takes place in the growth of tissues. Some develop to form nervous tissue, some cartilaginous, some bone, some muscle, and some the sex, or reproductive cells.

It is the sex or germ cells and not the other body tissues which pass on the characteristics of a species from one generation to the next. Theoretically, the germ cells are immortal.

Let us refer back to the importance of the nucleus of a cell. Recall that the nucleus contains chromosomes, which have been found to hold and determine the hereditary characteristics of a species.

In the simple fission type of reproduction of single-celled organisms, the nuclear material apparently divides in half and the rest of the cell protoplasm divides also to produce two new individuals—two daughter cells. In many-celled organisms, division takes place, but the cells remain attached.

MITOSIS

The process is not quite so simple as it seems. In order for nuclear material to divide in half, a series of changes must be undergone. These changes are known as mitosis.

While a cell is growing, its nucleus is in a resting stage so far as reproduction, or division, is concerned. When the cell is ready to divide, the network of nuclear material breaks up into little pieces known as chromosomes which are not apparent in the resting cell. Each species of plant and animal has a characteristic number of chromosomes in the nucleus of each of its body cells which is always the same for the specific species. For example, man's chromosome count is 23 pairs, or 46.

The stages of mitosis or preparation of the nuclear material for cell-division can be studied under a high-powered microscope. The growing tip cells of a radish seed root, or onion, usually provide a good specimen for this study.

The following phases outline the process of mitosis:

1 When the cell is ready to divide, the chromosomal material comes together to form the number of chromosomes characteristic of the species of plant or animal of which the dividing cell is a part.

2 A small body, the **centrosome,** divides into two equal parts, each of which migrates to opposite poles of the cell. The centrosome seems to be a chemical or electrical force that attracts a set of chromosomes to each end of the dividing cell.

3 A spindle of ray-like fibres of protoplasm appears between the centrosomes.

242 *Biology Made Simple*

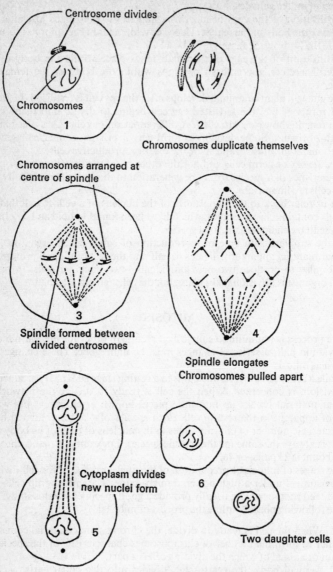

Figure 169 Mitosis in an animal cell

4 The chromosomes duplicate themselves to form pairs of **chromatids** and become arranged at the equator of the spindle.

5 The chromatids separate from each other, one member of each pair moving to the two poles of the nucleus.

6 The cell cytoplasm becomes constricted by the cell membrane.

7 The cell membrane between the daughter cells is completed. Nuclear membranes appear around each new nucleus. The chromosome material breaks up and becomes dispersed once more. Each daughter cell goes into the resting stage in which it grows. And the mitotic stages will start again in division of each full-grown daughter cell. Thus the body cells of a species retain their characteristic number of chromosomes from generation to generation, and pass on hereditary characteristics. See Fig. 169.

Now let us see how we are adapted to ensure the continuity of the number of chromosomes characteristic of a species and therefore ensure the continuity of the species.

We have mentioned previously in this chapter that the body cell chromosome number characteristic of the human animal species, Homo sapiens is 46, or 23 pairs. We know that new human beings are produced as a result of sexual reproduction. Two parents, one producing the female gamete or egg cell, and the other producing the male gamete or sperm cell, are involved. The union of a sperm cell with an egg cell results in a fertilized egg, which will develop into the new individual, the human being.

If each cell, by the nature of its species, has 46 chromosomes (46 in a sperm cell and 46 in an egg cell) then this union of egg and sperm would result in a total of 92 chromosomes or a doubling of the original specific number. And this would happen in each generation. But this is not so.

REDUCTION DIVISION

During the process called **gametogenesis,** during which gametes or sex cells are formed, there is a reduction division known as **meiosis** of the original number of chromosomes so that a single sperm or egg cell of man contains but 23 chromosomes. Then, during fertilization or union of egg and sperm cell, the resulting fertilized egg will contain the characteristic 23 pairs or 46 chromosomes.

The sperm and egg cell differ in many respects:

SPERM	EGG
Very small	Much larger
Motile (has a tail with which it moves)	Is stationary
No stored food	Contains stored food especially where the embryo develops outside the body
Many produced at a given time to ensure fertilization of as many eggs as possible	Many fewer than sperms produced at the same given time

The new individual or organism develops from the fertilized egg after a series of cell divisions The young organism that develops from the fertilized egg of an animal is called an embryo, as is the seed of a plant.

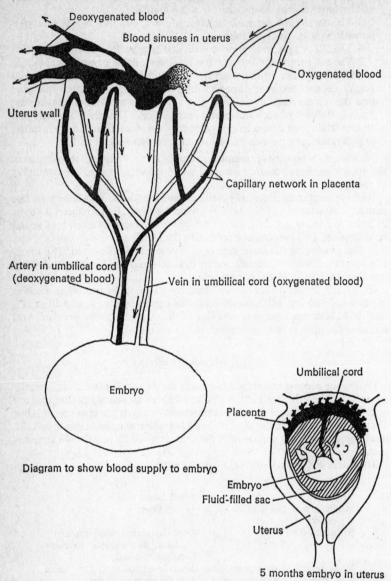

Deoxygenated blood

Blood sinuses in uterus

Oxygenated blood

Uterus wall

Capillary network in placenta

Artery in umbilical cord (deoxygenated blood)

Vein in umbilical cord (oxygenated blood)

Embryo

Diagram to show blood supply to embryo

Umbilical cord

Placenta

Embryo

Fluid-filled sac

Uterus

5 months embryo in uterus

Figure 170   Human embryo

In the development of a vertebrate embryo, including man, the single ferti-lized egg divides immediately to form a mass of cells called the blastula. These cells soon become rearranged into three definite layers, the primary germ layers, certain of which surround or enclose the others. It is from these three embryonic layers that all the tissues and organs of our bodies develop.

The outer layer of cells is called the **ectoderm**; the inner layer the **endoderm**; and the middle layer, the **mesoderm.** These tissues give rise to:

ECTODERM	MESODERM	ENDODERM
Brain	Blood vessels	Organs of digestive system
Spinal cord	Muscles	Organs of respiratory system
Nerves	Kidneys	Digestive glands (liver, pancreas)
Parts of the	Most bones	
sense	Reproductive	
organs	organs	
Skin		
Hair		
Nails		

THE HUMAN EMBRYO

It takes the human embryo about nine months within the body of the mother to develop all of the organs and systems it needs to carry on life's activities. While within the uterus of the mother the embryo, referred to as the **foetus,** receives oxygen and nourishment from the blood system of the mother through the umbilical cord, by which it is attached to the mother in the region of the **placenta.** It is surrounded by a fluid-filled sac which protects it from damage and allows freedom of movement. The heart of the foetus starts to function, circulating blood within its developing body, several months before the child is born. See Fig. 170.

The human baby is born helpless, and must receive constant parental care and protection in order to survive and grow successfully. Most mammals provide parental care to their offspring. The number of offspring is small, compared to the number born to animals lower in the scale of life. Among humans, multiple births (twins, triplets) are comparatively rare.

Insects produce many hundreds, sometimes thousands, of eggs to ensure the survival of at least some of them. Most species ignore their young immedi-ately after fertilization of the eggs takes place. Fish and frogs (with very few exceptions) also give their numerous young no parental care or protection.

Most birds, however, build nests, in which the eggs are laid and incubated by the warmth of either parent's body. Altricial birds (those born naked and helpless) are fed and protected and taught to fly and fetch food before their parents leave them to fend for themselves. Precocial birds are given less care than altricial birds, because shortly after they hatch from the eggs, they can take care of themselves.

Of all the animals, man provides parental care for the longest time. This helps ensure adaptation to all environments and continuity of the species.

SUMMARY

Redi and Pasteur proved that living things do not arise spontaneously but that all living things come from other living things of the same kind.

Reproduction is the process by which new individuals are produced by an individual or individuals (parents) of the same species.

Reproduction may be asexual (one parent involved) or sexual (two parents involved). Fission, budding, sporulation, regeneration and vegetative propagation are all methods of asexual reproduction.

Flowering plants reproduce sexually. The flower contains the male reproductive organ (stamen) and female reproductive organ (pistil).

A fertilized egg is the product of the union of an egg cell with a sperm cell. An embryo develops from a fertilized egg. All vertebrates reproduce sexually.

All tissues and organs develop in the embryo from three primary or embryonic layers: namely, ectoderm, mesoderm and endoderm.

VOCABULARY

mitosis	foetus	embryonic layers
centrosome	reduction division	placenta
zygospore	meiosis	umbilical cord
zygote	gamete	ectoderm
spindle	chromatids	endoderm
gametogenesis	blastula	mesoderm
	germ layers	

Exercise No. 48

Match a number in Column *A* with a letter in Column *B*.

A	B
1 spontaneous generation	a food poisoning
2 nucleus	b miniature plant within enlarged, food-filled leaves which grows into new plant
3 asexual reproduction	c type of asexual reproduction from part of a plant
4 sexual reproduction	d controls reproduction
5 binary fission	e attaching one part of a plant to a related plant
6 budding	f regrowth of a lost organ or tissue
7 sporulation	g combination of contents of two parent cells
8 gamete	h growth of living organisms from non-living matter
9 zygospore	i splitting of cell in two: asexual reproduction
10 botulism	j reproduction—involving one parent which splits off part of itself
11 vegetative propagation	k a cell that acts as a parent
12 regeneration	l reproduction by spore formation
13 bulb	m reproduction involving two parents
14 grafting	n asexual reproduction—projection of parent protoplasm to form new individual

Exercise No. 49

Complete the following statements:

1 Flowering plants reproduce ——.
2 The female organ of reproduction in the flower is the ——.
3 The male organ of reproduction in the flower is the ——.
4 —— is the name given to the structure in the flower in which the male gamete is formed.

5 The —— at the base of the pistil contains the egg cells.

6 —— is the term used to refer to the transfer of pollen from the stamen of one flower to the pistil of another flower of the same species.

7 The union of a sperm nucleus with an egg nucleus is known as ——, and results in a —— egg.

8 A seed of a flowering plant contains the —— and ——.

9 —— is the characteristic number of pairs of chromosomes in the body cells of man.

10 ——is cell division in which each daughter cell receives the same kind and number of chromosomes as were in the parent cell.

11 In the formation of gametes or sex cells, the process of —— takes place to reduce the number of chromosomes to half. This is to prepare for combination of male and female nuclei of the same species in fertilization.

12 The egg cell is much larger than the sperm cell because it contains ——.

13 The tissues and organs of an embryo mammal develop from the three ——.

14 The brain, spinal cord and nerve tissue develop from the original ——.

15 A human embryo is called a ——.

CHAPTER XV

GENETICS: HEREDITY

The previous chapter discussed the scientific basis for the existence of different species of plants and animals. Also we saw that a type of organism exists from generation to generation because each produces others of its own kind in the process of reproduction.

Everyone is aware of similarities and differences among the members of his immediate family. We are members of the human species so that, in general, we bear the characteristics of a male or female mammal (Homo sapiens).

There is probably a general resemblance among all the members of a given family. Specifically, there will be differences in physical traits; differences in emotional responses to a given circumstance.

Make a chart as follows and note a few of the obvious differences in the following characteristics:

CHARACTERISTIC	YOURSELF	PARENT A	PARENT B	OTHER MEMBERS OF THE FAMILY
Hair: colour, curly or straight				
Colour of eyes				
Adult height				
Shape of ear lobe				

Compare the results. Are there similarities? Differences? Any exact likenesses?

Have you ever seen how in a litter of new-born kittens or puppies each infant animal differs in colour, colour pattern or facial expression from the others and from its mother?

Study the leaves of a potted plant on your window ledge. Observe a number of full-grown leaves. Are they all identical so far as their outline, size, vein structure and colour are concerned? At a hasty glance all the leaves may look generally alike, but if you observe them closely you will see considerable differences.

VARIATIONS WITHIN A SPECIES

The differences in eye colour, hair colour, structure and so on, in a single family, and the differences in leaf structure on the same plant or tree are called **variations.** These variations, some due to heredity and some to influences in the environment, result in differences in species from one generation to the next, and changes in forms of life from the beginning of recorded time.

THE GENE THEORY OF HEREDITARY CHARACTERISTICS

Scientists have demonstrated that inherited characteristics are carried by chromosomes in the germ or reproductive cells, the germ plasm. PROFESSOR THOMAS HUNT MORGAN, working on genetics experiments (about 1930) with fruit flies in America, came to the conclusion that individual molecules of protein on the chromosomes, the **genes,** carry and produce the identifying individual characteristics of a species.

Many other scientists working with Morgan and subsequently have substantiated his **Gene Theory of Hereditary Characteristics.** In 1945 chromosomes were photographed from a pollen grain of corn using an electron microscope for magnification of the specimen. Small, dark masses in the chromosomes seemed to indicate the genes themselves or their location.

MENDEL AND THE LAWS OF HEREDITY

Many years before Morgan's experiments on heredity in fruit flies, an Austrian monk, Gregor Mendel, whose work covered the period of nine years between 1856 and 1865, became interested in the subject of heredity.

He wanted to understand why some children of brown-eyed parents were born with brown eyes, and others with blue eyes. His curiosity was aroused when in his parish he noticed that some children of red-headed parents or grandparents had red hair while a sister or brother did not.

Mendel knew he could not experiment with human beings to find the answers to his many questions. And, because in his years of gardening he noticed variations in inherited traits among plants he cultivated, he decided to experiment with plants. He called the study of inherited characteristics **heredity.**

Father Mendel chose the common garden pea for his experiments for several reasons. They are hardy plants and there are many different pairs of contrasting traits within a single strain or family. Among the pairs of inherited traits are: tall vines and short or dwarf varieties; coloured and white blossoms; green and yellow peas and smooth and wrinkled pea seed coats. Another important reason for his choice is the fact that peas are normally self-pollinating plants. He could then artificially pollinate them by hand when necessary as a measure of control.

After the nine years of experimentation, Mendel described his findings and conclusions in a paper he called *Experiments in Plant Hybridisation*. It was later published in the *Journal of Natural History* of the Brunn Society of the Moravian province in Austria.

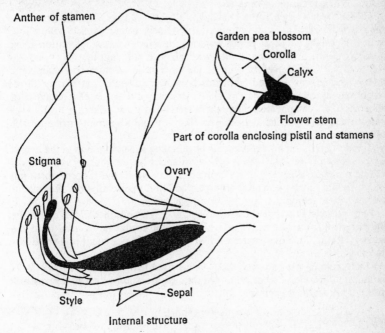

Anther of stamen

Garden pea blossom

Corolla

Calyx

Flower stem

Part of corolla enclosing pistil and stamens

Stigma

Ovary

Style

Sepal

Internal structure

Figure 171

The science of heredity, now called genetics, came into existence when Mendel discovered how characteristics of a species are inherited. He later established what are known as the **Mendelian Laws of Heredity.**

Little recognition was given to his published findings while Mendel was alive. It was not until 1900 that his observations were reviewed by other scientists and his laws of heredity were accredited.

MENDEL'S EXPERIMENTS

When Mendel first started cultivating garden peas, he noticed that there were many pairs of obvious contrasting characteristics, and he selected plants showing these. For example, he selected tall plants and short ones and observed them during their consecutive generations over a period of two years.

During this time he allowed the blossoms to be self-pollinated. A pea blossom is adapted for self-pollination by the nature of its structure. The pistil is shorter than the stamens which bend over it so that pollen drops from the anthers on to the stigma in self-pollination. Cross-pollination by any outside agent is prevented because two of the petals of the corolla form a sheath over the vital organs. See Fig. 171.

Mendel chose tall plants that always produced tall offspring and dwarf varieties which invariably produced short offspring. These plants he called pure breeds or strains, i.e. pure tall and pure short plants. After two years of pure breeding, he was convinced he had pure strains of this contrasting characteristic in the pea plant.

Then he went a step further. He carefully parted the two petals enclosing the reproductive organs and removed the stamens to prevent self-pollination. When the pollen on other plants was ripe, he effected cross-pollination using a fine paint brush to transfer pollen grains from a tall plant to a short one. He followed the same procedure with plants having other contrasting characters. The offspring that resulted from this cross were all tall, that is they all resembled only one of the parent plants. It seemed that the characteristic of shortness had disappeared altogether. He called these offspring **hybrids** because they were produced from crossing two unlike parent varieties. The hybrid offspring are referred to as the F_1 or first filial generation.

Mendel carried on his experiments by allowing self-pollination in the hybrid F_1 generation. This is known as **hybridization,** or the crossing of two hybrids.

The resulting offspring, the F_2 generation, were in the ratio of three tall plants to one short one. The short factor had not been totally lost after all but had only been temporarily masked for a generation.

The characteristic that showed up in the F_1 generation Mendel called the **dominant** trait; the characteristic which did not appear he referred to as the **recessive** trait. Thus he discovered that tallness was dominant and shortness recessive.

Once again Mendel allowed the F_2 generation their natural process of self-pollination. Resultant seeds produced the F_3 generation which were an assortment of tall and short plants as follows:

1 All offspring of short plants were short.
2 Offspring of tall plants were in the ratio of three tall to one short.

He got the same ratio of results in the F_4, F_5, etc., generations.

Mendel concluded that the gametes from each parent carried some factor responsible for the appearance, in the adult plant, of the particular character, while the offspring would carry two such factors, one from each parent. He maintained that these factors remained unaltered in the gametes even when the character did not appear in the adult (shortness in the F_1, generation).

From these experiments, Mendel drew his first law, the **Law of Segregation,** which states that characters are controlled by pairs of germinal units (we now call them genes) of which only one can be represented in a single gamete.

We can show symbolically the results of Mendel's experiments, representing the dominant factor for tallness as T, and the recessive factor for shortness as t.

Mendel's next task was to find out what happened when he crossed plants with two pairs of contrasting characteristics (dihybridization). He found that if he cross-pollinated flowers of pure breeding plants grown from round, yellow seeds and wrinkled, green seeds, all the resulting seeds were round and yellow. Round was dominant to wrinkled, and yellow to green. Self-pollination of this F_1 hybrid generation produced seeds showing all four characters

1 Crossing two pure strains.

| Parents | Tall | X | Short |

(two factors
for height)   TT   X   tt

Gametes
(one factor
for height)   Ⓣ   Ⓣ   ⓣ   ⓣ

F_1 hybrid generation
appears tall. Factor
for shortness is present
but masked (recessive)   Tt

2 Self-pollination of F_1 generation.

| Parents | Tt | X | Tt |

Gametes
Possible
combination of
gametes   Ⓣ   ⓣ   X   Ⓣ   ⓣ

F_2 generation   TT   Tt   tT   tt

3 tall (1 pure 2 hybrid)   1 pure short

in all possible combinations but in the definite numerical ratio of nine round yellow; three round green; three wrinkled yellow; one wrinkled green.

Represented symbolically, his results are as follows, where R=round (dominant); r=wrinkled (recessive); Y=yellow (dominant); y=green (recessive):

1 Crossing two pure
strains.

Parents   round yellow   wrinkled green
(2 factors each for   RRYY   X   rryy
shape and colour)

Gametes   ⓇⓎ   X   ⓇⓎ

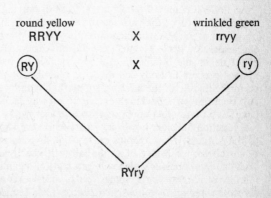

(1 factor each for
shape and colour)
Possible combinations
F_1 generation   RYry
all appear round and
yellow (dominant to
wrinkled and green)

2 Self-pollination of F_1 generation.

Parents   RYry   X   RYry

Gametes   (RY)   (Ry)   (rY)   (ry)   X   (RY)   (Ry)   (rY)   (ry)

It is usual, and simpler, to represent the possible combination of gametes as follows:

types of gametes	RY	Ry	rY	ry
RY	RYRY round yellow	RYRy round yellow	RYrY round yellow	RYry round yellow
Ry	RyRY round yellow	RyRy round green	RyrY round yellow	Ryry round green
rY	rYRY round yellow	rYRy round yellow	rYrY wrinkled yellow	rYry wrinkled yellow
ry	ryRY round yellow	ryRy round green	ryrY wrinkled yellow	ryry wrinkled green

F_2 generation: 9 round yellow (1 pure); 3 round green; 3 wrinkled yellow; 1 wrinkled green (pure).

Mendel's second law, **the Law of Independent Assortment** based on these results, states that each one of a pair of contrasted characters may be combined with either of another pair.

An understanding of reduction division or halving of chromosome number in the formation of the gametes and the knowledge that the genes carried on the chromosomes are the factors responsible for the transmission of inherited characteristics, make Mendel's conclusions easier to follow.

Let us review briefly mitosis and meiosis or reduction division. In the normal process of body-cell division, mitosis, the paired chromosomes line up in the middle of the nucleus, split in half lengthwise, and one of each split pair becomes part of a daughter cell. In this way each of the daughter cells will have the same number of chromosomes as the original parent cell. See Fig. 172.

Reduction division, however, occurs in the primary sex cells which give rise to the gametes. The daughter cells of this division receive only one of a pair of chromosomes instead of a split half from each one of a pair. This provides each daughter nucleus which will form part of a gamete with half the original number of parent chromosomes. This process occurs to prevent doubling of chromosomes *ad infinitum* each time a male gamete unites with a female gamete of the same species to form a new individual. See Fig. 173.

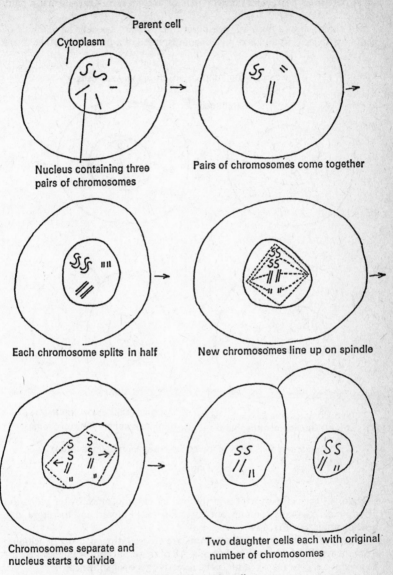

Nucleus containing three
pairs of chromosomes

Pairs of chromosomes come together

Each chromosome splits in half

New chromosomes line up on spindle

Chromosomes separate and
nucleus starts to divide

Two daughter cells each with original
number of chromosomes

Figure 172   Mitosis in body cell

Let us see how the presence of genes as transmitters of hereditary characters explains Mendel's laws.

Before gametogenesis (formation of gametes), each primary sex cell contains a pair of genes, each in one of a pair of like chromosomes, responsible for a particular characteristic. One pair of chromosomes carries many pairs of genes.

For example, in a pure tall pea plant, the primary sex cells have a pair of genes for tallness in a pair of like chromosomes. In a pure short plant, there

Meiosis (reduction division) in primary sex cells

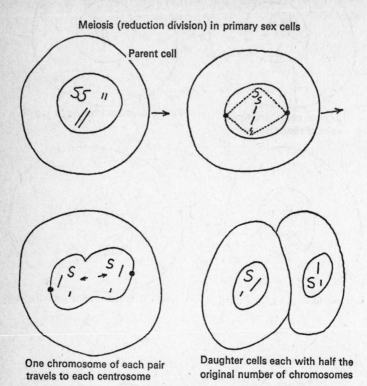

One chromosome of each pair travels to each centrosome

Daughter cells each with half the original number of chromosomes

(reduction division is followed by a normal mitotic division)

Figure 173

is a pair of genes for shortness in the pair of chromosomes. After reduction division, each gamete contains one chromosome of a pair, and therefore, one gene of a pair. See Fig. 174.

When pure tall and pure short plants are crossed, the offspring developing from the resulting seeds will be hybrids. All of these will appear tall because the dominant tall gene masks or hides the recessive gene for shortness.

Now if self-pollination of each of the hybrids occurs, or cross-pollination of two of them, the resulting F_2 generation will be 25 per cent pure tall (2 genes for tallness), 50 per cent hybrid (one gene each for tallness and shortness) and 25 per cent pure short (2 genes for shortness). See Fig. 175.

The Mendelian laws were later applied to the heredity of fur colour in guinea pigs. By using Mendel's method of mating pure breeds of guinea pigs

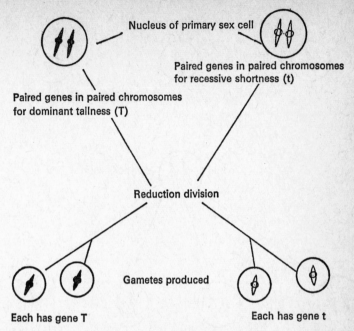

Nucleus of primary sex cell

Paired genes in paired chromosomes
for recessive shortness (t)

Paired genes in paired chromosomes
for dominant tallness (T)

Reduction division

Gametes produced

Each has gene T

Each has gene t

N.B. There are other genes and other chromosomes present in the nucleus,
but only one is indicated for the sake of clarity

Figure 174   Genes—reduction division

over a period of years, scientists concluded that black is the dominant, and
white the recessive colour, and that the F_1 generation is always 100 per cent
hybrid black.

Mating two hybrid black animals results in the 1 : 2 : 1 ratio of 25 per cent
pure black, 50 per cent hybrid black and 25 per cent pure white. See Fig. 176.

Another type of ratio results when a hybrid parent is back-crossed with a
pure recessive parent. The results are 50 per cent hybrid and 50 per cent pure
recessive. For example, when a hybrid tall pea plant (Tt) is crossed with a pure
short pea plant (tt) the results will be:

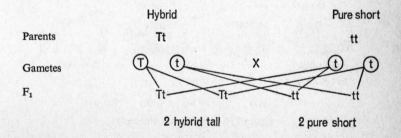

	Hybrid		Pure short
Parents	Tt		tt
Gametes	T t	X	t t
F_1	Tt——Tt——tt——tt		
	2 hybrid tall		2 pure short

Hybridization

T   Fertilizes   t   Tt (hybrid)

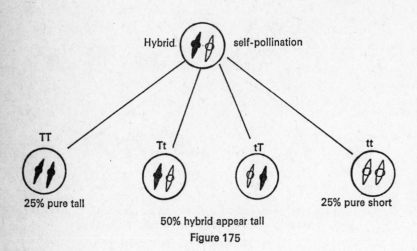

Hybrid.   self-pollination

TT   Tt   tT   tt

25% pure tall   25% pure short

50% hybrid appear tall

Figure 175

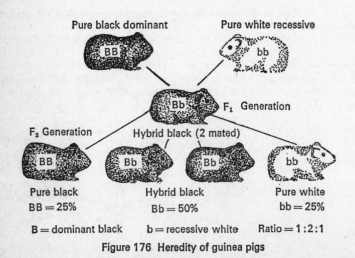

Pure black dominant   Pure white recessive

BB   bb

Bb   F₁ Generation

F₂ Generation   Hybrid black (2 mated)

BB   Bb   Bb   bb

Pure black   Hybrid black   Pure white
BB = 25%   Bb = 50%   bb = 25%

B = dominant black   b = recessive white   Ratio = 1:2:1

Figure 176 Heredity of guinea pigs

Of the pairs of characters which Mendel studied in pea plants, one was always completely dominant over the other.

BLENDING OR INCOMPLETE DOMINANCE

Although Mendel's laws still hold good, it now appears that complete dominance of one trait over another is by no means universal, and that individuals of F₁ generations may show an apparent **blending** of the two charac-

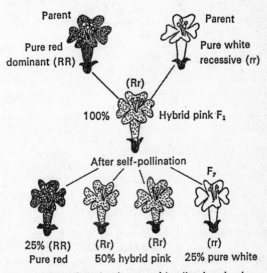

Incomplete dominance—blending in primula
Figure 177

ters, though not of course of the genes. Mendel's choice of characters was fortunate in that they did show complete dominance.

For example, the offspring of pure red and pure white star primulas are 100 per cent hybrid, but all appear pink. The F_2 generation resulting from self-pollination of the hybrid pink flowers, are 25 per cent pure red, 50 per cent hybrid pink and 25 per cent pure white. The new colour is due to complex causes, but the genes retain their identity and powers of segregation.

The same type of blending can be found in animals. The Andalusian fowl is a good example. When a pure, dominant, black-feathered fowl is crossed with a pure recessive white, the offspring in the F_1 generation are 100 per cent hybrid and appear blue-black in colour.

When two blue-black hybrids are mated, the resulting F_2 generation is 25 per cent pure dominant black, 50 per cent hybrid blue-black and 25 per cent pure recessive white.

The following is a list of some paired contrasting characters which are hereditary in several plants and animals:

PLANT OR ANIMAL	DOMINANT CHARACTER	RECESSIVE CHARACTER
Sweet pea	yellow seeds smooth seeds tall plant	green seeds wrinkled seeds short plant
Maize	yellow kernel	white kernel
Wheat	susceptibility to rust diseases	immunity to rust
Cattle	black colour hornless	red colour horned
Leghorn chickens	white plumage	pigmented plumage
Rabbits	short fur	angora fur
Mice	normal colouring of fur	albino (no colouring)

SEX DETERMINATION

One pair of chromosomes in the primary germ cell determines whether the organism is male or female. In the female human and some other animals, both members of the pair are alike; they are referred to as the XX chromosomes. In the male, the members of this pair differ from each other and are referred to as the XY chromosomes.

When reduction division occurs during gametogenesis, each of the daughter cells or eggs of the XX female primary germ cell receives an X chromosome.

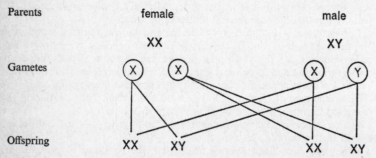

50 per cent male: 50 per cent female (scientists use the symbol ♂ for male and ♀ for female).

The daughter cells or sperms of the XY male primary germ cell receive either an X or a Y chromosome.

Thus when an egg unites with a sperm containing an X chromosome, an XX or female is produced. When an egg unites with a Y chromosome sperm, an XY or male is produced.

The reason why the sex of a human child, or any animal, cannot be predicted in spite of Mendelian ratios is that only one sperm of the large quantity which is produced actually succeeds in uniting with an egg cell. Also, not every egg cell that is produced becomes fertilized by a sperm cell.

LINKAGE

There are certain genes which are carried on one chromosome and are therefore not inherited independently, but linked to one another and transmitted in groups. This is known as **linkage.**

Morgan, working with the fruit fly, **Drosophila,** discovered that grey-bodied flies all had long wings, while black-bodied flies all had vestigial wings. He explained these results by postulating that the genes for grey colour and long wings were lodged on the same chromosome and thus transmitted together. The genes responsible for black colour and vestigial wings were similarly carried on a single chromosome.

The sex chromosomes, as well as carrying genes responsible for sex inheritance, also bear genes influencing other characteristics. These are referred to as sex-linked characters. Baldness, haemophilia and colour-blindness are sex-linked characters. They are recessive traits which can be transmitted by the female but are usually apparent only in the male of the species.

VOCABULARY

genetics	filial generation	back-cross
heredity	strain	blending
variations	hybrid	incomplete
gene	dominant	dominance
hybridization	recessive	linkage
pure breed	meiosis	sex-linked
	dihybridization	

Exercise No. 50

Select the correct word or phrase for each of the following:

1 The genes for colour-blindness are carried in the: (a) eye cells; (b) body cells; (c) sex cells; (d) sex chromosomes.
2 Mendel used —— for his experiments on heredity: (a) Andalusian fowl; (b) pea plants; (c) potatoes; (d) fruit flies.
3 The human animal which has an XY pair of chromosomes is: (a) male; (b) hybrid; (c) doomed; (d) female.
4 The science of heredity is known as: (a) biology; (b) embryology; (c) genetics; (d) physics.
5 The germ plasm refers to: (a) bacteria; (b) diseases; (c) blood; (d) reproductive cells.

6 A hybrid is a: (a) dominant trait; (b) pair of unlike genes in a trait; (c) recessive trait.

7 A gene is a: (a) hybrid; (b) heritable trait; (c) part of a chromosome that transmits a trait; (d) pure breed.

HEREDITY VERSUS ENVIRONMENT

We all recognize many differences among all living things. These differences may be due to variations in our genetic composition: that is, differences we inherited. They may also result from existing and changing factors in our environment: that is, they may be acquired characteristics.

It is common knowledge that each of us is born with inherited physical and mental traits, and that as we grow older and adapt ourselves to the environment, some of these characteristics are modified or changed. Some scientists used to believe that certain acquired characteristics were inherited.

In 1809 a French biologist, JEAN BAPTISTE LAMARCK, formulated his **Theory of Use and Disuse.** He held that some characteristics or traits are acquired by an organism in its efforts to adapt to its environment, and that these traits are passed on by heredity to the offspring. For example, he thought that originally all giraffes had short necks, and that circumstances forced them to reach into high tree-tops for food. Lamarck concluded that after many generations of neck-stretching, the long-necked giraffe came into being—the hereditary passage of an acquired character.

Further, Lamarck theorized that an organ of the body that was not used consistently for many generations ceased to function, decreased in size, or even ceased finally to exist. But towards the end of the nineteenth century, AUGUST WEISMANN helped to disprove Lamarck's **Theory of Inheritance of Acquired Characteristics** by experimenting with twenty-two generations of mice with normal sized tails. Weismann cut short the tails of every generation of the mice, mated them, and always got the same result—the mice in every generation were all born with normal sized tails. Thus Weismann concluded that cutting off the tails of the mice affected only the body cells and not the germ cells and that an acquired variation was not inherited.

In the second part of his experiment, Weismann selected mice with naturally short tails and mated them. The results were a strain of short-tailed mice. He concluded from this that only variations transmitted in the germ cells were inherited.

The conclusions drawn from both parts of his experiment led to the formulation of Weismann's **Theory of the Continuity of Germ Plasm**—that is, that germ plasm in reproductive cells continues from generation to generation, and is theoretically immortal.

MUTATIONS

Just after the beginning of the twentieth century, HUGO DE VRIES, a Dutch botanist, observed some evening primrose plants to be entirely unlike any he had ever cultivated or studied before. He carefully gathered and planted the seeds of many successive generations. The resulting offspring all resembled the parents which De Vries concluded to be pure types.

He gave the name 'sport' (something freakish) to the original different primrose. Later, after deciding that some change must have taken place in the germ plasm of the primrose to produce the variation, he renamed the organism a **mutant** and the variation a **mutation**.

De Vries proved with his experiments that a mutation may be either dominant or recessive, but is always a pure characteristic, and that it is a heritable variation.

In subsequent years, Morgan discovered that mutations arose in Drosophila because of genetic changes in the chromosomes or genes. Some of the changes were due to:

1 Loss of a piece of chromosome containing genes during cell division.

2 Detachment of part of a chromosome which may subsequently rejoin in an inverted position or attach itself to another chromosome.

3 An unexplained increase of original chromosome number by doubling or trebling.

4 A change within the gene itself.

PRACTICAL APPLICATION OF GENETICS

A plant or animal breeder must watch very carefully to spot a mutant. If he discovers one which has more favourable characteristics than the normal strain, he should make immediate use of it for breeding. If its offspring are like the parent mutants, then the breed is true, and the desirable trait can be passed on for generations. Here are some examples:

A large, juicy, seedless orange was spotted to be a mutant, superior in size and content to all seeded oranges. Since it could not reproduce itself, being seedless, the plant breeder grafted the buds from the tree which produced the seedless orange to a normal orange tree, thus creating a new, superior product.

A cattle breeder once spotted a mutant among his common long-horned cattle—a calf without horns. After the animal had matured, it was mated with a long-horned cow, and the hornless trait proved to be a dominant one. Since hornless cattle are safer to manage and less dangerous to the herd it was to the advantage of the cattle breeder to further the species.

A lamb with very short legs appeared among a herd of normal sheep. It bred true, and flocks of short-legged sheep were produced. The advantage lay in their inability to jump fences and escape the grazing fields.

Albinism, lack of all pigmentation, is a mutation which has appeared in plants, mice, rats, rabbits, birds and even human beings. It was discovered that this factor, produced by a combination of genes, is lethal in plants. The plant is doomed because, lacking green pigmentation, it cannot carry on the process of photosynthesis, and will therefore perish. In some animals, too, these genes have caused death to the offspring of mated albinos. Albinism is recessive in humans but not lethal.

INDUCED MUTATIONS

Scientists have discovered means of inducing the appearance of mutations in some plants and animals. Among the methods they use are:

X-rays—Exposure of germ plasm to X-rays produces changes in the genes.

This was discovered in 1927 by PROFESSOR H. J. MULLER, while he was experimenting with fruit flies. He was awarded the Nobel Prize in Medicine for his discovery.

Chemicals—Certain gases from smoke in industrial areas, and mustard gas in particular, seem to affect the genes of some insects, to result in the production of mutations. This was discovered by DOUGLAS C. HARRISON, a British biologist.

The use of a chemical called colchicine on some plant seeds produces plants with seeds which develop into plants with double the number of the original chromosomes. These mutants, self-pollinated, produce a new variety of plant. Improved types of fruit, tobacco and cotton have been produced by the use of colchicine. The chemical however, seems to be fatal to animal cells. In a few cases where animal cells have survived, the offspring have been short-lived and abnormal.

Atomic Radiation—This has produced mutations in many plants and animals. In time we shall know the effect of atomic radiation on the human beings who were exposed to them and still appear to be living normally.

PLANT AND ANIMAL BREEDING

Mendel's Laws of Heredity plus knowledge about heritability, induction of mutations and the continuity of germ plasm give us the working materials for modern plant and animal breeding practices. The basic steps to be followed in the course of plant and animal breeding are:

1 Selection of plants or animals with desired characteristics to be used as parents.

2 Self-pollination of the chosen plants and inbreeding of the chosen animals, mating closely related animals. There may be satisfactory results in inbreeding, or the results may be unsatisfactory, even disastrous. When desirable dominant features appear, results seem to be successful. On the other hand, close inbreeding may bring out recessive weaknesses which are undesirable. In human beings, such undesirable traits as feeble-mindedness, deafmutism, colour-blindness and haemophilia may be furthered.

3 Hybridization—mating plants and animals of different varieties resulting in a combination of the desired traits in their offspring. An example is the mating of a mare with a male donkey to produce a sterile mule. Although mules are not able to produce more mules, they have desirable characteristics as beasts of burden.

Another example of hybridization is the mating of domestic cows with bull buffaloes. The offspring, called cattaloes, are large and desirable for the firm quality of their beef.

One of the pioneers in scientific plant breeding was an American agriculturalist called LUTHER BURBANK, who conducted experiments on his farm and succeeded in producing many new varieties of plants and also hardier and more desirable varieties of existing species. By careful selection, spotting mutants, using controlled artificial pollination, inbreeding and hybridization, Burbank produced:

A variety of potato which is larger, meatier and has more eyes for vegetative propagation than the ordinary potato.

A stoneless plum, and a cross between a plum and an apricot known as a plumcot.

New varieties of plums, a cross between those grown in Europe, Asia and America, that are larger, juicier, meatier and hardier.

Spineless cacti that make good fodder for cattle in desert countries.

Many unusually large and beautiful flowers—variations of the Shasta daisy, Calla lily and others.

A finer type of corn has also been produced by self-pollinating corn with seemingly undesirable characteristics—long, stringy corn and dwarf varieties; then suddenly cross-pollinating two of the extreme specimens. The resultant sturdy, heavy-bearing specimens, when self-pollinated, perpetuate these good qualities since they are dominant.

In the plant world, disease-resisting varieties of cotton, wheat, chestnut, corn and several fruits have been developed. Hardier, superior fruit-bearing trees have been produced. Improvement in the quality and quantity of grains, herbs and tobacco has been accomplished. Entirely new types have been developed from mutations.

Among animals, disease-resisting varieties of cows, sheep, pigs and horses have been developed. Hardier meat-producing types of cows have been introduced—combinations of Hereford and Shorthorns. Cows producing larger quantities of milk (Holsteins); chickens that lay greater numbers of eggs (white leghorn); horses that are sleek, trim and swift—these are just some examples of inbreeding and hybridization. Also pedigree dogs and horses have been bred, chiefly for show purposes. Theoretically there is almost no limit to what can be achieved. But how can we apply these principles to improving the human race?

EUGENICS

SIR FRANCIS GALTON in 1885 was a pioneer in the field of eugenics—that is, the study of the improvement of the human race through the application of the laws of heredity. He believed that human beings could improve themselves by controlled marriages.

Galton's theoretical work was limited to statistics, as are all studies of eugenics, because of the nature of the science. People cannot be bred as we breed animals. The number of offspring in a given family is necessarily limited as compared with those of animals. Families separate geographically as well as economically, so that it is difficult to keep track of a family history. Statistics are often valueless because of inaccuracy of information.

Universal education in the principles of heredity and eugenics is necessary. Ideally, persons who are congenitally unfit, mentally or physically should be prevented from having offspring. Those in doubt can get expert advice from special clinics on the chances of their disabilities being passed on to their children.

HUMAN HEREDITARY TRAITS

Enough information has been gathered through the years to indicate which human traits are hereditary, and they appear to conform to the principles of heredity as set forth by Mendel. Among them are the following:

DOMINANT TRAIT	RECESSIVE TRAIT
Woolly hair	Straight hair
Brown eyes	Blue or grey eyes
White forelock	Normal hair colouring
Normal pigmentation	Albinism
Defective tooth enamel	Normal tooth enamel
Absence of incisors	Normal number of teeth
Supernumerary teeth	Normal number of teeth
Normalcy	Hare-lip and cleft palate
Normalcy	Deaf-mutism
Normalcy	Extra fingers
Normalcy	Epilepsy
Normalcy	Haemophilia
Normalcy	Adherent ear lobes
Night blindness	Normal vision

Blood groups or types are hereditary. There are four blood types: groups A, B, AB and O. Before a blood transfusion, tests must be made on the recipient and on the anticipated donor.

The Rh factor which appears, or is negative, in all blood groups is hereditary. About 85 per cent of human beings are Rh positive and the remaining 15 per cent are Rh negative.

There is much historical and statistical evidence that degrees of intelligence and special talents may be inherited.

MULTIPLE BIRTHS

Studies of multiple births (twins, triplets, etc.) are used to determine the influence of environment as well as heredity on individuals. See Fig. 178a and b.

There are two kinds of multiple births—one is called identical and the other fraternal. Identical twins develop from a single fertilized egg which has divided into two cells. Instead of these cells remaining attached to each other and dividing further to form a single blastula stage, and finally a single embryo, the two cells, from the first division, separate and each develops into an independent embryo. These result in two identical individuals, either two boys or two girls.

Fraternal multiple births occur when more than one egg cell is fertilized, each by a separate sperm, at the same time and each develops into an individual embryo to result in twins, triplets, etc. They may be all of the same sex or of both sexes, but are no more alike than normal brothers and sisters. See Fig. 179.

Studies have been made of the effects of environmental factors on pairs of identical and fraternal twins. The results show that not only are identical twins almost identical in physical appearance, but also that their emotional and rational responses to environmental conditions are almost identical even when the individuals of the pair are separated.

Fraternal twins, who resemble each other physically, seem also to be somewhat alike in intelligence and in emotional responses, but are not necessarily so.

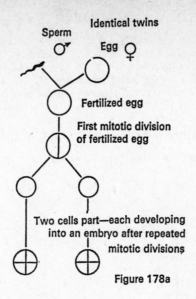

Identical twins

Sperm ♂   Egg ♀

Fertilized egg

First mitotic division
of fertilized egg

Two cells part—each developing
into an embryo after repeated
mitotic divisions

Figure 178a

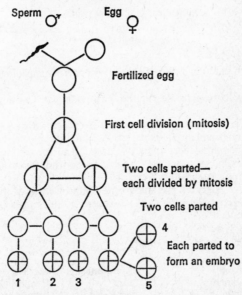

Identical quintuplets

Sperm ♂   Egg ♀

Fertilized egg

First cell division (mitosis)

Two cells parted—
each divided by mitosis

Two cells parted

Each parted to
form an embryo

1   2   3   4   5

Figure 178b

SUMMARY

No two individuals are exactly alike. Variations may be due to heredity or environment. Inherited characteristics are transmitted by the genes on the chromosomes in the germ cells.

Morgan is responsible for the gene theory of hereditary characteristics which explains Mendel's Laws of Heredity. A pair of genes (or sometimes a

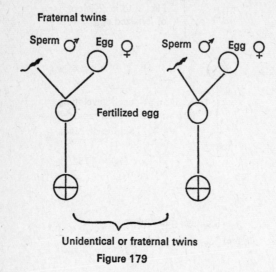

Figure 179

combination of pairs) in a pair of chromosomes is responsible for a character or trait.

Weismann was responsible for the Theory of the Continuity of Germ Plasm.

A mutation is an unexpected appearance of a new form, or an unanticipated genetic variation in a plant or animal strain. Mutations are heritable.

Plant and animal breeders apply the laws of heredity and mutations. They are able to develop new desirable variations and improvements of existing plants and animals by scientific breeding.

The science of eugenics, the study of the improvement of the human race by applying the laws of heredity was introduced by Sir Francis Galton.

VOCABULARY

mutant	hybridization	eugenics
mutation	mule	identical twins
lethal	inbreeding	fraternal twins
atomic radiations	pedigree	multiple births

Exercise No. 51

Identify each of the following scientists with a contribution listed below:

SCIENTIST	CONTRIBUTION
1 Thomas H. Morgan	a founder of laws of heredity and science of genetics
2 Gregor Mendel	b produced mutations in Drosophila by X-rays
3 August Wiesmann	c Gene Theory (heredity in fruit flies)
4 Hugo De Vries	d Theory of Continuity of Germ Plasm
5 Herman Muller	e famous plant breeder
6 Jean B. Lamarck	f father of eugenics
7 Luther Burbank	g Theory of Inheritance of Acquired Characteristics
8 Sir Francis Galton	h discovery of mutations among evening primroses

Exercise No. 52

Complete each of the following:

1 Physical and mental variations which occur in an individual during his lifetime are known as —— characteristics.
2 The seedless (navel) orange is an example of a beneficial ——.
3 A mutation is an —— character, either dominant or recessive. Mutations result from —— in germ plasm.
4 Hereford cattle are bred for their ——.
5 Burbank produced the spineless cactus by ——.
6 Albinism in plants is —— because the plant cannot carry on photosynthesis.
7 Professor H. J. Morgan exposed fruit flies to —— to produce mutations.
8 The chemical —— doubles the number of chromosomes in some plants.
9 Inbreeding often results in the appearance of recessive traits which are ——.
10 The process of mating selected, unrelated plants or animals to produce more desirable types is known as ——.
11 The offspring of a mare mated with a male donkey is a ——.
12 An example of ——, is the mating of a cow with a male buffalo. The resultant offspring is called a ——.
13 One result of hybridization in plant breeding is the development of ——.
14 A pedigree dog is produced from a —— line of descent.
15 A type of cattle, developed by animal breeders, which produces a great quantity of milk and is prized for superior beef is ——.
16 Twins which develop from a single fertilized egg are known as —— twins.

CHAPTER XVI

EVOLUTION: THE NATURE OF CHANGE

In the discussion of genetics we established the important concept that heredity of specific characteristics from generation to generation and variations among living things have brought about the existing forms of life on earth.

Scientists have gathered overwhelming evidence that life on earth 60 million years ago was quite different from what it was when man-like mammals first appeared about one million years ago and from what it is at present.

HISTORY OF THE EARTH

Geologists—scientists who study the history of the earth's surface—have been able to approximate the age of the earth and the various types of flora and fauna which inhabited the earth from its beginning.

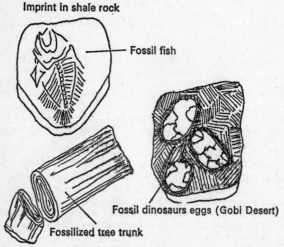

Imprint in shale rock

Fossil fish

Fossil dinosaurs eggs (Gobi Desert)

Fossilized tree trunk

Figure 180   Fossils

Palaeontologists—scientists who study fossil evidence of plant and animal life in layers of rocks—have contributed important data about life on earth in prehistoric times.

In regions such as the Grand Canyon in America and parts of central and east Africa, where sequential layers of rock are exposed, much evidence of life in the past has been unearthed.

Petrified remains—bones or imprints of animal and plant fossils found in the lowest layers (closest to the earth's core)—suggest the kind of plants and animals which first existed.

Fossils found in subsequent, higher layers of rocks indicate the absence of some that formerly existed, the change in some original forms, and the appearance of new forms.

It will be useful to describe briefly some major theories of the origin of the earth, and of life on earth.

THEORY OF EARTH'S FORMATION

Geologists and palaeontologists working together have estimated that the earth came into existence between eighteen hundred and three thousand million years ago. With the help of astronomy (the study of the heavenly bodies), scientists have evolved theories of the original formation of the planet.

Among rival theories, the one that has gained for itself the most substantial scientific support is the German astronomer, VON WEIZÄCKER'S **Turbulence Hypothesis.** This holds that the sun was once surrounded by a slowly rotating disc-shaped cloud of gas, from which—as a result of many factors—turbulence cells were formed. After several hundred million years, the planets formed in the dead-end region between the cells.

During the cooling process, cracks occurred in the hardening outer crust of the earth. The molten centre of lava tended to bubble over through these cracks. Upheavals took place during which folds formed in the crust—that is, mountains and valleys were formed.

CHANGES IN THE EARTH'S SURFACE

Because an atmosphere surrounds the earth, elements of wind and water, changes of temperature, chemical changes within the minerals of the earth brought about further changes in the earth's surface. This occurred even before the appearance of life.

We have daily evidence of the rate at which the surface of the earth changes. Erosion (wearing away) of rock and soil by the action of wind and water provides clues to prehistoric changes and to the age of the earth.

The rate of the formation of sedimentary rock from layers and layers of soil particles produced by erosion and packed down under the pressure of superseding layers helps to determine the approximate age of the earth.

A radioactive element called **uranium** provides another clue to the earth's age. An atom of this unstable mineral takes a certain length of time to change to lead. Geologists determine the age of a sample of rock layers containing uranium ore by the amount of lead it contains.

By determining the rate at which river water dissolves salts from the rocks and soil over which it passes on its way to the oceans, and by calculating the existing salt content of the oceans, geologists have another measure of the earth's approximate age.

The appearance of fossils in the sedimentary rock layers not only indicates the type of plant and animal life which existed at a given time but also reveals the gradual changes in living things from the time they first appeared on earth. Evolution refers to these gradual changes in life.

Palaeontologists using geological evidence in addition to their own have divided life on earth into several periods, using fossil evidence as criteria for the divisions.

Let us chart this record briefly (in reverse order):

ERA	CHARACTERISTIC FAUNA AND FLORA
Cenozoic (present day to 60,000,000 B.C.)	The age of man Modern plants and animals First appearance and development of mammals (except man). The prehistoric horse, Eohippus, appeared. Birds flourished
Mesozoic (60,000,000 B.C. to 230,000,000 B.C.)	Appearance of egg-laying mammals, bird-like creatures that somewhat resembled reptiles Era of huge reptiles, dinosaurs, etc. Modern insects flourished Lush growth of water plants Appearance of primitive seed-bearing plants
Palaeozoic. Era of coal formation. (230,000,000 B.C. to 505,000,000 B.C.)	Era of giant amphibians and insects Invertebrates predominant in the waters Primitive sharks and other primitive fish-like creatures Abundance of chain coral, trilobites Crustaceans appeared Rich and giant fern and horsetail growth on land
Proterozoic (505,000,000 B.C. to 2,000,000,000 B.C.)	No sign of land life Primitive marine invertebrates—algae, sponges, corals, small starfish
Archaeozoic ???	No fossils found Probable era of one-celled life

EVOLUTION OF LIFE—TO THE MODERN ERA

It is evident that there seems from the beginning to have been a gradual increase of specialization among plants and animals. See Fig. 181.

In the earliest layers of sedimentary rock (Archaeozoic) of the earth's crust, those closest to the earth's core, no fossils are evident. Since that part of the crust, as determined by the presence of salts and other minerals, was under water, scientists have theorized that simple, one-celled life existed.

It is probable that during the latter part of the Archaeozoic era, water-life began to advance somewhat in complexity of structure. Algae, some colonial forms and some with shell-like coverings of varied colours began to appear.

It is believed that sponges and coral animals with fibrous and stony skeletons appeared many millions of years after one-celled life began on earth. This second era has been named the Proterozoic era. Jellyfish and primitive marine worms appeared about this time.

Cenozoic era
Mammals, flowering plants, man

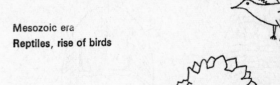

Mesozoic era
Reptiles, rise of birds

Palaeozoic era (coal age)
Giant amphibians and insects

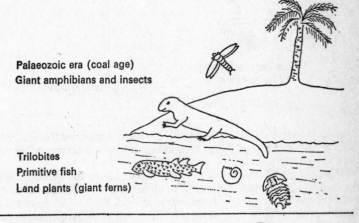

Trilobites
Primitive fish
Land plants (giant ferns)

Proterozoic era of marine
worms, corals, sponges

Archaeozoic era of one-celled life
  No fossil evidence

Figure 181

During the next long period, the Palaeozoic era, fossils indicate that most of the earth's surface was still under water but there is also some evidence of land forms, both plant and animal. During the latter part of the era vegetation was large and successful. In addition to existing organisms, jellyfish, corals and sponges, new water forms had appeared—**trilobites,** animals with hard exoskeletons, resembling modern shrimps, lobsters and most of all the modern horseshoe crab. They varied in size from an inch to three or four feet. Primitive fish mark the emergence of the vertebrates.

Trilobites—ancestor of modern horseshoe crab

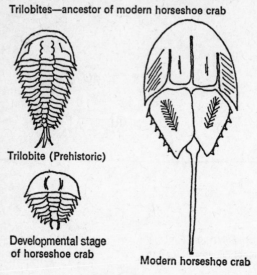

Trilobite (Prehistoric)

Developmental stage
of horseshoe crab

Modern horseshoe crab

Figure 182

In the middle strata of the Palaeozoic era rocks, land types of fossils of huge insects and giant amphibians resembling modern salamanders but much larger have been found.

It was in the Palaeozoic era that lush tree-like ferns and horsetails existed in land which was very swampy. The climate must have been hot and exceedingly moist. During the latter part of the era, the foundation of our coal beds was formed. For that reason it is referred to as the carboniferous period of the Palaeozoic era.

Coal is almost pure, solidified carbon. Softer coals still retain traces of other elements which composed the living stuff from which coal originated. The harder the coal, the purer the carbon composition, until under the most extreme pressure over aeons of time, a diamond may be formed.

Geologists believe that the giant ferns and other plant forms died and were covered with water and sediment from eroded land. Two hundred million years passed during which decay and chemical changes occurred. Heat from the atmosphere and as the result of chemical changes, and the tremendous pressure of the weight of sedimentary rock were responsible for the conversion of organic matter into coal beds.

Towards the end of the era, there must have been a drastic change in climate all over the world. Bodies of water dried up. Vast continents of land seem to have been raised. A decided change in dominant plant and animal life took place during the next era, the Mesozoic era, often referred to as the Age of Reptiles.

During this time both flora and fauna seem all to have been on a vast physical scale. Tremendous seed-bearing land plants seem gradually to have come into existence. It is during this era that gigantic prehistoric reptiles ruled the air, waters and the land. Monstrous dinosaurs, brontosaurs and other such creatures, crowded the earth. Some fed on vegetation, others were carnivorous (flesh-eaters) and destroyed one another, still others were omnivorous, eating both plants and animals. Most of them were apparently lumbering, slow-moving, and dull-witted, with tiny brains compared to the hugeness of their tough, scaly-skinned bodies. A few flying reptile species were able to eat

Draco (native of Malaya)

Pouch

Modern flying lizard
Figure 183

seeds and foliage of the trees and some ate animals smaller than themselves such as insects.

There is current a tiny descendant of the flying reptiles (**pterodactyls**), which is native to Malaya. It is called the Draco lizard, and measures up to ten inches from nose to tail. There is a pair of spreading membranes of skin between the limbs and supported by elongated ribs which enables it to glide from tree to tree, as far as 60 feet, in search of insects.

In the Mesozoic era there is evidence (a fossil imprint) of a bird-like animal which has been given the name, **Archaeopteryx.** It had features of both reptiles and modern birds. The imprint shows the presence of plumage but the skull is reptilian and contains teeth in the jaws, unlike the beak of a modern bird. Perhaps the Archaeopteryx was a stage in the evolution of birds from a reptile-like ancestor. See Fig. 184.

The Mesozoic period seems to have lasted for about 130 million years. Then the climate over the entire earth began to change again and the Cenozoic era began. Periods of extreme cold occurred, resulting in scarcity of food and killing off numerous huge reptiles and large plants. The surface of the earth changed. Mountain ranges such as the Himalayas and Alps appeared, as well as more continents of land.

Fossil and rock formations provide evidence that there was probably a land connexion between North America and the northern part of Europe, and also between North America and Asia. The North and South Americas were probably entirely separated.

Mammals, similar to those now in existence, began to appear. Many modern birds inhabited the sky and treetops. There were all types of invertebrates on land and in the air. Ancestors of every modern type of vertebrate inhabited

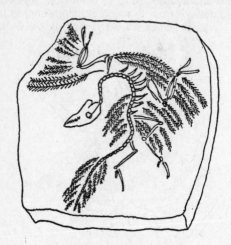

Fossil—Archaeopteryx
ancestor of modern bird   (imprint)
Figure 184

the part of the earth's crust to which it was best adapted for survival. Flowering plants of every variety, not nearly as huge as their predecessors, grew in all habitats.

Later in the Cenozoic era, man-like mammals began to appear in various parts of the earth (about 1 million years ago). Fossil skulls and other skeletal structures have been discovered. These indicate that earliest man, our ancestor, resembled modern man physically but also bore some resemblance to less highly specialized primate mammals, the anthropoid apes.

Again drastic changes in climate occurred. Huge glaciers spread from the poles, melting and retreating at intervals. Each time the land surface was covered by the massive sheets of ice, vegetation and some animal life died. Other animals fled before the oncoming glaciers to an environment in which they could adapt themselves to live. During the warm periods between glaciers, other plants and animals grew and flourished.

Fossils of prehistoric elephants some whole and with flesh and fur intact,

Mammoth—prehistoric elephant
Figure 185

have been found preserved, frozen solid in ice that has never melted since the glacial period.

In the most recent part of the Cenozoic era came the ancestors of modern man who had the ability to adjust to their environment and to control the factors in this environment. Later in the chapter, we will attempt to show how man, the most highly specialized animal, has changed in structure through the ages.

VOCABULARY

geologist	uranium	Archaeopteryx
palaeontologist	radioactive	Draco lizard
fossil	evolution	anthropoid
erosion	trilobite	pterodactyl
sedimentary	carboniferous	

Exercise No. 53

Select the correct word or phrase for each of the following:

1 Scientists who study the age of the earth from rocks and minerals are: (a) biologists; (b) palaeontologists; (c) astronomists; (d) geologists.
2 The layer of air surrounding the earth is called its: (a) gravity; (b) atmosphere; (c) orbit; (d) blanket.
3 Wind and flowing water wear away rock in an action called: (a) rotting; (b) sanding; (c) erosion; (d) blasting.
4 The radioactive mineral in the earth's crust which changes to lead is: (a) uranium; (b) aluminium; (c) platinum; (d) silver.
5 The rate at which the radioactive mineral changes to lead helps the geologist to judge the: (a) use of lead; (b) weight of the mineral; (c) age of the earth.

6 A gradual change, over a long period, in a form of life is known as: (a) erosion; (b) evolution; (c) revolution; (d) reduction.
7 Our coal beds were formed during the era known as: (a) Cenozoic; (b) Palaeozoic; (c) Mesozoic.
8 Scientists believe that all life originated in: (a) the sea; (b) the soil; (c) the ground; (d) the air.
9 Scientists have found plant fossils in coal beds. These are evidence of prehistoric: (a) giant oaks; (b) Sequoia; (c) thick vines; (d) fern forests.
10 The most recent group of plants to appear on earth is the: (a) flowering plants; (b) ferns; (c) pines; (d) bacteria.

Just as science has presented us with evidence of the gradual and constant changing of the earth's surface, so has it given evidence of the gradual changes in plant and animal life. Thus, also, it has given evidence of the gradual change of one particular species of plant or animal to another.

Scientists have found evidence that all living things have common ancestors. It is believed that each plant or animal branched off from the common ancestor to form a species that still retains characteristics resembling those of the original ancestral form. This belief or theory is known as evolution.

EVIDENCE OF EVOLUTION

The evolutionist bases his theories of relationships on evidence from many sources. Let us enumerate them:

Evidence from fossils (Palaeontological): Bones, teeth, shells and woody plant-parts are found in rocky layers petrified.

Whole animals are preserved in ice (mammoth); in amber, a hardened tree resin (prehistoric insects, spiders and some amphibians); in tar pits (prehistoric or primitive camels, sabre-tooth tigers, giraffes); in peat bogs and quicksand (mastadon and huge insects); and in coal beds (giant ferns, etc.).

Impressions, imprints and moulds (preserved outlines of an animal or plant, the soft parts of which have disintegrated) have been discovered.

Evidence from successive rock formations (Geological): The simplest forms of life appear to be in the lowest or oldest layers of rock. Logical sequence indicates the gradual change from a simple form to the more highly specialized form of plant or animal.

Evidence shows that the oldest forms of life were all sea dwellers. Life then, it has been deduced must have originated in the sea.

Fossils in adjoining rock layers are more closely alike than those with layers of rock separating them.

Some forms of plants and animals which existed in prehistoric periods, ceased completely to exist after drastic changes in climate, natural food supply and changes in the earth's crust.

Fossils have been found which show characteristics of two successive plant or animal groups (successive in specialization of structure).

Fossils in successive rock layers indicate gradual changes (evolution) in the structure of a specific animal or plant from the time it first appeared to the present. For example, the primitive horse, **Eohippus,** was about the size of a dog, with a short skull, four-toed front feet and three-toed hind feet. Fossils have been found which reveal a gradual change in the size and structure of the horse. The present modern horse, **Equus,** is much larger, has a long skull, and a single toe on each foot which has become enlarged, solid and horny—a hoof.

Evidence from comparative anatomy: Structural similarities among different and apparently unrelated plants and animals yield additional significant evidence.

The arm of man, the flipper of a whale, the wing of a bat, and the wing of a bird are similar in skeletal structure. All are organs that aid in locomotion. See Fig. 187.

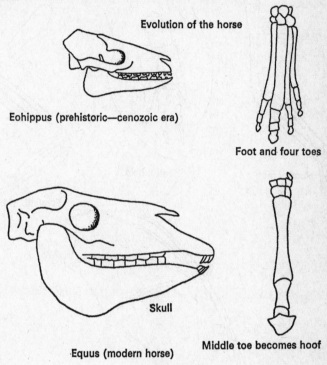

Evolution of the horse

Eohippus (prehistoric—cenozoic era)

Foot and four toes

Skull

Equus (modern horse)

Middle toe becomes hoof

Figure 186

The bony backbones of vertebrates are similar; and that of all mammals, even more so.

The digestive systems, and other systems of vertebrates are structurally and functionally similar. They are particularly similar within a group of like vertebrates. For example, all mammals, including man, have very similar brains and central nervous systems.

Evidence from vestigial structures: There are a few structures found to exist in animals which are useless to a specific species. These are called vestigial structures. Similar structures are found to exist and to be useful in other related species of animals. These tend to suggest common ancestry; and also to show a common genetic relationship among even apparently unrelated animals.

For example, small bones representing the pelvic girdle and hind limbs are

found in the snake. Since snakes have no limbs, these bones are useless structures, but show that snakes are descended from normal reptiles with functional limbs.

Evidence from biochemistry: There is evidence also from the similarity of
the chemical composition of all protoplasm. Scientists have been able to determine the elements, the compounds and their proportions, which compose

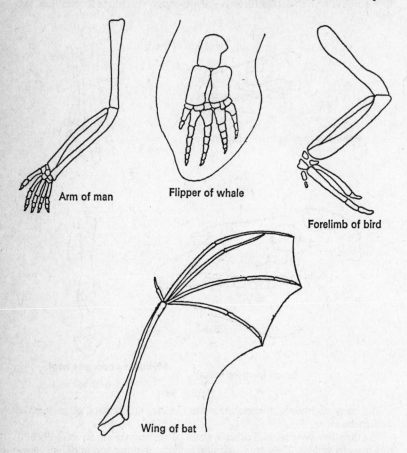

Arm of man

Flipper of whale

Forelimb of bird

Wing of bat

Evidence of evolution (comparative anatomy of forelimb structure).

Figure 187

all protoplasm. Although the basic composition is known, scientists are as yet
unable to combine the chemicals in a test tube to produce protoplasm.

Another point of chemical evidence is the fact that all plant and animal cells
carry on the basic life processes (e.g. respiration, digestion, excretion, etc.).

Evidence also shows close blood relationships among vertebrate animals.
It also shows cell sap relationships among plants.

Different citrus fruits (orange, lemon, grapefruit, lime) are structurally similar and produce the same type of cell sap, citric acid.

In vertebrate animals, all red blood corpuscles contain haemoglobin.

The chemical nature of blood serum of all mammals is almost the same.

The closer the groups of animals which are structurally related, the more nearly alike is the chemistry of their blood.

Evidence from a comparative study of the developmental stages of plants and animals, **embryology** further proves that there is a relationship between the most highly specialized form of life and the most simple. Let us consider vertebrate animals:

They start life as a fertilized egg cell, the result of the fusion of a male gamete with a female gamete. The embryos of all vertebrates are very similar in their early stages. The early embryos of mammals contain structures which

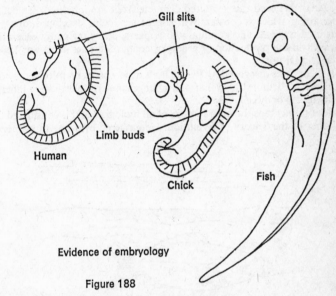

Gill slits

Limb buds

Human

Chick

Fish

Evidence of embryology

Figure 188

resemble the embryonic forms of less highly developed animals. These structures sometimes disappear as an embryo reaches maturity, or remain as vestigial structures.

For example, the human embryo has paired gill slits (which later disappear) in an early stage. This seems to be evidence of a common water-living ancestor. The human embryo has a small tail, the coccyx (which becomes vestigial)—possible evidence of a common ancestor with a tail.

The study of genetics and its practical application to plant and animal breeding provides further evidence of evolution.

The production of new varieties by careful selection, inbreeding and hybridization show how plants are able to change from one generation to another.

The inheritance of physical variations furnishes further proof of this.

Scientific tables of classification of all plants and animals have been devised by taxonomists, as based on structural resemblances among the existing

forms and fossil evidence of prehistoric and extinct forms. General divisions
in the classification of plants and animals are based on general or basic similarities in structure. Specific groups within a general division are based on
closer, more detailed similarities of individual plants or animals.

Many scientists have studied the evolutionary changes among plants and
animals. A few have attempted to explain how these changes come about.
Among the most prominent are JEAN LAMARCK, CHARLES DARWIN and HUGO
DE VRIES. Present experimenters in genetics and breeding favour a combination of the theories of Darwin and de Vries and tend largely to discount the
theories of Lamarck.

THEORIES OF EVOLUTION

Let us summarize the theories of each of the following scientists:

LAMARCK believed that acquired characteristics are inherited. He believed
that an organ which is constantly used becomes highly developed, one which
is not used weakens and eventually disappears, and after many generations,
will result in the production of a new or changed species. This was his Law
of Use and Disuse.

His theory was disproved by Weismann's experiments on mice and by other
scientists who demonstrated that only changes in germ plasm were inherited,
not changes in body cell plasm.

DARWIN is perhaps the most famous of all biologists and is considered to be
the father of the Theory of Evolution. He gathered evidence to support his

Figure 189   Struggle for existence

theories during twenty years of experimentation and research all over the
world. Darwin's theories of evolution, published in *The Origin of Species* in
1859, follow a specific pattern:

All living things produce more offspring than can normally live to maturity
(over production). A competitive struggle for existence takes place among
them to secure sufficient food, water and shelter for survival.

No two animals or plants are alike. There is variation even within an immediate family.

The organisms which survive are those with variations that best fit them or adapt them to their environment. (Natural selection.)

These organisms best adapted to cope with the factors in the environment will survive and reproduce themselves (survival of the fittest). The others will perish.

This will result in the evolution of a new species. Darwin's theories are accepted as sound by scientists generally. His theories, however, are now known to contain certain weaknesses.

Some characteristics which adapt an organism for survival may have been acquired because of more favourable environmental factors in a natural habitat; these characteristics are not heritable; new species do not necessarily develop from inheritance of variations.

HUGO DE VRIES, after his many experiments with mutations in evening primroses, formulated his theories on the nature of evolution. He stated that new species developed in nature only after a mutation appeared which was favourable to the survival of the organism. Since a mutation results from a sudden variation in germ plasm, it is therefore heritable. Organisms which possess the favourable variation pass it on from one generation to the next and a new species comes into being.

VOCABULARY

fossil	mastodon	taxonomist
amber	mammoth	morphology
tar pit	Eohippus	natural selection
peat bog	Equus	survival
quicksand	hoof	

Exercise No. 54

Match a number in Column *A* with a letter in Column *B*.

A	*B*
1 fossil	a famous evolutionist
2 probable origin of life	b petrified remains of prehistoric life
3 vestigial organ	c medium for fossils
4 a theory of evolution	d prehistoric horse
5 probable ancestor of birds	e pelvic girdle of snake
6 Charles Darwin	f classification
7 amber	g one-celled organism
8 mastodon	h Archaeopteryx
9 taxonomy	i survival of the fittest
10 Eohippus	j prehistoric elephant-like animal

THE EVOLUTION OF MAN

It is generally recognized that:

Man belongs to the Animal Kingdom.

Man is a vertebrate animal.

Man is a mammal.

Man is a member of the Primate group of mammals (flexible-fingered, well-developed brain, nails on fingers and toes) to which monkeys, and apes belong.

Man is the only member of a family group called Hominidae of which there is but one known species, Homo sapiens (wise man).

It is believed that man and monkeys are related indirectly through a common ancestor.

Fossil evidence, parts of skulls, teeth and a few skeletal bones, indicates that man-like mammals first appeared on earth about a million years ago and modern man, Homo sapiens, about 25,000 years ago.

The discovery of tools and other artifacts (implements) and primitive paintings obviously used and made by man, as well as fossil remains, gives us some

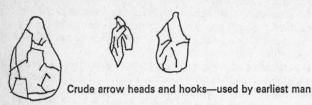

Crude arrow heads and hooks—used by earliest man

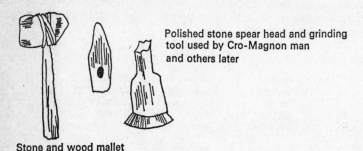

Polished stone spear head and grinding tool used by Cro-Magnon man and others later

Stone and wood mallet

Artifacts—(tools and implements used by prehistoric man)

Figure 190

indications of evolutionary changes in the physical structure of man and in his mode of living.

The implements used for hunting food, for protection against natural enemies, for building shelter, for fashioning body coverings and finally for means of transportation are all indications of man's attempt to adapt himself to his environment, of his struggle for survival.

Fragmentary fossils of several types of prehistoric man have been found in various parts of the world. Anthropologists and palaeontologists have worked together and reconstructed, using the fossil fragments, what they believe to be approximate representations of each type of man. For this difficult task, it is necessary to have an unerring knowledge of human anatomy.

FROM PREHISTORIC TO MODERN MAN

Among the outstanding types of prehistoric man (each was named after the geographical location in which fossils were found) are the following:

Java Ape-Man. Fossil remains of the skull and teeth were discovered by Dubois in 1891. A fragment of a thigh bone was subsequently found. Upon reconstruction, it was estimated that this primitive man-like creature, who lived about a half million years ago, was about five and a half feet tall. Because he apparently walked erect he was named Pithecanthropus erectus. The skull cavity indicates a small brain (but larger than that of an average adult ape), narrow forehead, protruding brow, wide and flat nose and a heavy jaw with no distinct chin. No artifacts were found which might give some clue to the mode of living or culture of the creature.

Heidelberg Man. Very fragmentary fossils of this type of man were found in Heidelberg, Germany (only a lower jaw including teeth). Fossils of animals found with the jawbone indicate this early man lived about 300,000 years ago. He was named Homo heidelbergensis.

Peking Man. Fossil remains of at least forty different individuals of the same species have been unearthed. This primitive man who lived about a quarter of a million years ago, appears to have been similar in physical structure to the Java Man except that the size of the skull cavity indicates a larger brain. The discovery of crudely fashioned stone tools, charred animal bones and fire dugouts seems to indicate a primitive culture. It seems also to indicate

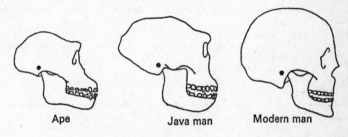

Figure 191   Evolution of man from apes (skulls)

the discovery of fire for cooking and for warmth. The increased size of the brain substantiates the fact that this primitive man (Sinanthropus pekinensis) developed the beginnings of a culture.

Neanderthal Man. (Homo neanderthalensis.) Many skulls and other skeletal structures (some complete) were found in various parts of Europe, Asia and Africa. Evidence is conclusive that they were a species of Homo—existing, apparently, about 25,000 to 50,000 years ago. They were about five feet tall, of stocky muscular development and large heavy head. These were cave dwellers (cave men) who used implements of flint and bone for protection, hunting and eating. They obviously used fire for cooking and warmth, and fashioned and used animal skins for body coverings. The discovery of burial grounds in caves is further evidence of a culture. Neanderthal Man was too specialized, and too recent in time to be our direct ancestor. He represents an offshoot of the main evolutionary line which became extinct with the increasing competition of Homo sapiens.

Cro-Magnon Man. Many fossil remains of what were probably the direct ancestors of modern Homo sapiens were found in Southern France and Spain. In physical structure, they were tall (about six feet for the average adult), well-proportioned, with a high forehead and a large, well-developed brain. Cro-

Magnon Man was artistic as well as practical, as indicated by the excellent coloured paintings on the stone walls of his caves (some in Lascaux, France) and skilful carvings on tools and other artifacts. His implements were fashioned of stone, bone, horn and ivory. There is evidence that needles made of bone were used to sew clothing. There is also evidence that male and female wore carved jewellery as well as leather body-coverings. It is believed that they cooked their food in hot water as well as over an open fire. Household utensils,

RACE	HEREDITARY PHYSICAL TRAITS	NATIVE GEOGRAPHIC LOCATION
Negroid	Skin colour: grey-brown to dark brown and black Hair: dark brown to black; frizzy to woolly Eyes: generally dark brown to black Nose: broad Lips: generally thick	Many islands in Pacific Ocean, in Africa, Australia Members of the race: African Negroes, Ethiopians, Hottentots, Bushmen, Pygmies (very short in stature)
Mongoloid	Skin colour: yellow to reddish-brown Hair: black, straight, coarse Eyes: dark brown, generally almond-shaped Nose: low-bridge, smallish except for American Indian Head: broad, small	North American, eastern Asia, Malaya, Siberia Members of the race: Eskimos, Chinese, Filipinos, Japanese, American Indians
Caucasian	Generally fair-skinned with blond, fine hair and light blue or grey eyes; generally tall, large-framed with long, narrow head	Northern Europe (Nordic) Norwegians, Swedes
	Generally ruddy-skinned with straighter, darker hair than those in northern Europe. Eyes usually light to dark brown; body structure generally shorter than northern Europeans with shorter, broader heads	Central Europe (Russia, Poland, Germany and Northern Italy) (Alpine stock) Russians, Polish, some Italians
	Generally olive-skinned, with dark-brown to black, wavy hair. A tendency towards more slender body structure than central Europeans	Southern Europe (Italy, Greece) Mediterranean stock
	Generally olive or darker skinned than southern Europeans. Dark, fine hair. Lighter body structure than southern Europeans	Southwestern Asia (northern and central India) Asian Indians and Arabs (Hindu stock)

(Notice that the Caucasian race is subdivided to represent members whose geographical location seems to have some effect on external characteristics.)

pots, spoons and a type of fork, have been found. This was truly a culture of modern man.

'Piltdown Man.' A skull and lower jaw were found in England which seemed to indicate a definite advance in the higher forehead and straighter brow of the skull. The jaws and teeth still had an apelike appearance. It was estimated that this primitive man must have existed about 300,000 years ago. He was still not classified as a human being.

Research scientists were suspicious of the circumstances under which the fossils were found and also the patness with which they fitted into the theoretical evolution of man. Intensive investigations and study were undertaken. It was discovered, as a result, that the Piltdown fossils were not authentic, that they were in fact a hoax.

RACES OF MAN

Originally scientists who concentrated on the study of man (anthropologists) divided all Homo sapiens into three major groups which they called races, based on similarities of inherited physical structures. This artificial classification was made to simplify the study of the evolution of man and variations among men.

Fossils and artifacts of early man have been found scattered all over the world. From recorded history, we know that the species, man, has travelled much, developed cultures and destroyed cultures. In most habitats, he has adapted himself successfully.

Since the beginning of man's time on earth, there has been constant intermingling and inter-marriage of all representatives of the human species. As a result, there is no absolutely pure race among the three stock races into which scientists have catalogued man.

A race of man refers to a group in the species of Homo sapiens which shares certain hereditary physical traits. The three major races of mankind are: Negroid, Mongoloid and Caucasian. See the chart on page 284.

SUMMARY

The age of the earth has been estimated by studying the rate of sedimentation, the formation of sedimentary rock, the rate of change of radioactive uranium to lead, and the degree of saltness of seas.

Fossils found in various rock strata indicate the type of life which existed on earth throughout the ages, the gradual changes organisms have undergone (evolution) and the relationships of all living organisms.

Life appears to have originated as a simple, one-celled organism in a salt-water environment. The simplest forms of life have been found in the oldest and deepest rock strata.

All living things have probably descended from a common ancestor and are therefore related to one another.

Theories of evolution are based on evidence from fossils, similarities of body structures, vestigial structures, embryonic development, common structure and function of protoplasm, blood relationships and results of breeding experiments.

Classification (taxonomy) of plants and animals is based on similarities of structure.

The one known species of man, Homo sapiens, fits into his place in the animal kingdom as a vertebrate, a mammal, and a Primate with hands for grasping and fingers and toes with nails.

There is evidence that man and other primates stem from a common ancestor.

VOCABULARY

primate	Caucasian	Peking man
Hominidae	anthropologist	Heidelberg man
Negroid	race	Neanderthal man
Mongoloid	Java ape-man	Cro-Magnon Man

Exercise No. 55

Complete each of the following:

1 Man belongs to the group of mammals called ——.
2 The scientific name of modern man is ——.
3 A scientist who studies man and his place on earth is called an ——.
4 A group of human beings with similar hereditary physical traits is known as a ——.
5 The three stock races of mankind are ——.
6 It is believed that modern man originated about —— years ago.
7 All races of man have —— blood groups.
8 Anthropologists believe that man and other primates are related because they arose from a ——.

CHAPTER XVII

CONSERVATION

As we traced life from the beginning, from pre-history onwards as recorded in the rocks of the earth's crust, we have witnessed the interdependence of all plants and animals. Each discovery of fossils reinforced the law that where there were animals, there were plants. We know that a large variety of flora and fauna survived, and that some have ceased to exist (become extinct). Examples of the latter are the great auk and the dodo. Only living organisms which can adjust to the environment in their natural habitats can survive and produce offspring for many generations.

We have discovered that specific kinds of plants and animals live together in mutual interdependence, and will not be found in the same grouping anywhere else.

We know the importance of green plants in the cycle of living organisms. In the process of photosynthesis, where there is an exchange of the gases vital to all living plants and animals, we locate the original source of all food.

BALANCE IN NATURE

In the cycles of elements (carbon cycle, oxygen cycle, nitrogen, mineral and water cycles) we saw the frugality of nature in using and reusing all of the

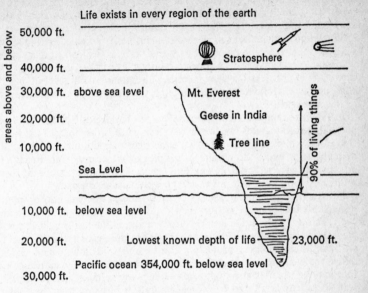

Figure 192

Figure 193 Migration of Canadian geese

existing elements—never destroying matter, only changing its form. The symbiotic, parasitic and saprophytic relationships take on new significance in the scheme of maintaining a balance in nature.

This important balance in nature remains undisturbed after thousands of years, except when interrupted by natural catastrophic phenomena such as volcanoes, earthquakes, tornadoes, typhoons, hurricanes and floods. Unfortunately, man has it in his power to upset the balance of nature. But man, if he chooses, has also the knowledge and ability to restore, by slow degrees, what he has destroyed.

In 1869 ERNST HAECKEL introduced the new science of **Ecology,** which is at present one of the fields most open for research. It is the study of the relationship of each plant and animal to all other plants and animals in their natural habitats. It provides the guiding principles by which man can create a programme of conservation of our natural resources, and thus restore the successful balance of nature without which he would cease to exist.

For hundreds, if not thousands of years, and in many countries, man has given some sort of protection to those wild animals he has used for food and sport. But it is only in the last 150 years or so that he has sought to preserve plants and animals for their own sake and for future generations. Today there are many national laws protecting forests and wild flowers and providing refuge for wild animal life such as deer, wildcats and many species of birds. International treaties also exist to preserve many animals such as whales and seals from extinction and to protect migratory birds such as the Canadian geese. See Fig. 193.

CONSERVATION OF FORESTS

The value of forests is immeasurable. Some trees provide timber for building homes, wood for furniture, and pulp for the manufacture of rayon, paper and paper products. Other trees are valuable for their turpentines, resins and

Figure 194 Denuded forest area

dyes. By-products of the timber industries produce in turn large quantities of alcohol. Forests provide natural habitats for wildlife. They serve to prevent erosion of soil, and so to prevent floods. Not least, they are beautiful.

Destruction of forest lands, by man and plant disease, can be prevented by well-planned conservation programmes set up by Forestry commissions in

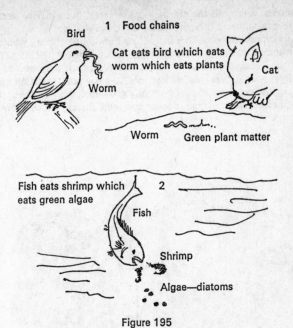

1   Food chains

Cat eats bird which eats worm which eats plants

Bird

Worm

Cat

Worm   Green plant matter

Fish eats shrimp which eats green algae

2

Fish

Shrimp

Algae—diatoms

Figure 195

Figure 196   Animals protected by game laws

most countries, and with the aid of local services, both private and public. Here are several valuable measures in forest conservation:

Wise forest management. This includes planned tree-cutting which should be done in such a way as to avoid injury to the undergrowth. This will make it easier for the young seedlings to grow quickly. Scientifically trained men go periodically through areas from which trees have been cut: (a) to cut out shoots from the cut ends of stumps, which usually grow into inferior trees; (b) to get rid of weed trees such as birch, poplar and wild cherry, which grow rapidly,

Conservation of wildlife (beavers building dam)
Figure 197

but which are not good for timber; and (c) to thin out undesirable seedlings so as to ensure enough space and nourishment for the best growth of the desired ones.

Reafforestation: This refers to the planting of new trees in areas badly denuded by fire or disease, where the natural plant successions will not appear. Varieties of young trees that would grow together normally are planted.

Protection of young growing trees.

Limiting cutting of trees to those which are mature.

Combating and preventing plant diseases.

Preventing careless fires, and controlling accidental forest fires, with forest fire fighting equipment.

Education of the public to the value of forests and the significance of conservation.

By conserving forests, wildlife is also conserved, thus helping to keep the balance of nature. Wildlife refers to all manner of animals that live in the forests and in its streams and rivers.

An important branch of ecology is the study of food chains—the sequence of animals, each of which eats, or lives on (as a parasite or saprophyte) the next organism in the series, thus helping to preserve the natural balance in a given habitat. All food chains end with or begin with a green plant, the original source of all food. Examples of food chains are:

Man eats cattle; cattle eat grass.

Cat eats bird; bird eats worm; worm eats tiny green plants in soil.

Fish eat shrimp; shrimp eat green algae. See Fig. 195.

Golden eagle

Avocet

Figure 198 Protection of birds

CONSERVATION OF WILDLIFE

The economic importance of wildlife is manifold. Water-living animals such as clams, oysters, lobsters, shrimp, squid and fish are used extensively as food. Some fish produce vital oils, others, fertilizer. Oysters produce pearls. Useful insects destroy insects which damage our crops, and some which harbour disease-producing organisms. Birds destroy harmful rodents and man's insect-enemies. Seed-eating birds tend to restrict the spread of weeds.

We secure meat, leather and furs from some animals. The beaver is useful for its fur, and for preventing soil erosion and floods through the building of dams. Many fur farms breed silver fox, mink, muskrat and beaver for commercial reasons, and serve to prevent a possible extinction of the species.

Fish hawk or osprey

Various laws to protect natural wildlife have been put into effect:

Game laws limit seasons for hunting and fishing, specify kinds of animals, minimum size of animal and maximum quantity which may be hunted and caught. Closed seasons are declared during the breeding seasons of each animal.

Nature reserves and national parks are found throughout the world for the encouragement of the growth of wildlife, and areas of land set aside where no killing is allowed. In Scotland, one such reserve protects the Scots pine, arctic-alpine plants, deer, wild-

**Bird of valuable plumage
Figure 199**

cats, golden eagles and buzzards. In Suffolk, avocets have been able to re-establish breeding colonies. Huge tracts of country in East Africa give freedom and safety to large game animals including the white rhinoceros, dangerously close to extinction. Koala bears, pelicans, lyre birds and rare orchids are protected in Australian reserves.

Governments have also done much to protect their own fishing and shell-

Figure 200   Salmon leaping falls—to spawning grounds

fish industries. Fish hatcheries, have been set up where many different species of fresh- and salt-water fish are reared under natural conditions.

Public lakes and rivers are stocked from the hatcheries, for example, with trout and salmon.

Wildflowers grow profusely in country fields. But in wooded areas, there are few wildflowers, for many species have become extinct. Private organiza-

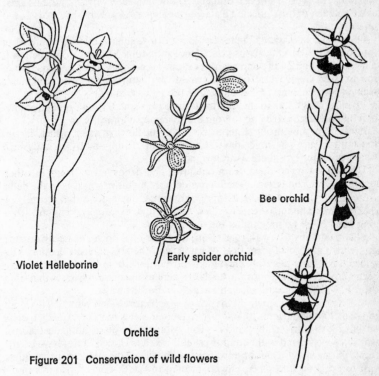

Violet Helleborine

Early spider orchid

Bee orchid

Orchids

Figure 201 Conservation of wild flowers

tions such as the Wild Flower Preservation Society help in the conservation of already rare natural-growing blossoms.

CONSERVATION OF SOIL

Soil is the source of life, providing raw materials and point of anchorage for our vast variety of plant food and other plant products. It is approximately a 7-inch layer of invaluable, yet greatly abused, natural resource.

All soil originated from rocks. Atmospheric conditions of alternating cold and warmth, chemical changes and erosion by the wind, running water and moving sheets of ice (glaciers) over a long period of time break up surface rocks into the small particles that form top-soil.

Plants living in top-soil, from which they get water containing dissolved minerals and nitrates, contribute to the formation of the soil. The excreta of animals which live in the soil (almost all wild animals spend all or part of their lives in and on the soil) contribute to the fertility of the soil. Bacteria of decay feed on dead plants and animals, and return to the soil elements vital to living, growing plants. Top-soil contains organic matter known as humus.

Top-soil is varied in texture from coarse to fine, and varied in the amount of organic materials and water it contains. Soils also vary in the amount and kinds of minerals and nitrates. Some soils are basically acid; others, basically alkaline. The type of soil determines the flora and fauna which inhabit its area, and the soil is, in turn, affected by the type of living organisms that grow in and on it.

Obviously, damage or depletion (loss of organic and mineral content) of top-soil will result in a serious imbalance of nature. Widespread depletion is a menace to human life and man's economic security. Causes of depletion of soil may be chemical or physical, caused by natural phenomena or man's recklessness. Damage to the soil may be brought about by:

Erosion. This refers to the wearing away of top-soil. It is a natural phenomenon that has been taking place from the beginning of time.

Erosion may be brought about by falling or flowing water, which carries top-soil particles with it. Rain water, water from streams and rivers, and ocean waters pounding the shore wear away soil.

Top-soil is carried away from one area, and deposited in heaps in other regions, which sometimes benefit considerably by the process, as in the delta areas of the Nile and the Mississippi. Water running in areas that are hilly or rocky or mountainous creates gullies, ravines and, eventually, canyons. Running water levels off mountains and fills in valleys.

Where land is thick with vegetation, the roots hold down the richly organic soil, which absorbs a great deal of water, and thereby prevents erosion. Denuded forest land therefore encourages erosion. Fields in which animals have been allowed to graze until the fields are bare of the natural grasses that bind the soil, will be subject to erosion by rain and flowing water.

Much erosion is caused by the wind, which carries and blows away loose top-soil. 70 million acres of land in the United States have been made useless or difficult to cultivate, by wind erosion. Many of the devastating dust storms which have occurred in the south-west and western United States have been a result of man's contribution towards the imbalance of nature. Cutting down vast forest lands for timber, unwise farming and cattle-raising methods result in exposure of more and more top-soil to the ravages of the elements.

Depletion of soil. This occurs when top-soil loses its natural minerals and organic content over a period of years. This makes the soil useless for growing most crops—hence more vulnerable to erosion by wind and water.

Man is usually the cause of soil depletion. Unscientific raising of crops—for example, planting the same crop in one field year after year, thereby requiring the same minerals, will result in chemically worn out and useless soil. Subsequent erosion of the remaining minerals by water renders the soil almost valueless.

Man has come to realize the ultimate danger to top-soil, our basic source of food, shelter and clothing. Agricultural scientists have experimented with methods of repairing top-soil damage. They have also developed scientific methods for preventing such damage in the future. The knowledge of ecology has been responsible to a great extent for the formulated methods of preserving rich top-soil.

SCIENTIFIC FARMING

There are several scientific methods of farming which will help in the conserving of soil. Among them are the following:

To prevent erosion by rain, flowing water and wind:

Planting of soil-binding grasses, shrubs and trees on a part of land where prevailing winds will be blocked, thus helping to prevent erosion by wind. Soil-binding plants also help prevent erosion by rain, because of the absorbent mat they form.

Contour planting of crops on slopes and hillsides helps prevent erosion by run-off rain-water, and helps absorb rain-water.

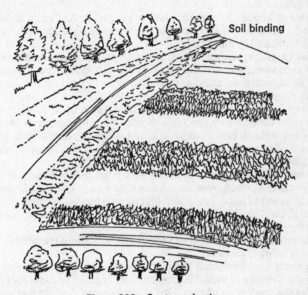

Soil binding

Figure 202 Contour planting

Strip cropping—that is, planting alternating rows of soil-binding and non-soil-binding crops in contour planting. This helps prevent erosion by both wind and run-off water.

Digging trenches or channels to catch and direct run-off water helps in terrace planting on hillsides (steps around a slope).

Reafforestation of areas of land around sources of rivers helps prevent erosion by river water and floods.

The use of soil-binding plants in projects other than farming is most important. Areas of dust storms (Dust Bowl of the south-west United States) can be controlled to some degree. Roads are protected from washouts by soil-binding vegetation planted in rows in strategic areas.

To prevent depletion of fertile soil:

Crop rotation—that is, planting alternating crops, each needing different

minerals or amounts of minerals and other soil-bearing substances, in successive years.

Replacing depleted organic matter by adding fertilizers, crop residues (stalks
of corn and cotton, straw from wheat and rye, pods of beans and peas—in
other words, unused crop parts that might be otherwise disposed of as
waste). The soil in domestic back gardens can be replenished by keeping a
compost heap: that is, grass cuttings, vegetable parings, leaves, etc., in a pile
to decay, and then adding in to your garden soil in the spring.

Mixing phosphate fertilizer and bone meal (ground animal bones) to replace
used, vital phosphorus in the soil.

Planting leguminous plants (with nitrogen-fixing nodules) such as clover,
alfalfa, lupin, etc., in rotation with wheat, corn and oats helps to replenish the
used nitrate compounds.

Addition of lime or lime compounds to counteract basically acid soil in which
legumes do not grow. This replaces the calcium and magnesium which has been
taken from the soil by other crops.

Ministries of Agriculture issue scientific and practical bulletins to all
farmers concerning scientific farming for their particular type of farmland.

How do conservation and control of our water supply help to maintain the
vital balance of nature?

All plants and animals, including man, need water, in varying amounts, to
carry on the functions or processes of life. Water-living plants or animals
cannot exist on land. Land-living plants and animals cannot exist in water for
any length of time—but they cannot exist without water. Amphibious forms
are adapted to live in both habitats. Man needs water to live.

A farmer whose land does not border on a pool, lake or stream, or contain
some swampland, must rely on artificial irrigation (man-made means of
supplying water) of some sort to keep his crops and cattle, and himself, alive.

In addition to its being essential to life, water, with its power provides us
with energy (either as such, or converted into electricity).

Water provides us directly with sources of food, being the natural habitat
of so many living organisms.

Huge dams have been built in order to control swift-flowing rivers and to
prevent the flooding of valuable farm and city lands. The dams also provide
power for the production of electricity. It is in times of drought that we realize
just how important water is to life, and why we must conserve and control it.

SUMMARY

Living organisms exist in communities in and on the earth, in fresh and salt
water, and in the atmosphere around the earth.

All plants and animals, including man, are dependent upon one another.

Green plants provide the original source of all food for all living organisms.
The process of photosynthesis is perhaps the key to all life.

The interdependence of plants and animals with their symbiotic, parasitic
and saprophytic relationships results in the balance of nature.

Matter is never wasted, destroyed or lost; it is only changed in form. We
recognize this in the various cycles of life: carbon, oxygen, mineral and water
cycles.

Man has helped to create an imbalance in nature by destroying forests and wildlife, damaging and depleting soil, and wasting and polluting water. An active, concentrated programme of conservation of natural resources will help restore the balance of nature, which is vital to the successful living of plants and animals, and therefore to man.

VOCABULARY

extinct	bone meal	irrigation
ecology	compost heap	depletion of soil
game law	food chain	conservation
insectivorous	fur farm	soil binding
reafforestation	closed season	contour planting
wildlife	migratory	terracing
crop rotation	stock	strip cropping
crop residue	hatcheries	

Exercise No. 56

Complete the following definitions:

1 The science that deals with the interrelationships of living things with one another and their environment is called ——.
2 The specific environment of a given group of plants and animals is known as the ——.
3 A series of organisms, each of which feeds on the next organism, the beginning or ending of which is a green plant, is called a ——.
4 The interdependence of plants and animals that tends to maintain each species, and at the same time keep it from overwhelming another, is called the —— in nature.
5 Animals growing in natural habitats are known as ——.
6 Replacing cut mature trees in forests is known as ——.
7 The manufacturing of food within a green plant is known as ——.
8 Animals which eat insects are called ——.
9 Filling lakes, ponds and streams with young, cultured fish is known as ——.
10 The wearing away of top-soil is known as ——.
11 The using up of natural minerals, nitrates, etc., in the soil is known as —— of the soil.
12 Plants like alfalfa and clover, which harbour nitrogen-fixing bacteria on their roots, are known as —— plants.

Exercise No. 57

Which one term in each of the following includes the other three?

1 crop rotation, scientific farming, terracing, replenishing soil
2 control of plant diseases, reafforestation, fire protection, forest conservation
3 natural resources, forest land, wildlife, top-soil
4 song birds, beavers, wildlife, deer
5 ducks, migratory birds, geese, swallows
6 minerals, calcium, phosphorus, sulphur
7 humus, sand, top-soil, loam

APPENDIX A

CLASSIFICATION OF THE ANIMAL AND PLANT KINGDOMS

NOTE: The details provided in this Appendix are not to be taken as complete or as permanently fixed. They are only approximate, and an attempt has been made to make them consistent with the consensus of the most reliable scientific opinion. As must be expected, there is substantial difference of opinion among scientists, and of course the details are always subject to change as scientific knowledge is modified and expanded by new findings.

Classification

All living things are divided into two major divisions: the Animal Kingdom and the Plant Kingdom. Each of the Kingdoms is further subdivided into smaller and more detailed groups, finally reaching the individual plant or animal.

The Animal Kingdom has ten major divisions, each of which is called a **Phylum.** The subdivisions of phyla (pl.) are known as **Classes;** the subdivisions of Classes are **Orders;** and of orders, **Families.** Families are subdivided into **Genera** and then into the individual animal, called the **Species.**

The following classification is simplified. We will present the detailed subdivisions only in the last Phylum.

THE ANIMAL KINGDOM

Phylum: Protozoa. Simple, one-cell animals, living independently or in colonies; found in water, air, land, and in other living organisms; about 20,000 known species. Examples: Amoeba, Paramecium, Plasmodium.

Phylum: Porifera. Animals with two-layered bodies; found most commonly in salt water, attached to rocks or other objects; cellular support of lime, silica or spongin; about 3,000 known species. Examples: Grantia, Venus flower basket, common natural bath sponge.

Phylum: Coelenterata. Generally, salt-water animals; mouth surrounded by tentacles; central hollow digestive cavity; about 9,500 known species. Examples: Hydra, coral, jellyfish, sea anemone.

Phylum: Platyhelminthes. Flatworms; three-layered animals with bilateral symmetry; mostly parasitic; about 7,000 known species. Examples: Planaria, tapeworm, liver fluke.

Phylum: Nematoda. Roundworms; have long slender bodies with digestive tube which opens at both ends; about 3,500 known species. Examples: hookworm, porkworm (Trichinella), vinegar eel.

Phylum: Annelida. Segmented worms; bilateral symmetry; closed circulatory system; about 6,500 known species. Examples: earthworm, sandworm, leech.

Phylum: Mollusca. Unsegmented, soft bodies, covered with calcareous shells; soft ventral foot for locomotion; about 80,000 known species. Examples: clam, oyster, snail, squid, octopus, cuttlefish.

Phylum: Arthropoda. Animals with jointed, paired appendages; exoskeletons of chitin or lime; about 75,000 known species. Examples: centipede, millipede, crab, lobster, mite, tick, scorpion, king crab, all insects, spider.

Phylum: Echinodermata. Marine animals with spiny skins; skeleton of limestone plates sometimes covers body; radial symmetry; organs of locomotion operated by a water system; about 6,000 known species. Examples: starfish, sea cucumber, sea urchin, sea lily, brittle star.

Phylum: Chordata. Vertebrates; animals with internal notochord (primitive backbone); bilateral symmetry; dorsal nerve cord; gill slits at some time during the life cycle; about 70,000 known species.

Class: Pisces. Fish; breathe by means of gills; two-chambered hearts; bodies covered with scales; about 20,000 known species. Examples: lamprey eel, all fish including sharks.

Class: Amphibia. Breathe by means of gills in larval stage, through lungs in adult; cold-blooded; three-chambered heart; complete metamorphosis; about 4,000 known species. Examples: frog, toad, salamander, mud puppy, newt.

Class: Reptilia. Breathe by means of lungs throughout life; three-chambered heart (except in crocodiles and alligators four-chambered); body usually covered with scales; eggs laid in leathery shells; about 5,000 known species. Examples: turtle, horned toad, chameleon, Gila monster, snake, alligator, crocodile.

Class: Aves. Birds; warm-blooded with high body temperature; body covered with feathers; front limbs modified to form wings; hollow bones; eggs laid in lime shells; breathe by means of lungs; about 23,000 known species. Examples: all birds.

Class: Mammalia. Warm-blooded; body covered with hair or fur; diaphragm separates chest from abdominal cavity; young born alive and nourished from mammary glands; about 13,000 known species.

Order: Monotremata. Egg-laying mammals. Examples: duck-billed platypus, spiny ant-eater.

Order: Marsupialia. Mammals with pouches. Examples: opossum, kangaroo, koala bear.

Order: Edentata. Although some are toothless, most lack front teeth only; live on ants and termites. Examples: sloth, hairy ant-eater, ant-bear, armadillo, aardvark.

Order: Insectivora. Insect-eating mammals; usually nocturnal in habits. Examples: hedgehog, mole, shrew.

Order: Cetacea. Marine mammals; fore-limbs modified into paddles; hind-limbs absent. Examples: whale, dolphin, porpoise.

Order: Carnivora. Flesh-eating mammals; canine and molar teeth well developed in strong jaws. Examples: aquatic forms—seal, walrus, sea lion; Terrestrial—bear, raccoon, wolf, cat, dog, lion, weasel, otter, mink, etc.

Order: Rodentia. Gnawing mammals, adapted for gnawing with long, chisel-shaped incisor teeth; lack canine teeth. Examples: rat, mouse, beaver, squirrel, porcupine.

Order: Lagomorpha. Herbivorous mammals with two pairs of large incisors. Examples: rabbit, hare.

Order. Artiodactyla: Even-toed hoofed mammals. Examples: cow, goat, sheep, camel, deer, giraffe.

Order: Perissodactyla. Odd-toed hoofed mammals. Examples: horse, tapir, rhinoceros, zebra.

Order: Subungulata. Trunked mammals; incisors elongated to form tusks; broad molars heavily enamelled for grinding plant food. Example: elephant.

Order: Chiroptera. Flying mammals; fore-limbs modified for flight; nocturnal in habit. Examples: bats.

Order: Primates. Mammals with flexible fingers and opposable thumbs and big toes for grasping; large, well-developed brain; mammals that walk erect or semi-erect. Examples: lemur, monkey, chimpanzee, man.

Complete classification of the dog would be as follows:
Kingdom—Animal
  Phylum—Chordata
    Class—Mammalia
      Order—Carnivora
        Family—Canidae
          Genus—Canis
            species—familiaris

THE PLANT KINGDOM

Division: Thallophtya. Plants without stems, roots or leaves; single-celled, colonial or many-celled; lack of hard, woody tissue; about 110,000 known species.

  Sub-Division: Algae. Usually aquatic, may be on moist land; possess chlorophyll; about 20,000 known species.

    Class: Cyanophyceae. Blue-green algae; contains blue pigment as well as green; no distinct nucleus. Examples: Oscillatoria.

    Class: Chlorophyceae. Green algae; contains only green pigment; well-developed nucleus; found in fresh water and moist, shaded areas. Examples: Pleurococcus, Spirogyra, desmids.

    Class: Phaeophyceae. Brown algae, brown pigment masks chlorophyll; chiefly salt water, seaweeds. Examples: kelp, rockweed.

    Class: Rhodophyceae. Red algae; red pigment masks chlorophyll pigment; mostly found in warm, marine waters. Examples: Irish moss, agar agar.

    Class: Bacillariophyceae. Diatoms; single-celled encased in box-like shell composed of silica. Examples: diatoms.

  Sub-Division: Fungi. Lacking all chlorophyll; parasitic or saprophytic; may be colourless or have a variety of colours; about 90,000 known species.

    Class: Phycomycetes. Moulds with hyphae without cross walls; reproduce with spores in spore-cases. Example: potato blight and bread mould.

    Class: Ascomycetes. Hyphae have cross walls and spores are produced in a special sac-like organ or ascus, e.g. yeast, chestnut blight, potato blight, Penicillium, mildews.

    Class: Basidiomycetes. Includes both saprophytes and parasites; spores produced on a special structure. Examples: mushrooms, bracket fungus, puff balls, rusts and smuts.

  Sub-Division: Slime moulds. Plant body a naked mass of protoplasm, reproduced by spores but not forming hyphae.

  Sub-Division: Fission Plants. One-celled plants reproducing by binary fission, e.g. bacteria and viruses.

Division: Bryophyta. Multicellular green plants; may reach about 6 inches in height; possess root-like rhizoids; usually found on moist and shady land areas; about 23,000 known species.

  Class: Hepaticae. Possess a flat, leaf-like body; resemble the lobes of a liver; no true stems or leaves. Examples: liverworts.

  Class: Musci. True mosses; possess rhizoids, true stems and leaves. Examples: sphagnum moss, pigeon wheat moss, peat moss.

Division: Pteridophyta. Flowerless green plants with true leaves, stems and roots; about 9,000 species.

  Class: Equisetineae. Found in sunny areas on banks of streams, railway embankments; contain glass-like silica; used commercially for scouring purposes. Examples: common horsetail, scouring rush.

  Class: Lycopodineae. Perennial, evergreen creeping forms with scale-like leaves; club-shaped spore-bearing structures. Examples: ground pine, ground cedar, club moss.

Class: Filicineae. Usually found in shaded, mossy places; have long leaves. Examples: Christmas fern, maidenhair fern, bracken.

Division: Spermatophyta. True seed-bearing plants; have true stems, leaves, roots and flowers which develop into seed-producing fruit bodies; well developed conducting and supporting tissue; contains familiar trees, shrubs and flowers; about 250,700 known species.

Sub-Division: Gymnospermae. Plants with naked seeds (not enclosed in ovaries) often in scales of cones; no true flowers. Examples: conifers.

Sub-Division: Angiospermae. Plants with seeds enclosed in a fruit or nut; includes common grasses, grains, trees, shrubs and plants with true flowers.

Class: Monocotyledons. Usually parallel veined leaves; single cotyledon in seed. Examples: corn, onion, grasses, jack-in-the-pulpit, palms.

Class: Dicotyledons. Usually netted veined leaves; two cotyledons in seed. Examples: rose, buttercup, potato, aster, apple, beech, oak, maple, etc.

Complete classification of a wild rose would be as follows:

```
Kingdom—Plant
  Phylum—Spermatophyta
    Sub-Phylum—Angiospermae
      Class—Dicotyledons
        Order—Rosales
          Family—Rosaceae
            Genus—Rosa
              species—carolina
```

APPENDIX B

CONCISE GLOSSARY OF BIOLOGICAL TERMS

NOTE: Roman numeral is a chapter reference

A

abdomen, VIII. Posterior section of the body; between diaphragm and pelvis in vertebrates.

absorption, X. The passage of liquids through a cell membrane.

adaptation, II. Fitness of structure for function; fitness for environmental conditions.

adrenal, X. Ductless glands above the kidneys.

adrenalin, X. A hormone secreted by the adrenal glands.

adventitious, VII. Roots from any part of plant other than primary root.

afferent, XII. Nerves which receive stimuli and send impulses to the brain or spinal cord; sensory nerves.

agar agar, VI. Gelatin material obtained from seaweed; used in bacteriology.

algae, IV, VI. Simplest green plants.

alternation of generations, VI. Life cycle in which an asexual generation follows a sexual generation.

altricial, IX. Born helpless.

Amoeba, II. Simple (one-celled) animal.

amphibian, IX. Vertebrates which live part of their lives in water and may live part of their lives on land.

anal pore, IV. Weak point in cell membrane for elimination of solid wastes (Paramecium).

anaemia, VIII. Deficiency of red blood corpuscles or haemoglobin in red blood corpuscles.

antennae (sing.: **antenna**), VIII. Sense organs or feelers on heads of insects and related arthropods.

anther, VII. Pollen-producing structure of the stamen of flowering plants (part of male reproductive organ).

anthropologist, XVI. One who specializes

in the study or science of man and his activities as a rational animal.

antibiotic, VI, XIII. Chemical substance produced by a living organism which can stop growth of some disease-producing bacteria, viruses and protozoa.

antibodies, VI. Chemical substances in blood which fight bacteria, toxins and other foreign substances.

antiseptic, XIII. A substance which prevents growth of some bacteria and destroys others.

antitoxin, XIII. A substance produced in animal bodies which counteracts harmful effects of disease-producing organisms; may provide immunity to certain diseases.

aphid, III. Ant-cow; provides nourishing fluid for ants; receives shelter and protection from ants.

appendage, VIII. A structure or organ attached to the main body.

appendix, X. Vestigial organ in man; part of digestive tube.

aquatic, III. Water-living.

arboreal, III. Tree-living.

Archaeopteryx, XVI. Fossil bird-form showing relationship to reptiles.

artery, X. Blood vessel which carries blood away from the heart to all parts of the body.

aseptic, XIII. Free of micro-organisms; sterile.

asexual, XIV. Reproduction without the union of two unlike parent cells.

assimilation, X. Process by which digested food is changed into protoplasm.

astigmatism, XII. Defect in the curvature of the eyes; results in indistinct vision.

atoll, VIII. Coral reef in the form of a ring.

atom, V. The smallest quantity of an element that enters into chemical combination.

auricle, IX, X. Upper chamber of the heart which receives blood from the veins.

auxin, XII. Plant hormone which controls plant growth.

axon, XII. Main, long fibre or branch leading from a neuron; carries impulses away from neuron cell body.

B

bacillus, VI. Rod-shaped bacteria.

backbone, IX. Bony, internal vertebral or spinal column.

bêche-de-mer, VIII. Sea cucumbers, dried and used for food (related to starfish).

beriberi, XI. Deficiency disease caused by lack of thiamin (B_1 of vitamin B complex).

binary fission, II. Simple splitting of a parent cell into two daughter cells.

bivalve, II, VIII. Mollusc having two shells (clam, oyster).

botulism, XIV. Food poisoning caused by specific bacteria.

bronchi, X. Bronchial tubes branching from the trachea and leading into each lung.

budding, VI. Form of asexual reproduction; growth from mother cell which remains attached to or separates from mother cell.

C

calcareous, VIII. Made of calcium.

calorie, XI. A heat measuring unit used in reference to foods.

calyx, VII. Sum total of sepals or outermost leaf-like structures of a true flower.

capillary, X. Smallest blood vessel in the body; between and connecting an artery and a vein; in closest contact with body cells for exchange of digested food, gases and waste fluids.

carnivorous, IX. Meat-eating.

cartilage, X. Soft, flexible, pre-bone tissue; gristle.

castings, VIII. Undigested solids containing soil (eliminated from the earth-worm); enriches the top-soil.

catalyst, II. Activating agent which brings about changes but is not itself changed during the processes.

caterpillar, VIII. Larval stage in the metamorphosis of butterfly and moth.

cattaloes, XV. Hybrids resulting from cross-breeding of a buffalo and a cow.

cell, II. The unit of protoplasmic structure and function of all living things.

cellulose, II. Organic substance found in the cell walls of plant cells.

cerebellum, XII. Part of the vertebrate brain behind the cerebrum; regulates muscular activity and controls body balance.

cerebrum, XII. Largest area of brain;

centre of conscious mental processes and voluntary muscular activity.

chemotherapy, XIII. Branch of medical science; study of the use of drugs and other substances of chemical nature in the treatment of specific diseases.

chlorophyll, II. Green colour pigment in plant cells; necessary for photosynthesis.

choroid coat, XII. Membrane around the eyeball which contains blood vessels for nourishment and pigmentation.

chromosome, II. Body in nucleus which contains genes; carrier of hereditary characteristics.

chrysalis, VIII. Pupal stage of butterfly (similar to cocoon of moth); quiescent stage before adulthood.

cilia, VIII. Threads of protoplasm surrounding entire cell of Paramecium; used for locomotion.

coccus, VI. Round type of bacteria.

coccyx, X. Bone at end of spinal column consisting of four fused vertebrae; tail-like vestigial structure in man.

cochlea, XII. Snail shell-like portion of inner ear which contains nerve endings of auditory nerve.

cocoon, VIII. Pupal stage in the metamorphosis of a moth; quiescent stage.

colchicine, XV. Plant extract (drug-type) used in experiments on plants to induce formation of mutants.

cold-blooded, IX. Having the same body temperature as that of the immediate environment.

compound, V. A substance resulting from the chemical combination of two or more elements.

conditioned reflex, XII. An acquired response; a response to a stimulus other than the usual or inherited one.

conjugation, IV. Temporary union of two similar cells during which there is an exchange of nuclear material.

cornea, XII. Transparent layer covering the front of the eyeball.

corolla, VII. The sum total of the petals of a flower.

corpuscle, X. Blood cell (red or white).

cotyledon, VII. Part of a seed which often contains stored food for the embryo plant.

cretin, X. One who was born with a serious deficiency of the thyroid gland.

cutin, VII. Transparent, waxy secretion which protects outer surface of some leaves.

cytoplasm, II. Protoplasm of the cell minus the nucleus.

D

dendrite, XII. A branching process of a neuron which carries impulses to the cell body.

dental caries, X. Tooth decay.

dentine, X. Bony portion of the tooth beneath the enamel.

diaphragm, IX. A layer of muscle tissue which separates the chest from the abdominal cavity in mammals; important in breathing process.

diatom, IV. A species of algae; cell is enclosed in box-like shell containing silica.

diffusion, V. Spreading of molecules of gas or liquid from an area of greatest density towards an area of less density.

dinosaur, IX, Extinct, prehistoric reptile.

disinfectant, XIII. A substance used to destroy harmful bacteria; usually too strong to be used on the body.

dissemination, VII. Distribution (as of seeds).

dominant, XV. Referring to hereditary characteristics or traits which show in a hybrid.

E

ecology, XVII. The study of the relationships of living things to each other and their environment.

ectoderm, XIV. The outer layer of cells; one of the three germ layers of an embryo.

efferent, XII. Referring to nerves which carry impulses away from the brain to glands or muscles; motor nerves.

electrocardiograph, X. A machine used to make a recording of electrical waves from the heart; used in diagnosis of heart conditions.

element, V. A substance which cannot be further simplified by chemical means.

embryo, II, VII. A young plant or animal before germination or birth.

endocrine, X. Referring to ductless glands which secrete hormones or body regulators.

endoderm, XIV. The inner layer of cells; an embryonic layer.

endoskeleton, X. Bony skeleton within the body of vertebrate animals.

enzymes, II. Chemical substances in plants and animals which induce or hasten chemical changes as in digestion, without being themselves changed.

Eohippus, XVI. Prehistoric horse.

epiglottis, X. A flap of tissue which covers the opening of the trachea during the act of swallowing.

epiphyte, plant which grows upon another plant but obtains no nourishment from it.

erosion, XVI. The wearing away of soil by the action of water, wind, etc.

eugenics, XV. The study of the improvement of the human race by applying the laws of heredity.

evolution, XVI. Succession of gradual changes that take place in an individual plant or animal or species of plant or animal or form of life, over a long period of time, usually from the simple towards the more complex.

excretion, X. The process by which waste products are eliminated from a living organism.

exoskeleton, VIII. An outer or external skeleton (shell of crayfish).

F

faeces, X. Indigestible, solid waste materials.

fauna, III. Animals within a given life zone or natural habitat.

fertilized egg, II. Result of the union of male cell with female cell.

fibrinogen, X. A substance in the blood plasma which is changed to fibres to form a clot under certain conditions.

fins, IX. Organs of locomotion, steering and balance of fish.

flaccid, VII. A soft or relaxed condition of a cell, usually due to lack of water within the cell.

flora, III. Sum total of all plants within a given life zone or natural habitat.

foetus, XIV. Unborn young of mammals, after it has assumed the appearance of the parents.

fossil, XVI. Petrified remains, imprints, tracks or other markings of prehistoric plants or animals.

fraternal twins, XV. Twins which develop from two separate eggs

fertilized at approximately the same time.

frond, VI. The leafy part of a fern.

fruit, VII. A ripened ovary and its contents (seeds) plus any parts of the flower adhering closely to the ovary.

fry, IX. Young fish with yolk sac still attached but almost used up.

function, II. The use or work of any living organism or part of an organism.

fungus, III, VI. Plant which lacks chlorophyll; a thallophyte (simplest group); dependent on dead or living organic food.

G

gamete, XIV. A sexual reproductive cell; female gamete is an ovum or egg cell and a male gamete is a sperm cell.

gametogenesis, XIV. Process during which gametes or sex cells are formed.

ganglion, VIII. A mass of nerve cells.

gene, XV. A unit in a chromosome which carries hereditary characteristics.

genetics, XV. The science of heredity.

geologist, XVI. One who studies the science of geology, the study of the earth's crust, past and present.

gills, II, IX. Organs of breathing of fish.

gizzard, IX. Muscular organ of earthworms, birds and some other animals in which food is crushed and partly digested.

glycogen, X. Animal starch; a carbohydrate sorted in the liver and present in muscles.

grafting, XIV. Joining a twig or scion to another plant stem called a stock.

guard cells, VII. Cells on either side of a stoma which regulate the size of its opening.

gullet, VIII. Oesophagus or food tube extending from the back of the mouth to the stomach.

H

haemoglobin, X. Red colouring matter in red blood corpuscles of vertebrates; an organic compound which carries oxygen.

haemophilia, X. Hereditary disease in which the blood will not clot normally even after a slight injury.

herbivorous, IX. Plant-eating animal.

heredity, XV. The passing on of traits or characteristics from parent to offspring through the gametes.

hibernate, IX. Prolonged sleep-like inactivity during a winter season (bears, frogs, etc.).

Homo sapiens, IX. Scientific name of present-day man.

hormone, X. Substance which is secreted by ductless or endocrine glands directly into the blood stream; which controls actions in some part of the body or some body process; chemical messenger.

humus, VI. Substances in soil formed by decay of plants and animals.

hybrid, XV. A plant or animal carrying unlike genes in the same pair of chromosomes.

hybridization, XV. Crossing individuals in breeding, that carry contrasting traits.

I

identical twins, XV. Twins which result from the fertilization of a single egg cell which splits into two like parts in early cell division.

immunity, XIII. Ability to resist a certain disease because of a previous attack or natural ability to resist it or by preventative inoculations, vaccinations, etc.

incisor, IX, X. The cutting teeth with chisel-like edges; front teeth in jaws of mammals.

ingestion, II. Process of taking in food.

inorganic, V. That which is not alive, nor ever was alive, nor came from anything alive.

insectivorous, VII, XVII. Insect-eating animal or plant.

insulin, X. A hormone secreted by the islets of Langerhans of the pancreas; controls oxidation of sugars.

invertebrate, VIII. An animal without a backbone.

iris, XII. The coloured part of the eye of vertebrate animals.

irradiation, XI. Exposure of food, human skin, etc., to ultra-violet rays.

K

kelp, VI. Brown algae seaweed; used for food in China and Japan; burned to produce iodine.

kidney, IX, X. Paired organs in vertebrates which extract nitrogenous wastes from the blood for elimination.

L

lacteal, X. Small lymph vessel in the centre of each villus; absorbs digested fats from the small intestines.

larva, VIII. Worm-like, eating stage in the complete metamorphosis of some insects (caterpillar of moth and butterfly, maggot of fly).

larynx, X. Voice box (Adam's apple) in the trachea; contains vocal cords.

lateral line, IX. Line of nerve cells on sides of fish; indicate depth of water for the fish.

legume, V, VII. Plant which has pod fruits (peas, beans).

lens, XII. A transparent body in the eye which is biconvex; light rays pass through the lens and are bent to focus on the retina.

lichen, III. A symbiotic relationship between a fungus plant and a green alga; common on moist rock surfaces.

ligament, X. A band of tissue which connects bone to bone.

linkage, XV. Referring to the grouping together of genes on a chromosome which are transmitted together to the offspring.

lungs, IX. Organs of breathing of vertebrate animals from adult amphibians to mammals.

lymph, X. Part of the blood serum which is outside the blood vessels; bathes the cells.

M

maggot, VIII. Larval stage in the metamorphosis of the common house-fly.

malaria, XIII. Disease caused by a parasitic protozoan (Plasmodium) which is carried and transmitted by the Anopheles mosquito; Plasmodium lives in blood stream of man (alternate host).

mammals, IX. Vertebrates which have hair on their bodies, breathe by means of lungs, bear their young alive and nourish their young with milk from mammary glands.

mammary gland, IX. Milk-secreting gland of mammals.

medulla oblongata, XII. Posterior part of the brain, connecting the spinal cord; controls respiration and heartbeat.

meiosis, XVI. Reduction division; reduction of original number of chromosomes so that each sex cell (egg or sperm) has half the original number of chromosomes characteristic of the species.

mesentery, IX. Tissue which holds the intestine in place in the abdominal cavity.

mesoderm, XIV. The middle layer of cells formed during embryonic development.

metamorphosis, VIII. The changes in form some organisms undergo during their development from a free-living larval form to the adult stage.

mitosis, XIV. Cell division during which the chromosomes duplicate themselves.

mixture, V. The physical combination of two or more elements or compounds each of which retains its original characteristics and can be separated from each other.

molecule, V. Smallest particle of a compound capable of having the properties of the compound.

morphology, XVI. The study of the structure of plants and animals.

mutation, XV. A sudden appearance of a new trait or variation which is heritable.

myxoedema, X. A disease in adults resulting from a deficiency of thyroid hormone.

N

nacre, VIII. Mother-of-pearl; substance which forms a pearl in the irritated bivalve.

neuron, XII. A nerve cell.

nitrate, V. A compound containing nitrogen, oxygen and at least one other element.

nucleus, II. Specialized protoplasm in a cell which controls all cellular activity in general and governs heredity in reproduction in particular (contains chromosomes).

O

oesophagus, IX. The gullet or food tube leading from the mouth to the stomach.

organ, IV. A group of different tissues working together to perform a specific function.

organic, V. Pertaining to something living, or which was at one time living, or which was produced by something living.

organism, IV. Any living plant or animal.

osmosis, V. Diffusion of water through a semipermeable membrane.

ovary, VII. Organ of the female reproductive system of flowering plants and higher animals in which eggs are produced.

oviduct, X. Tube down which mammalian egg passes after leaving ovary.

oxidation, II, V. The chemical combination of oxygen with another element.

P

palaeontologist, XV. One who studies fossils.

pancreas, IX. A digestive gland which pours digestive juice into the small intestine; also a ductless gland which controls sugar oxidation.

parasite, III. An organism which takes its nourishment from another living organism without giving any benefits to its host.

parathyroid, X. Ductless or endocrine glands near the thyroid glands in the neck; regulates calcium assimilation in the body.

Pasteurization, XIII. Process of treating milk by heating it to 145° F. and rapidly cooling it, killing most of the harmful bacteria.

pathogenic, III, VI. Referring to disease-producing bacteria.

pelvis, X. Broad bones which support the organs of the abdomen.

penicillin, VI, XIII. An organic chemical product isolated from a common mould; used in treating diseases caused by certain types of bacteria; now synthesized.

pericardium, X. A membrane surrounding and protecting the heart.

pericarp. Fruit wall.

peristalsis, X. Wavelike, muscular motion of the food tube of higher vertebrate animals which forces food along alimentary canal.

phagocyte, X. White corpuscles of the blood which act as scavengers.

photosynthesis, II. Manufacture of carbohydrates by the green plant in the sunshine.

pistil, VII. The female reproductive organ in the flowering plant.

pituitary, X. Ductless or endocrine gland; called the master gland because it controls all other endocrine glands.

placenta, XIV. Organ in mammalian uterus containing maternal and embryonic blood vessels.

plankton, IV, VI. Minute forms of plant and animal life floating near the surface in the ocean.

plasma, X. The liquid portion of the blood of vertebrates.

platelets, X. Small bodies in blood which aid in clotting.

Pleurococcus, IV. Single-celled (alga) green plant which grows on the shady side of tree trunks.

plumule, VII. Part of the plant embryo which develops into the shoot with its leaves.

pollen, VII. Grains formed in the anther of a flower or the male cone of a conifer; contains male sex cells.

pollination, VII. Transfer of pollen from the anther of a flower to the stigma.

precocial, IX. Young born relatively independent of their parents.

primate, IX, XVI. Order of mammals which include monkeys, apes and man.

protein, V. A food nutrient necessary for the building of protoplasm; contains nitrogen in addition to oxygen, hydrogen, and carbon.

protoplasm, II. The living substance of all plants and animals.

pseudopodium, IV, VIII. Projection of protoplasm; aids in locomotion of Amoeba.

pulp, X. Innermost section of a human tooth; contains blood vessels and nerves.

pulse, X. Rhythmic wave of motion indicating beat of the heart felt in an artery.

pupa, VIII. Quiescent stage in the complete metamorphosis of an insect; stage during which the adult develops.

pupil, XII. The round opening in the iris of the eye through which light rays enter the eye.

Q

quinine, XIII. Drug used in the treatment of malaria.

R

radicle, VII. Part of a plant embryo which develops into the root.

recessive, XV. A hidden trait or characteristic in a hybrid contrasting pair.

rectum, X. Terminal end of large intestine; functions in the elimination of solid wastes from the body.

reduction division, XIV. See **meiosis.**

reflex, XII. Simple, involuntary action in response to a stimulus; no thought involved.

regeneration, VIII, XIV. The act of growing a new body part for one which has been injured or lost.

reproduction, XIV. The process by which new individuals of the same kind are produced by a plant or animal; producing offspring.

respiration, X. A life function in which oxygen is taken into the cells to release energy from food and the waste gas, carbon dioxide is given off.

retina, XII. Innermost layer of tissue in the eyeball; contains nerve endings (from optic nerve) which receive light stimulus.

rickets, X, XI. Deficiency disease resulting from an insufficiency of vitamin D in the diet, or inadequate assimilation of it.

roe, IX. Fish eggs.

root hairs, VII. Elongated epidermal cells of a root; for absorption of soil water and mineral salts.

S

saliva, X. Digestive juice secreted by glands in the mouth.

saprophyte, III. Plant or animal which lives on dead organic matter (some fungi).

sclerotic coat, XII. Tough, outer protective layer of the eye.

scurvy, XI. Deficiency disease caused by lack of vitamin C in the diet.

scutes, IX. Scales on the under or belly surface of snakes; aid in locomotion.

secretion, X. A chemical substance produced by a living cell (enzyme or hormone).

sedimentary, XVI. A type of rock which is formed by materials deposited from suspension in water.

semicircular canal, XII. Part of the inner ear, functions as organ of balance.

Sequoia, VII. Oldest living organism on earth; a giant redwood tree in the conifer group.

serum, X. Blood plasma from which the fibrinogen has been removed.

sex-linked, XV. Refers to a hereditary trait whose gene is in the sex chromosome.

sexual, XIV. Reproduction in which the new individual is a result of the union of male and female gametes.

soluble, II. That which can be dissolved in a fluid.

spawn, IX. To deposit eggs or roe (as fishes).

specialization, IV. The adaptation of cells or groups of cells to perform a particular function.

sperm, II. The male sex cell or gamete in an animal.

sphygmomanometer, X. Instrument used to measure blood pressure.

spinal cord, X. The main nerve cord of all vertebrates.

spiracles, II, VII. Openings on the bodies of insects through which they breathe.

spirillum, VI. A spiral-shaped bacterium.

Spirogyra, IV. A filamentous green alga; commonly known as pond scum.

spore, II, VI. Non-sexual reproductive body, common to fungi, bacteria, mosses and other plants and some protozoa.

stamen, VII. Male reproductive organ in flowering plants.

stethoscope, X. Instrument used to listen to heart and lung sounds.

stigma, VII. Top of a pistil of a flower, part which receives pollen.

stoma, II, IV, VII. Opening on lower surface of a green leaf through which there is an exchange of gases and water vapour.

streptomycin, VI. An antibiotic used in the treatment and control of tuberculosis and other pulmonary diseases, infections of the urinary tract and other diseases.

symbiosis, III. A state in which two dissimilar organisms live together to mutual advantage (lichen).

synapse, XII. The space over which a nerve impulse passes from the dendrites of one neuron to the dendrites of another.

system, IV. A group of organs working together to perform a particular function (digestive system).

T

tadpole, IX. The fish-like stage in the metamorphosis of frogs and toads.

taxonomist, XVI. One who specializes in classification of plants and animals.

tendon, X. Tissue which attaches a muscle to a bone.

tentacles, V, VIII. Flexible arm-like projections of jellyfish and related animals; used in food getting and locomotion.

testis, X. Male organ of reproduction in mammals; produces sperms.

thorax, VIII. The middle division of an animal's body; between the head and abdomen.

thymus, X. An endocrine or ductless gland.

thyroid, X. An endocrine or ductless gland in the neck, just below the larynx; controls rate of metabolism in the body.

tissue, IV. A group of similar cells that perform the same function.

toxins, VI. Poisons released by disease-producing bacteria.

trachea, II, VIII, X. Windpipe; tube which delivers air from throat to lungs in vertebrates; air passage in insects.

transpiration, V, VII. Loss of water by evaporation through the stomata of the leaves of plants.

trichocysts, IV, VIII. Dart-like substances ejected by Paramecium as a means of anchorage.

tropism, II, VIII, XII. Growth response of plants to external stimuli.

U

umbilical cord, XIV. Attaches mammalian embryo to placenta; contains blood vessels.

univalve, VIII. Mollusc with a single shell (snail).

urea, X. Nitrogenous waste collected and excreted by the kidneys.

uterus, X. Muscular organ in which mammalian embryo develops.

V

vaccine, XIII. Substance used in preventive inoculation; (virus of cowpox used in inoculation against smallpox).

vacuoles, II. Small spaces in cytoplasm of a cell, containing liquid or solid food or waste matter.

vein, X. Blood vessel in which blood returns to the heart from all over the body; liquid-conducting vessels in leaves.

venom, IX. Poison secreted by glands of poisonous snakes, lizards, etc.

ventricle, IX, X. Lower, muscular chamber of a vertebrate heart; pumps blood through arteries to the rest of the body.

vertebrae, X. Bones of the backbone.

vertebrates, II, VIII. Group of animals which have internal backbones.

vestigial, X. Referring to a remnant of a once useful organ or a structure formerly more complete in function.

villus, X. A small (microscopic) projection in the lining of the small intestine; organ of absorption of digested food.

virus, XIII. Sub-microscopic substance which has characteristics, both organic and inorganic; causative agent of some diseases.

W

warm-blooded, IX. Referring to an animal which maintains a constant body temperature.

Y

yolk sac, IX. Stored food material for embryo vertebrate.

Z

zygote, XIV. The result of the fusion of two gametes.

ANSWERS

Exercise No. 1

2 d   3 c   4 a   5 b

Exercise No. 2

2 animal kingdom   4 protoplasm
3 plant cell   5 inorganic

Exercise No. 3

1 b   2 d   3 g   4 a   5 e   6 c   7 h   8 i   9 j   10 f

Exercise No. 4

2 vacuoles   4 anatomy   6 microscope
3 cell   5 protect and support the
        plant cell

Exercise No. 5

1 ingestion   4 digestion   7 enzyme
2 carbon dioxide, water   5 absorption   8 circulation
3 photosynthesis   6 food vacuole

Exercise No. 6

1 oxidation   3 soluble   5 circulation
2 life process   4 waste products

Exercise No. 7

1 By the oxidation of food; the sun.
2 Through the stomata.
3 The elimination of waste products resulting from metabolism.
4 A form of reproduction by splitting into two halves.
5 Feeding, respiration, growth, reproduction, excretion, sensitivity and movement.
6 The method of obtaining food substances.

Exercise No. 8

1 h   2 d   3 a   4 g   5 f   6 b   7 e   8 c   9 i

Exercise No. 9

Ocean:	animals:	whale, jellyfish, sea turtle, shark, oyster
	plants:	diatoms, kelp, blue-green algae, rockweed, some bacteria
Pond:	animals:	fish, snakes, snails, leeches, crayfish
	plants:	green algae, blue algae, water lilies, water cress, duck weed
Desert:	animals:	rattlesnake, horned toad, rabbit, lizards, vulture
	plants:	yucca, cactus, sagebrush, grasses
Polar regions:	animals:	penguin, whale, seal, walrus, polar bear
	plants:	moss, lichen, dwarf poppy, forget-me-not, grasses

Exercise No. 10

1 e   2 b   3 d   4 a   5 c

Exercise No. 11

1 environment
2 environment
3 protective adaptation
4 barriers
5 photosynthesis

Exercise No. 12

1 protective
2 symbiosis
3 parasite
4 mistletoe
5 symbiosis
6 symbiosis
7 scavenger
8 pathogenic
9 scavengers

Exercise No. 13

1 cell
2 Amoeba
3 contractile vacuole
4 shells
5 binary fission
6 Protozoa
7 Euglena
8 pseudopodia

Exercise No. 14

1 c   2 g   3 a   4 e   5 b   6 h   7 f   8 d

Exercise No. 15

1 has weight, occupies space
2 element
3 atom
4 physical
5 mixture
6 energy
7 oxygen, hydrogen
8 H_2O, CO_2
9 104
10 solid, liquid, gas

Exercise No. 17

1 d   2 g   3 h   4 c   5 a   6 b   7 i   8 j   9 e   10 f

Exercise No. 18

1 chlorophyll
2 brown algae—Sargassum
3 plankton
4 symbiotic, alga
5 seaweeds
6 kelp
7 agar agar
8 diatoms
9 plankton
10 chlorine
11 Spirogyra

Exercise No. 19

1 d   2 b   3 e   4 h   5 i   6 c   7 j   8 g   9 f   10 a

Exercise No. 20

2 a   3 b   4 d   5 b   6 d   7 a   8 c, d   9 d

Exercise No. 21

1 Extreme temperatures, dryness, bright light, some chemicals.
2 An antibiotic made from a mould.
3 It produces carbon dioxide which, when warmed, expands and pushes up the dough.
4 Typhoid, diphtheria, tuberculosis.
5 Decaying organic matter in soil; it is a source of nitrates for plants, and aids soil to retain warmth and moisture.
6 Hyphae penetrate the food, produce enzymes to digest it and then absorb it. It reproduces: (a) by spore formation; (b) by conjugation.

Exercise No. 22

1 pine	5 embryo	9 cones
2 cones	6 Sequoia	10 pod, tomato
3 vascular	7 fir	
4 conifer	8 seeds	

Exercise No. 23

1 h 2 l 3 b 4 a 5 c 6 e 7 m 8 k 9 f 10 d
11 i 12 j 13 g

Exercise No. 24

1 manufacture food	6 parallel	11 sun
2 arrangement	7 veins	12 carbon dioxide
3 simple	8 insectivorous	13 stomata
4 compound	9 photosynthesis	14 transpiration
5 rosette	10 starch, oxygen	15 guard cells

Exercise No. 25

(a) Protection of flower bud.
(b) Protection of reproductive organs; attracts insects.
(c) Contains pollen (male gametes).
(d) Female reproductive organ; contains ovules.
(e) Supports flower parts.

Exercise No. 26

1 fruit	6 key fruit (e.g.	11 radicle
2 dispersal	sycamore)	12 cotyledon
3 fleshy fruit (e.g.	7 embryo	13 plumule
apple)	8 barbs	14 pod
4 drupe (e.g. cherry)	9 germination	15 testa
5 nut (e.g. walnut)	10 dicotyledon (e.g. pea)	

Exercise No. 28

1 invertebrate	4 segmented worms	6 bivalves
2 parasite	5 molluscs	7 oyster
3 reproduction		

Exercise No. 29

1 h 2 g 3 e 4 o 5 b 6 k 7 n 8 i 9 a
10 f 11 c 12 l 13 j 14 p 15 m 16 d

Exercise No. 30

1 gills	8 nymph	14 destroy their breeding
2 four	9 incomplete	places
3 black widow, tarantula	10 larval	15 mouth parts
4 spider	11 complete	16 vertical, horizontal
5 tick	12 night, daytime	17 swarm
6 spider	13 it transmits bacteria	18 cellulose
7 insects		

Exercise No. 31

1 c 2 f 3 g 4 h 5 b 6 d 7 a 8 e

Exercise No. 32

1 oxygen
2 cold
3 fins, tail
4 vibrations and temperature changes
5 swimming
6 (a) lungs, (b) skin
7 mesenteries
8 ventricle
9 tadpole
10 yolk
11 hibernation
12 scutes
13 shell
14 chameleons
15 fangs
16 dinosaurs
17 lungs
18 four

Exercise No. 33

1 d   2 a   3 i   4 b   5 j   6 l   7 k   8 c   9 e   10 h
11 f   12 g

Exercise No. 34

1 mammals
2 diaphragm
3 lays eggs
4 kangaroo
5 aquatic
6 grain, disease
7 incisors
8 canines
9 rat flea
10 cud

Exercise No. 36

1 m   2 g   3 d   4 j   5 a   6 h   7 l   8 i   9 o   10 c
11 k   12 f   13 e   14 n   15 b

Exercise No. 37

1 c   2 a   3 c   4 d   5 a   6 d   7 d   8 b   9 c   10 a
11 b   12 d   13 c   14 a

Exercise No. 38

1 lungs
2 air sacs
3 asphyxiation
4 (a) epiglottis, (b) trachea, (c) choking
5 tuberculosis
6 bladder
7 sweat glands
8 kidneys
9 large intestine
10 skin

Exercise No. 39

1 endoskeleton
2 joint
3 tissue
4 muscles
5 bone
6 ductless gland
7 pancreas
8 glandular malfunctioning
9 hormone
10 secretions

Exercise No. 40

1 f   2 j   3 g   4 a   5 e   6 h   7 b   8 i   9 c   10 d

Exercise No. 41

1 d   2 c   3 c   4 b   5 b

Exercise No. 42

1 positive geotropism
2 auxin
3 heliotropism
4 neuron
5 brain, spinal cord, nerves
6 reflex
7 afferent or sensory neuron
8 to maintain balance
9 antennae
10 efferent or motor neuron
11 Pavlov
12 Amoeba
13 reflex
14 learned response

Exercise No. 43

1 Protective.
2 Contains blood vessels for nourishment.
3 Transparent; allows light rays in.
4 Carries impulse to brain.
5 Coloured; controls size of pupil.
6 Opening through which light rays pass.
7 Focuses light rays on to the retina.
8 Receives and responds to light rays; (contains nerve cells).
9 Keeps lens moist.
10 Maintains shape of eyeball.

Exercise No. 44

1 c   2 h   3 f   4 a   5 i   6 g   7 j   8 d   9 e   10 b

Exercise No. 45

1 d   2 c   3 f   4 b   5 e   6 a   7 g

Exercise No. 46

1 immune   4 diphtheria toxin   7 Widal
2 antibody   5 toxins   8 antiseptic
3 acquired   6 diphtheria; scarlet fever

Exercise No. 47

1 c   2 c   3 a   4 c   5 a   6 c   7 a   8 b   9 a   10 c

Exercise No. 48

1 h   2 d   3 j   4 m   5 i   6 n   7 l   8 k   9 g   10 a
11 c   12 f   13 b   14 e

Exercise No. 49

1 sexually   7 fertilization, fertilized   12 stored food
2 pistil   8 embryo, stored food   13 embryonic layers
3 stamen   9 Twenty-three   14 ectoderm
4 pollen   10 mitosis   15 foetus
5 ovary   11 meiosis (reduction
6 cross-pollination   division)

Exercise No. 50

1 d   2 b   3 a   4 c   5 d   6 b   7 c

Exercise No. 51

1 c   2 a   3 d   4 h   5 b   6 g   7 e   8 f

Exercise No. 52

1 acquired   7 X-rays   12 hybridization, cattaloe
2 mutant   8 colchicine   13 rust-resistant wheat
3 inheritable; changes   9 undesirable   14 pure
4 beef   10 hybridization   15 Holstein
5 selection   11 mule   16 identical
6 lethal

Exercise No. 53

1 d   2 b   3 c   4 a   5 c   6 b   7 b   8 a   9 d   10 a

Exercise No. 54

1 b   2 g   3 e   4 i   5 h   6 a   7 c   8 j   9 f   10 d

Exercise No. 55

1 Primates
2 Homo sapiens
3 anthropologist

4 race
5 Negroid, Mongoloid, Caucasian

6 25,000
7 four
8 common ancestor

Exercise No. 56

1 ecology
2 natural habitat
3 food chain
4 balance

5 fauna
6 reafforestation
7 photosynthesis
8 insectivorous

9 stocking
10 erosion
11 depletion
12 leguminous

Exercise No. 57

1 scientific farming
2 forest conservation
3 natural resources

4 wildlife
5 migratory birds
6 minerals

7 top-soil